IMAGES
of America

SACRAMENTO'S

GREENHAVEN/POCKET AREA

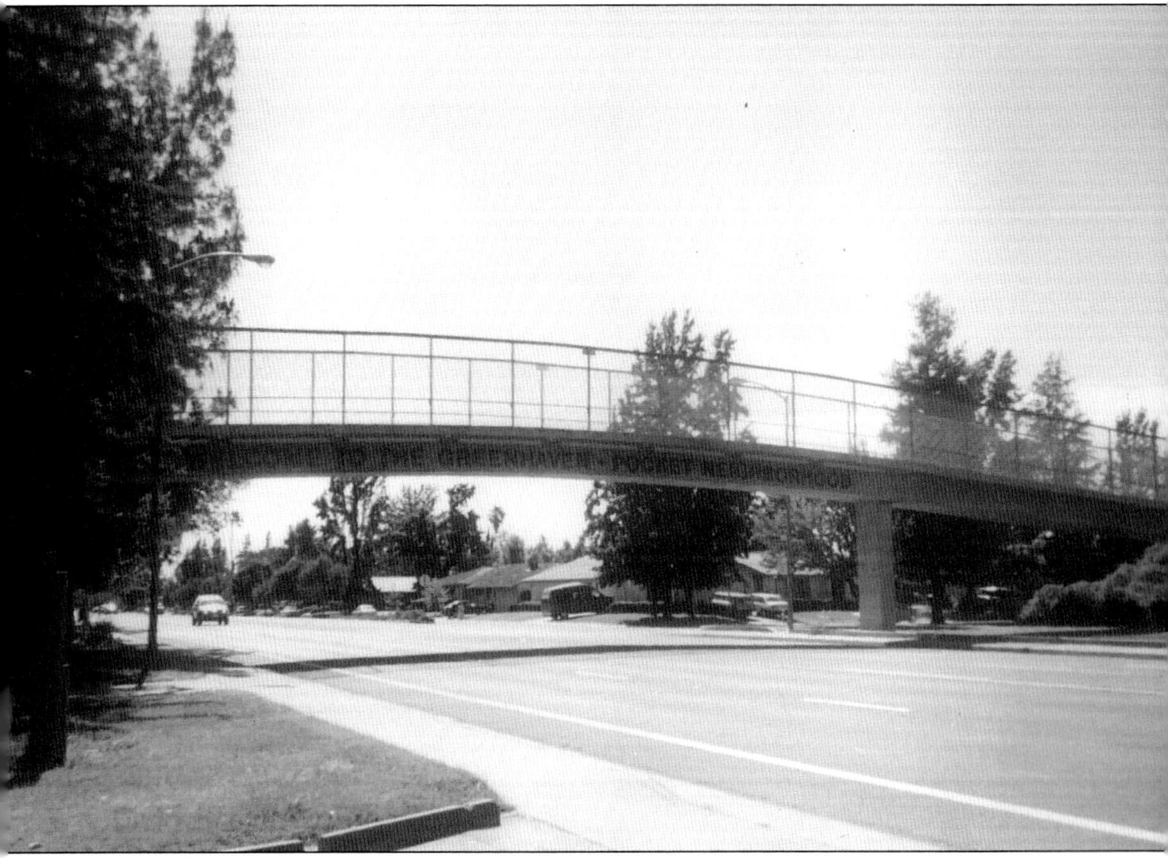

GREENHAVEN/POCKET NEIGHBORHOOD. A sign recently added to the pedestrian overpass in Greenhaven welcomes people to the Greenhaven/Pocket neighborhood. The Pocket area has a distinct community name based on its geographic location in a large meandering bend of the Sacramento River. It has historically been referred to as the Pocket, commonly associated with nearby Riverside (now South Land Park). The Greenhaven community name refers to the North Pocket area where development in the Pocket first began. It is named after the innovative Greenhaven 70 plan development by the Lincoln and Parker Development Company in the 1960s.

IMAGES
of America

SACRAMENTO'S GREENHAVEN/POCKET AREA

Carol Ann Gregory

ARCADIA
PUBLISHING

ISBN 978-0-7385-1909-8

Published by Arcadia Publishing
Charleston, South Carolina

Printed in the United States of America

For all general information contact Arcadia Publishing at:
Telephone 843-853-2070
Fax 843-853-0044
E-mail sales@arcadiapublishing.com
For customer service and orders:
Toll-Free 1-888-313-2665

Visit us on the Internet at www.arcadiapublishing.com

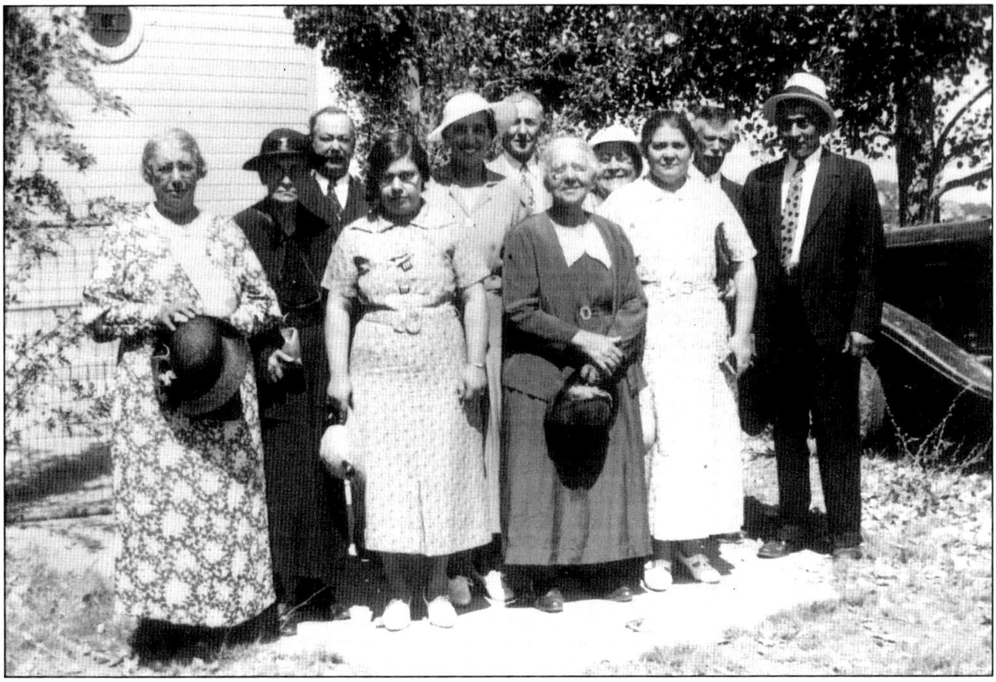

These Pioneer Pocket Family Descendants Gathered in Front of the Church of St. Mary's in 1940. From left to right are as follows: (front row) Mary Garcia, Annie Luiz, and Mary Lewis; (second row) Mary Perry, Mary Lewis, Louise Lewis, and Manuel Lewis; (back row) Antone Dutra, Manuel Silveira, unidentified, and Jessie Lewis. (Courtesy of the Portuguese Historical and Cultural Society)

Contents

About this Book

This photographic history book of the Sacramento's Greenhaven/Pocket area ultimately started in 1997, as I began doing research on the community for college term papers and later my master's thesis project. When I began my research, there was no book published solely on the history and development of the Greenhaven/Pocket area. I hope this book can be used as a guide and reference for future studies on the community.

First and foremost, this book would not be possible without the photo collection of the Portuguese Historical and Cultural Society (P.H.C.S.), based in Sacramento, California. The local organization began gathering pictures on the history of the Portuguese settlers in the Pocket area over 20 years ago. Without their efforts and permission, the majority of the pictures in this book would not be made available for publication. Special thanks to Dolores Silva Greenslate, a local historian and life-long resident of the Greenhaven/Pocket area. Dolores has kept and maintained the P.H.C.S. photo collection and her knowledge and original research on the area provide the basis for this book. The pictures of the Pocket area from the P.H.C.S. photo collection are noted in this book along with the individual that originally donated the photos to them.

Due to the majority of photos in this book from the P.H.C.S. photo collection, the book has an overwhelming focus on the historic Portuguese settlement that settled in the Greenhaven/Pocket area today. The Portuguese were an extremely important aspect to the history of this area and were once the primary population in the community. However, it should be noted that a few non-Portuguese families also settled in the area, and a sizeable number of Japanese families settled and co-existed with the Portuguese community after World War I. Information on the non-Portuguese groups of the Pocket area is extremely scarce and original pictures are even more difficult to locate.

Hopefully, Chapter 4 on schools will give the reader a sense of the diversity that existed in the Pocket area at one time and continues today. I also included a number of photos found in Chapter 6 that I took myself of the community today. This chapter should illustrate how unique the Greenhaven/Pocket area is in terms of its development and community character.

I apologize for any inaccuracies, errors, or omissions found in this book and take full responsibility for them.

Carol Ann Gregory

Introduction

This is a photographic history book of Sacramento's Greenhaven/Pocket area, with photos spanning from the 1870s to 2001. The goal of this book is to provide the reader with a visual sense of how the Pocket area has evolved over the years to become the community that it is today.

Sacramento's Greenhaven/Pocket area is located roughly 5 to 7 miles southwest of downtown Sacramento. It is within the city limits of Sacramento, having been annexed by the city in 1959. Geographically, its unique location is within a meandering bend of the Sacramento River, thus termed "the Pocket" because it is bounded by the Sacramento River to the north, west, and south. To the east it is bounded by Interstate 5. Before Interstate 5 was built, the Pocket had historical ties with "the Riverside" community, today's South Land Park neighborhood. Riverside was also termed for the northern Pocket area (present day Greenhaven), named after the only road that went through it, Riverside Road.

The first inhabitants of the Pocket area are believed to be the Miwok Native American tribe. Native American mounds of burial grounds and artifacts were commonly found by early day settlers and construction crews during its suburban development. Physical geography of the community before initial settlement was usually tule-filled swampland in the center of the Pocket and forest like broad leaf trees, mainly oak trees, growing along the Sacramento River banks. Elevation tended to be higher along the Sacramento River and gradually decrease towards the center of the Pocket. This "bowl-like" feature dictated how early settlement in the Pocket was established. Homes were commonly found next to or along the Sacramento River banks while farming was done further inland.

The Greenhaven/Pocket area was a rural farming community for 110 years before suburban development. The northern part of the Pocket was in the Sutter Township while the southern part was in the Franklin Township. The most significant group of people that contributed to the Greenhaven/Pocket area's history and identity were Portuguese immigrants from the Azores Islands of Faial, Pico, Sao Jorge, and Terceira. They began arriving a few years after the Gold Rush and by 1880, 38.4 percent of the Portuguese population in Sacramento County was within these townships that encompassed and surrounded the Riverside/Pocket area. The Riverside/Pocket area was part of a general region, constituting Clarksburg and Freeport, that identified itself as "Little Portugal," the "Lisbon District," or "Portuguese Bend." These historic landscape names reflect the fact that the majority in this area were Portuguese, one of the most intensive early day settlements of this ethnic group in California.

Some non-Portuguese families also settled in the Pocket area, a few being early day families as well. A sizeable Japanese community settled in the Pocket area after World War I. When many of the Japanese families in the Pocket area were forced into internment camps during World War II, their property and homes were watched by Portuguese families until they returned. Reflections of early day settlers, work life, family homes and ranches, community life, and the area's schools are in Chapters 1–5 to provide a visual sense of the Pocket area before its initial development.

After the annexation of the Pocket area in 1959 by the City of Sacramento, the area was slated for residential and commercial development. Suburban development of the Pocket area was inevitable because of its close proximity to downtown Sacramento and its general location in a growing metropolis. The construction of Interstate 5 in the 1970s also gave greater access and links to the community from other areas in Sacramento, further increasing the development potential for the area. Land was accessed and zoned for urban use, causing higher property taxes for farmers in the area. This forced many to sell their land to developers although some farmers did hold out for a higher price or because they wanted to continue farming for as long as they could.

The first stages of planning in the Pocket area were begun by the Lincoln and Parker Development Company in the early 1960s and were extremely innovative for their time in an age of sprawl and growth. Their plan, Greenhaven 70, signifying the future decade at that time, the 1970s, was designed to meet the social needs of people. Greenbelts with schools located along them, pedestrian overpasses and underpasses, and underground utilities were the common features of this plan to be established throughout the entire Pocket area. Over time, bankruptcy by the development company, the passage of Proposition 13, and citizen participation in the planning process led to many changes from this initial plan. Chapter 6 displays pictures of the Greenhaven/Pocket area today, reflecting its unique community character because of what took place during its development process.

One

Early Day Settlers

After the Gold Rush, families began to settle in the Pocket area, purchasing land for farming. Many had to drain the swampy land to create a suitable place for farming. The following Portuguese family names settled in the Pocket area, many of which are pictured in this chapter: Alvernaz, Amaral, Brazil, Brown, Camacho, Cambra, Correy, Curry (Correia), Da Costa, De Costa, Duarte, Dutra, Enos (Inacio), Fernandes, Ferria, Fortado, Foster, Frates (Freitas), Garcia (Gracia), Gomes, Lee (Leal), Lewis (Luiz), Lopes, Machado, Mauricio, Mello, Nevis (Neves), Pedro, Perry (Pereira), Pimentel, Pine, Prady, Rico, Rogers (Rodrigues), Rose (Rosa and Da Rosa), Sarmento, Silva, Silveria, Simas, Souza, Tash, Vargas, Waxon, and Williams. Non-Portuguese family names who settled in the Pocket area include Berkencamp, Coleman, Curran, Gosling, Lods, Klotz, Mc Nassal, Meier, Reed, and Zacharias. A sizeable number of Japanese families also settled in the Pocket area after World War I, and the children of these families can be seen in the school pictures in Chapter 4. Intermarriage between families who settled in the Pocket area was common, especially among Portuguese families who settled in the community.

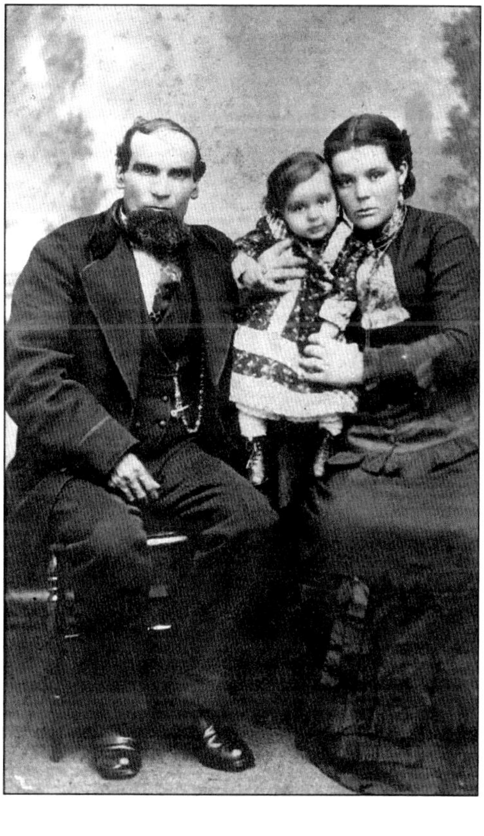

Manuel da Rosa Garcia and Lenora Silveria Garcia With Their Daughter Mary, c. 1879. Mr. Garcia, whose original name was Gracia, bought a ranch of 70 acres with his brother Jose (Joe), located at the first turn of Old Pocket Road. Garcia Bend Park in the South Pocket area is named after these early day Pocket settlers. (Courtesy of P.H.C.S., donated by Iva Womble)

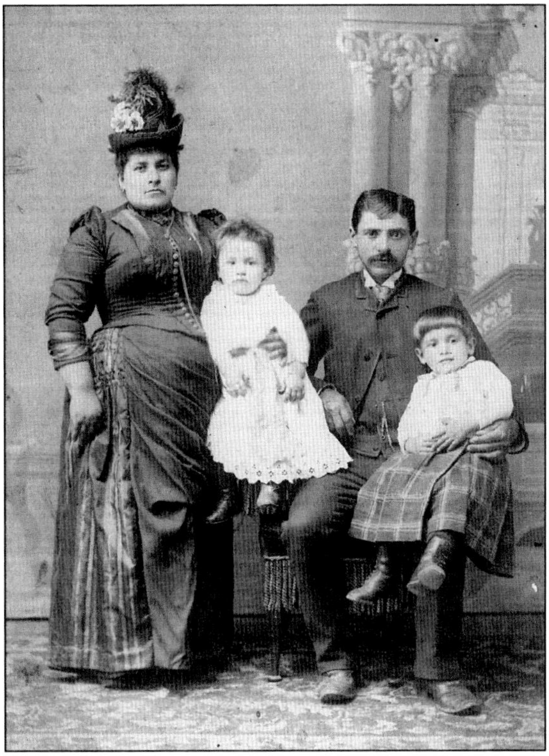

Francisco J. Luiz with His First Wife Mary Florence Rose, Who Died at 46 Years of Age. Mr. Luiz came to California at age 19, settling in the Pocket area. The family name was subsequently changed to Lewis. The children in the photo may be their grandchildren from their daughter Minnie (Lewis) Vargas. (Courtesy of P.H.C.S.)

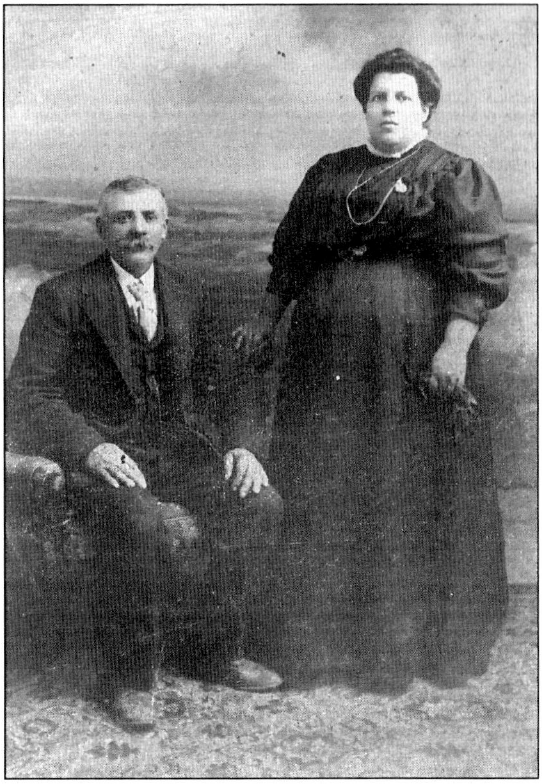

Francisco J. Luiz (Lewis) in Later Years with His Sister Anna. Frank Lewis at one time had three ranches in the Pocket area: one was 200 acres next to the Dutra ranch, the second was 100 acres, and the third was 36 acres. He also had a 300-acre home ranch. He donated two acres of his ranch land for the Portuguese hall and church. (Courtesy of P.H.C.S., donated by Tony Dutra)

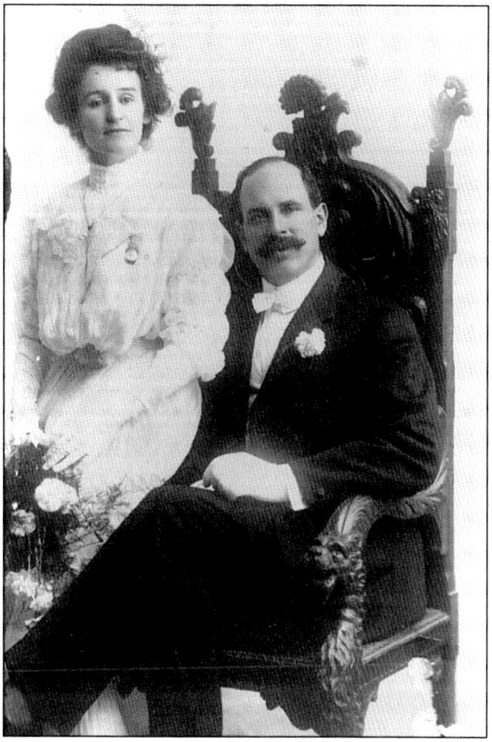

Manuel Lewis with His Wife Anna Seamas, Whose Family Owned Grangers Dairy in the Pocket Area. Manuel was the son of Frank Lewis. He owned a bar on the corner of Second and L Streets in downtown Sacramento. (Courtesy of P.H.C.S.)

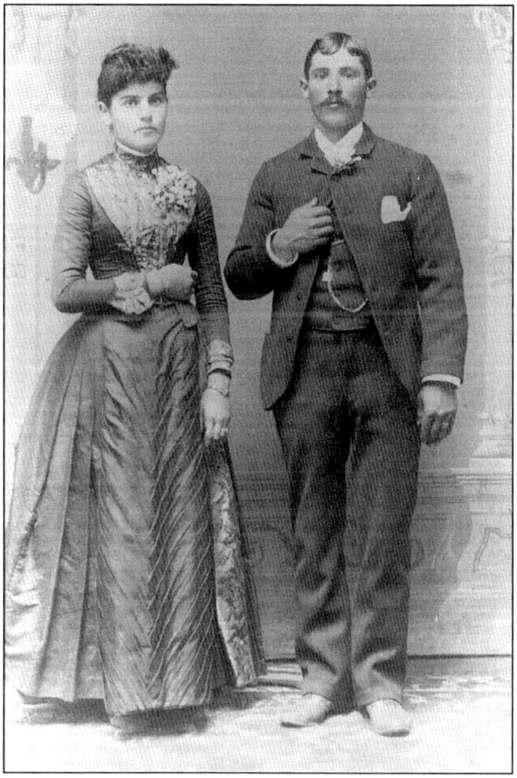

Manuel Lewis, Brother of Frank Lewis, at 23 Years of Age with 14-Year-Old Emma Perry in 1889. Emma was the daughter of pioneer Pocket settler Antone Perry. Lewis Park, located in the northern Pocket area on Park Rivera Way is named after this couple. (Courtesy of P.H.C.S.)

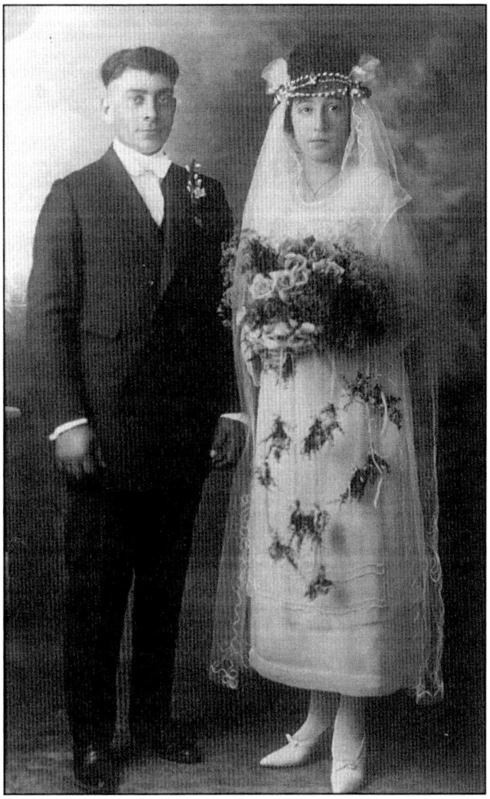

Manuel Joseph Lewis, the Son of Frank Lewis, with Mary Alice Souza on Their Wedding Day on June 17, 1920. Manuel acquired his father's second Pocket area ranch of 100 acres. Mary Alice Souza's father, Antone Machado Souza, had a 15-acre ranch next to Frank Lewis' pear orchard and a small ranch of 17 acres next to the Pocket canal. Mr. Souza helped farm the Lewis home ranch. (Courtesy of P.H.C.S., Mary Souza Lewis collection)

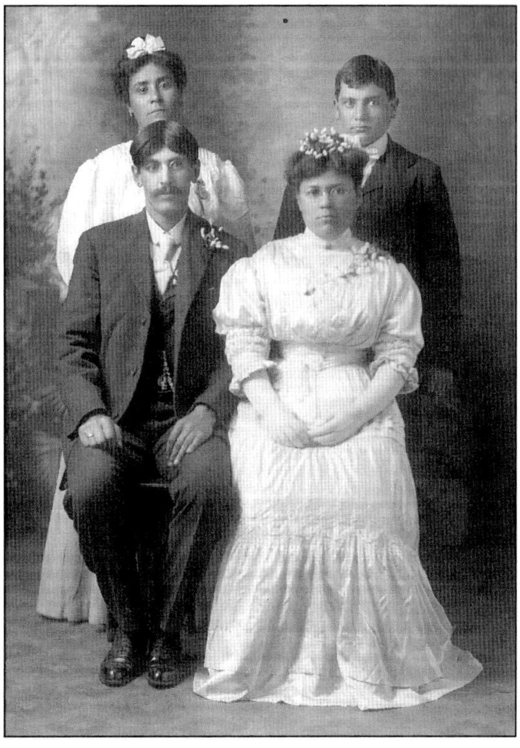

Mary Lewis Frates and Joe Lewis (standing) with Frank Vargas and Minnie Lewis (seated) in 1900. Mary, Joe, and Minnie were the children of Frank Lewis. Joe Lewis acquired his father's 200-acre property next to the Dutra ranch. (Courtesy of P.H.C.S.)

Jess (Jessie) Lewis, the Brother of Frank Lewis Sr. He was a neighbor next to the Joe F. "Milhomens" Silva ranch in the South Pocket area. Dolores Silva Greenslate remembered that he gave a goose every Christmas to her family and was very well known in the community. (Courtesy of P.H.C.S., information provided by Dolores Silva Greenslate)

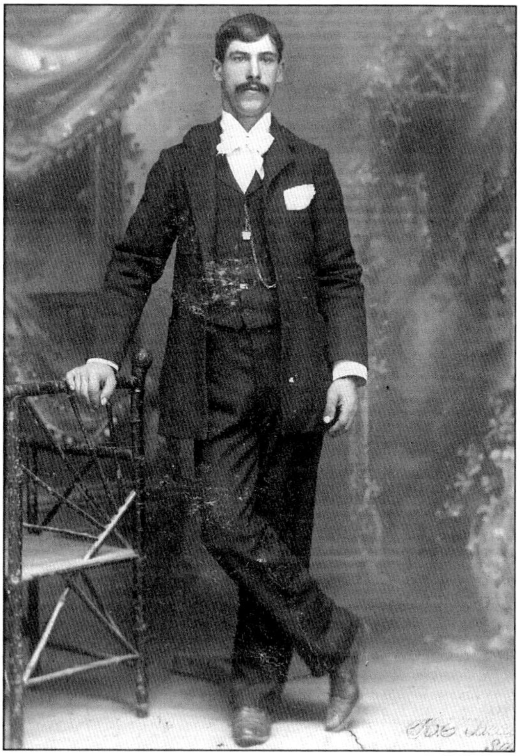

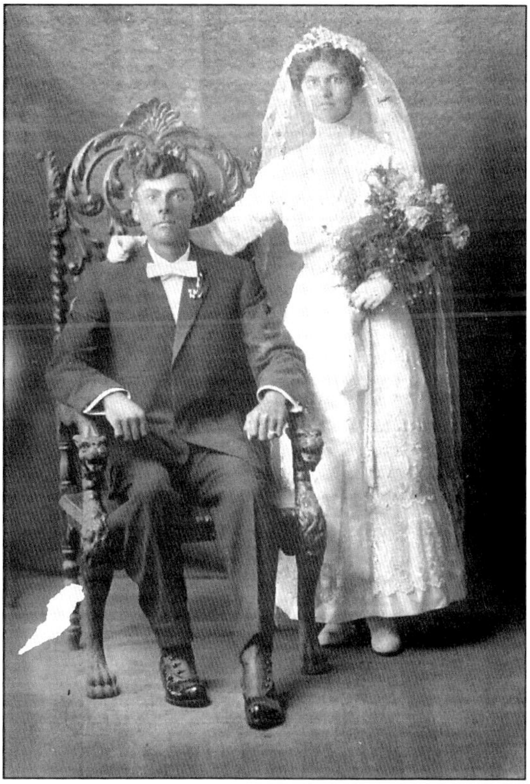

Margaret Rodgers, Daughter of Albert Rogers and Rose Gear, with Her First Husband From the Lee Family. She later married into the Machado family. Her parents had a small ranch of 18 acres where today Park Riviera Way intersects with Pocket Road. Margaret kept four of the acres, including her parent's home, an old wooden structure that stood in the area, for many years after suburban development. All of her children were born there and she lived there until her death. (Courtesy of P.H.C.S.)

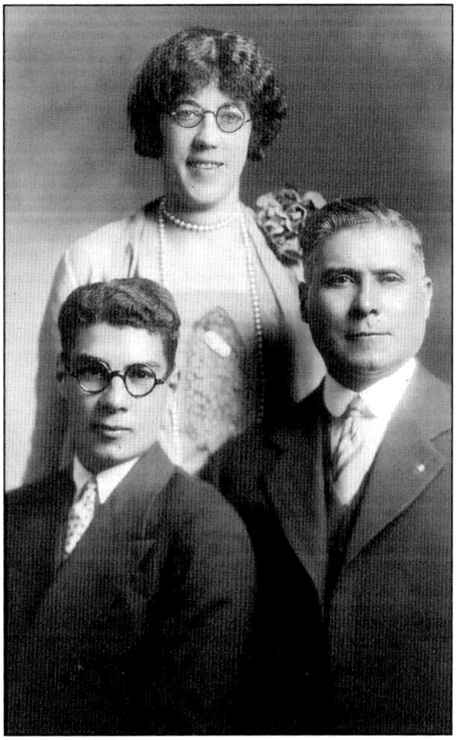

Frank J. Lewis Jr., Son of Frank Lewis Sr., with His Wife Clara Marshall Lewis From Newcastle and Son Jack About 1925. Frank J. Lewis Jr. was born in the Pocket area on August 11, 1879. After his father's death in 1918, Frank and his brother Manuel bought a 285-acre ranch in the Pocket, which was part of the old McNassal ranch. It is located where Renfree Park is today. (Courtesy of P.H.C.S.)

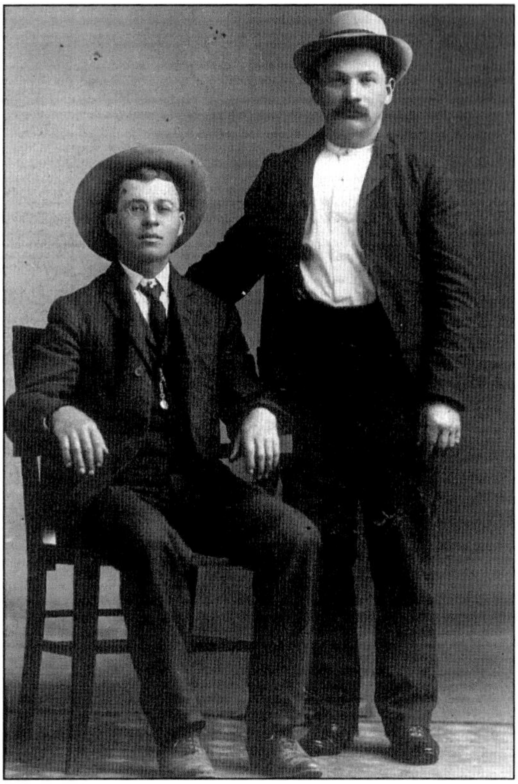

At Right, the Carpenter of the Riverside/Pocket Area, Manuel Faria Dutra, Nicknamed "Chopinho." Chopinho was a builder, repairman, and general handyman who used length of sticks to measure instead of a ruler. He also used many nails on his projects so nothing he built ever came down. He was known to build oratorios, or small chapel shrines in local Portuguese families homes. (Courtesy of P.H.C.S., donated by Tony Dutra)

John Luiz Silva with his Wife Nancy on Their Wedding Day in December 17, 1904. Mr. Silva purchased 100-plus acres from Frank Rico in the Pocket area in 1916. He farmed the property into the 1950s, when he ultimately retired and his sons took over. The property is located on the present day Casa del Sol housing development. (Courtesy of P.H.C.S., Emily Silva Souza collection).

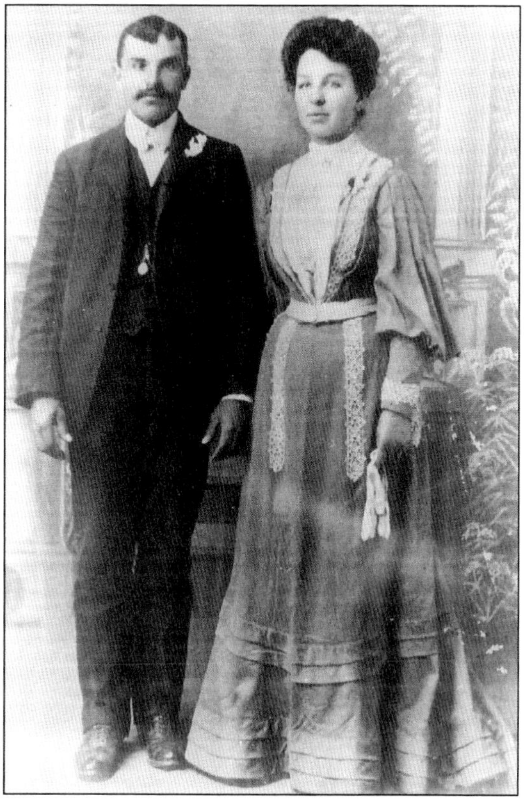

John L. and Nancy Silva Around 1922 with Their Children. From left to right, the children are Mary, Tony, Manuel, King, Dolores (on Mr. Silva's lap), John Jr., Anna, and Madeline. (Courtesy of P.H.C.S., donated by Emily Silva Souza).

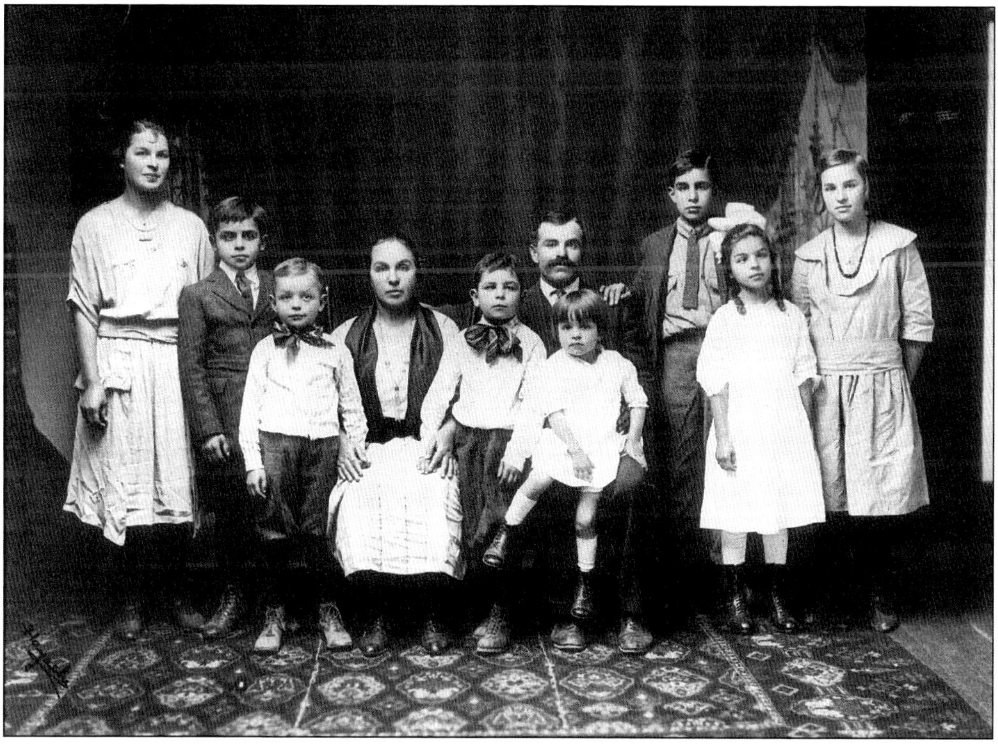

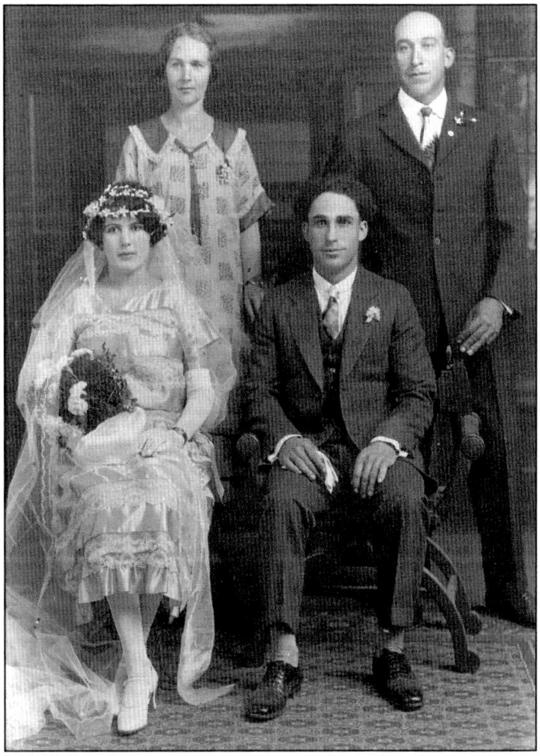

Mr. and Mrs. Tavares (Back Row) with Mary Marks and Faustino Silva on Their Wedding Day in November 7, 1925. Faustino Silva had a slaughterhouse near the northern intersection of where Riverside Blvd. and Park Riviera Way is today. He put in the first pipe-irrigation system in the area. (Courtesy of P.H.C.S., donated by Marie Zampathas)

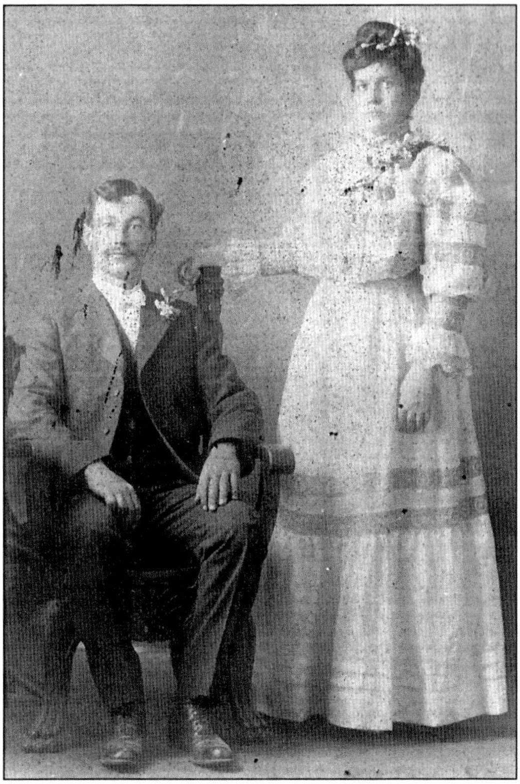

Antone Perry Dutra with Wife Louise Florence Lewis c. 1908. Louise Florence Lewis was the daughter of Frank Lewis Sr. Mr. Dutra bought 10 acres of land in 1907 in the Pocket area near the pumping station from Manuel Peters. He was nicknamed "Peru" (Portuguese for turkey) because he raised them on his ranch. (Courtesy of P.H.C.S., donated by Mary Dutra Rosa)

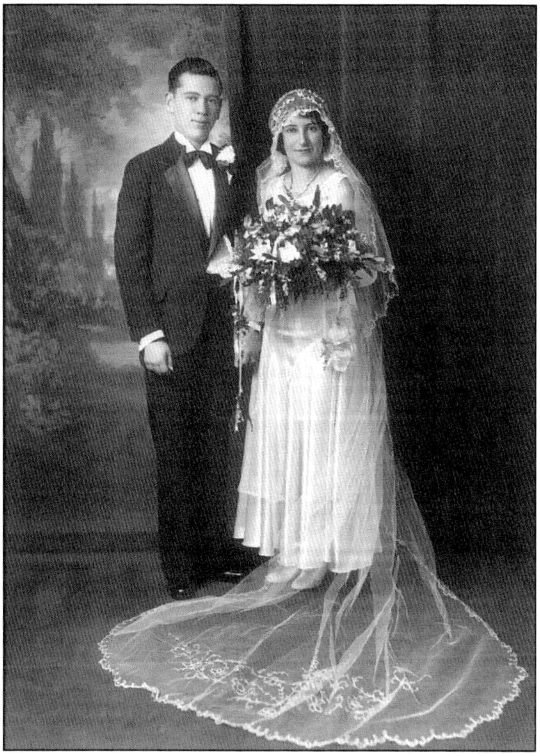

Manuel Garcia Rosa Jr. With Wife Mary F. Dutra on Their Wedding Day in October 19, 1930. Mary is the daughter of Antone Dutra and Louise Lewis. Manuel Rosa Jr.'s father, Manuel Garcia Rosa, farmed land on the property originally known as Munger Lake. Today, this is Reichmuth Park. (Courtesy of P.H.C.S., donated by Mary Dutra Rosa)

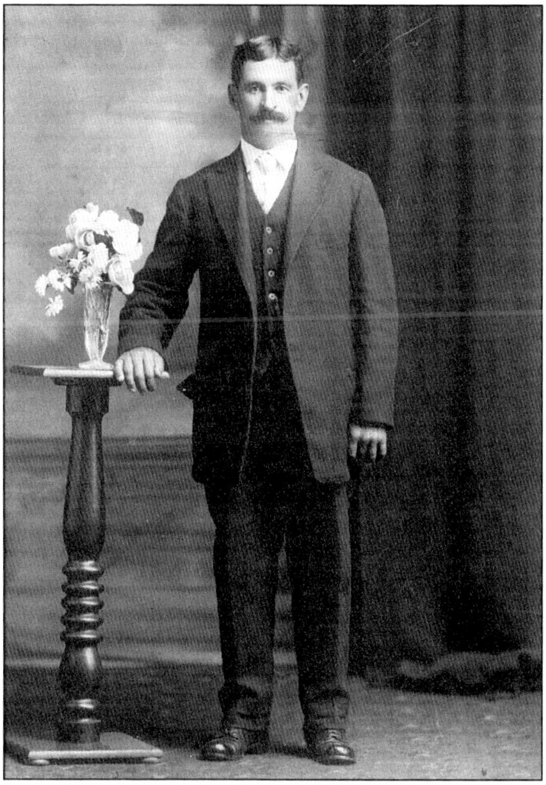

John R. Silva, c. 1915. A settler in the Pocket area, he was nicknamed "Joao do Pico," John of the Pico or "Peak" (one of the nine Azores Islands). Mr. Silva was a bachelor who drowned in the nearby Sacramento River in 1923. He was in his 40s. (Courtesy of P.H.C.S., donated by King Silva)

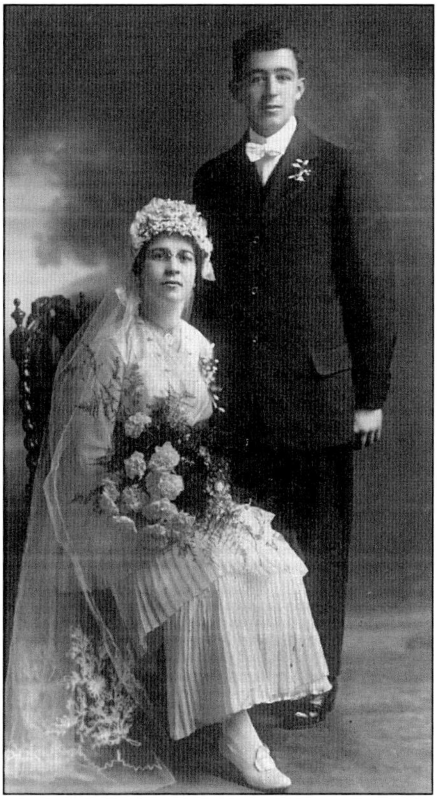

Tony Pimentel and Maggie Valine on Their Wedding Day on June 21, 1916. Mr. Pimentel was the son of Antone Pimentel and Anna Leonora Silveria, widow of Manuel da Rosa Garcia. Tony operated Pimentel's Ingelside Café, later known as Pimentel's Saloon, which today is known as The Trap. (Courtesy of P.H.C.S., donated by Maggie Pimentel)

Antone Pereira Rodrigues (Perry) and Maria de Gloria Silva Perry in 1890. A year after they were married in 1867, they joined the Da Rosas in a joint purchase of 45 acres of river bottom swampland in the Pocket area for $2000. Both families, through hard work and dedication, were able to clear and drain the swampland to produce fertile land. (Courtesy of P.H.C.S.)

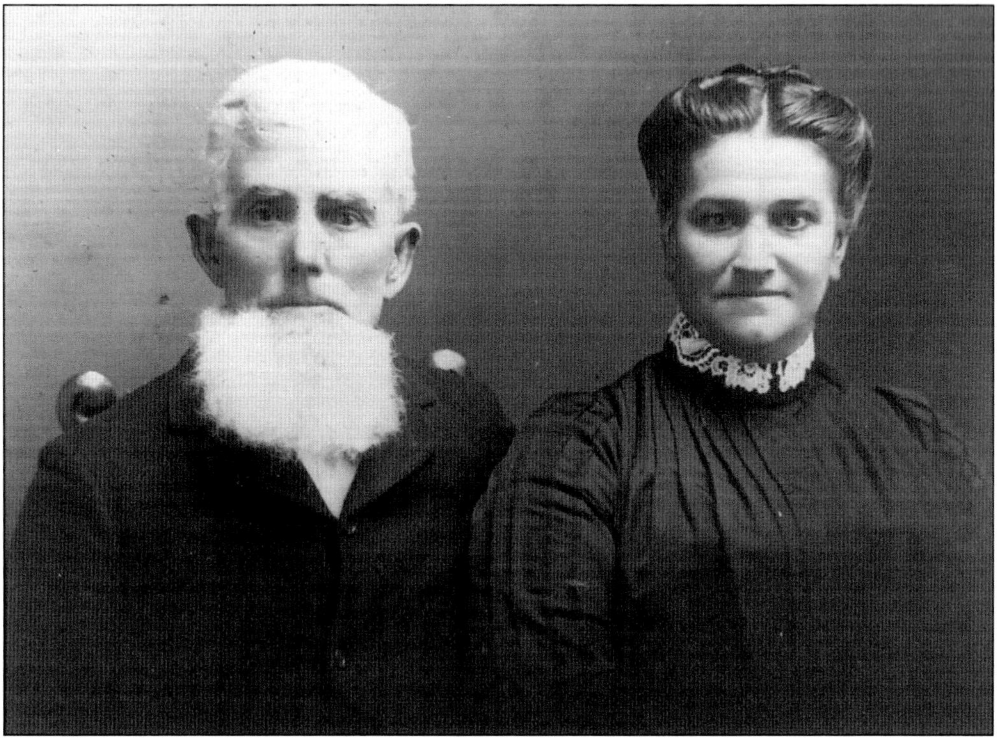

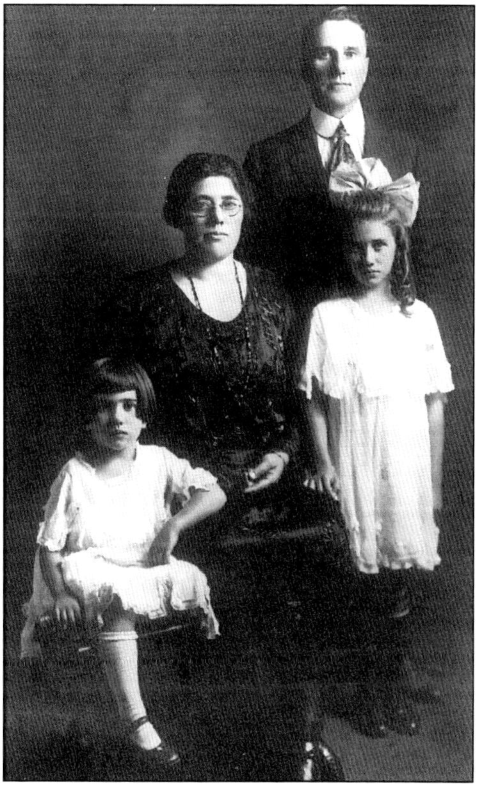

Mr. and Mrs. Joseph Perry with Their Daughters Evelyn (standing) and Lorraine (sitting), c. 1919. Mrs. Josie Perry was from the Marshall family in Newcastle. Joseph Perry was the son of Antone and Maria Perry and worked with his father on their Pocket area ranch. (Courtesy of P.H.C.S)

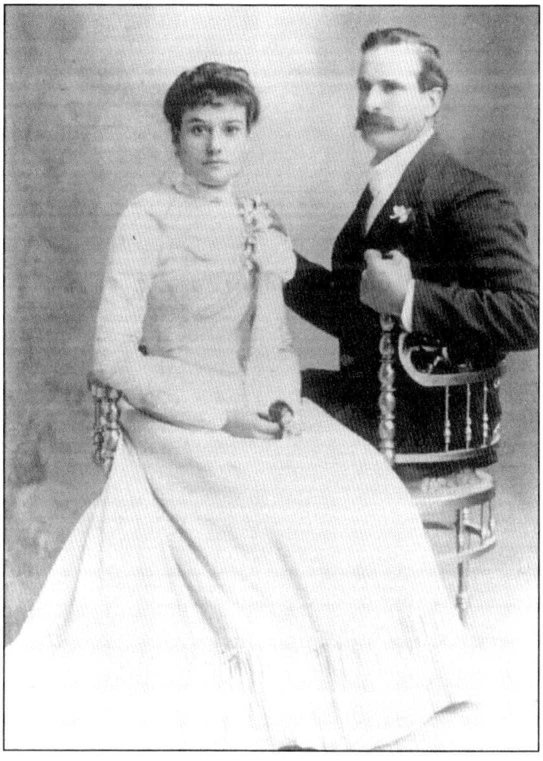

The Wedding Portrait of John Joseph Machado and Clara Perry on November 17, 1900. Clara Perry was one of the daughters of Antone and Mary Perry. John first worked on a haypress in the Pocket area and later purchased 53 acres of land with his brother-in-law Joseph Azevedo Sr. in the Riverside area. (Courtesy of P.H.C.S., donated by Dolores Silva Greenslate)

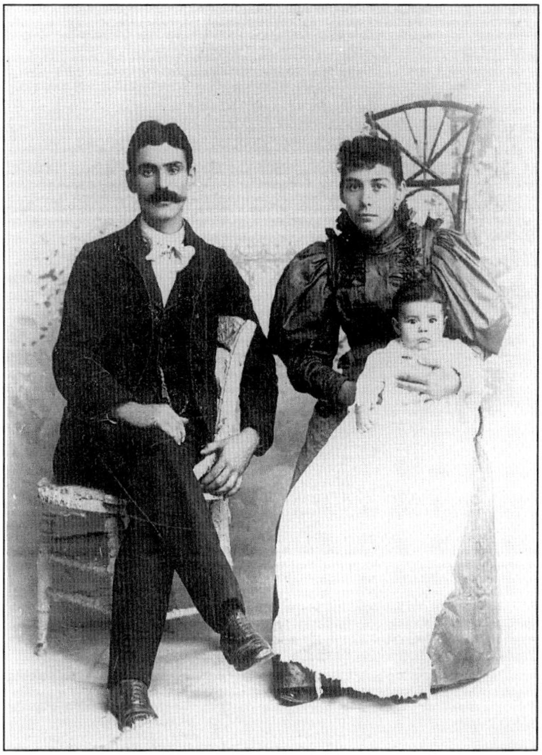

Antone Perry Jr. with His Wife Amelia Bettencourt and Their First Child, Minnie. This photo was taken in 1896. Antone Jr. was the son of Antone and Mary Perry. (Courtesy of P.H.C.S., donated by Lawrence Perry)

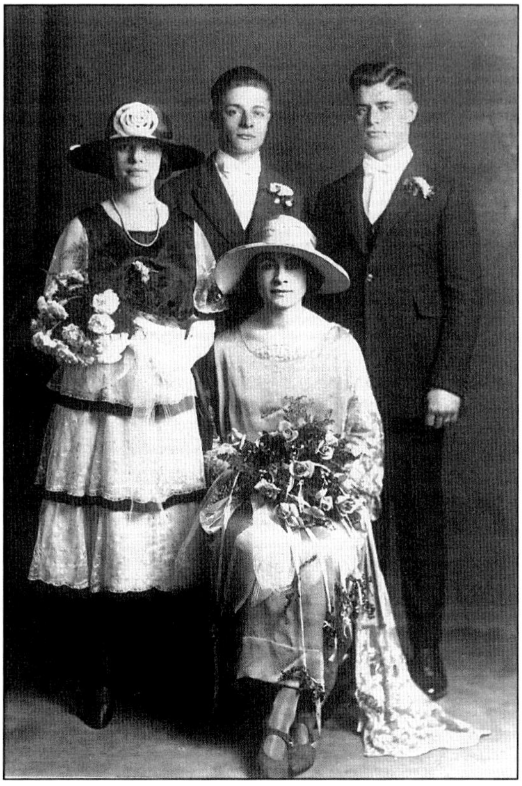

A Wedding Photo. Pictured here, from left to right, are Marie Silveria Teixeira, John M. Silva, Mamie G. Machado, and Victor D. Silva in 1923. Mamie G. Machado, daughter of Clara Perry and John Machado, married Victor Silva. (Courtesy of P.H.C.S.)

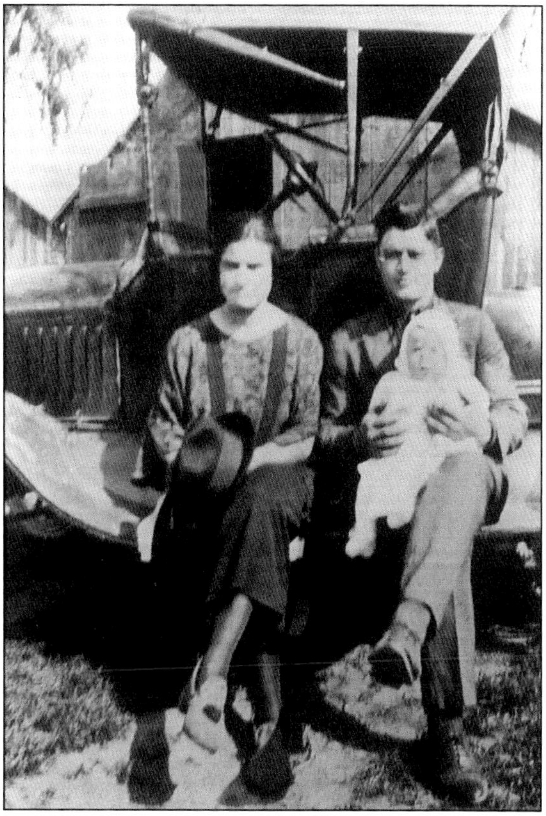

Victor Dias Silva with His Wife Mamie Machado Silva and Son Marvin. This picture was taken at the home ranch of John Joseph Machado where Mr. Silva and his family lived in the second house. In the background is their 1922 Model T Ford. (Courtesy of P.H.C.S.)

The Machado Family on Their Ranch in 1925. Pictured here, from left to right, are Albert, Clara, John, Rosaline, and Joseph. (Courtesy of P.H.C.S.)

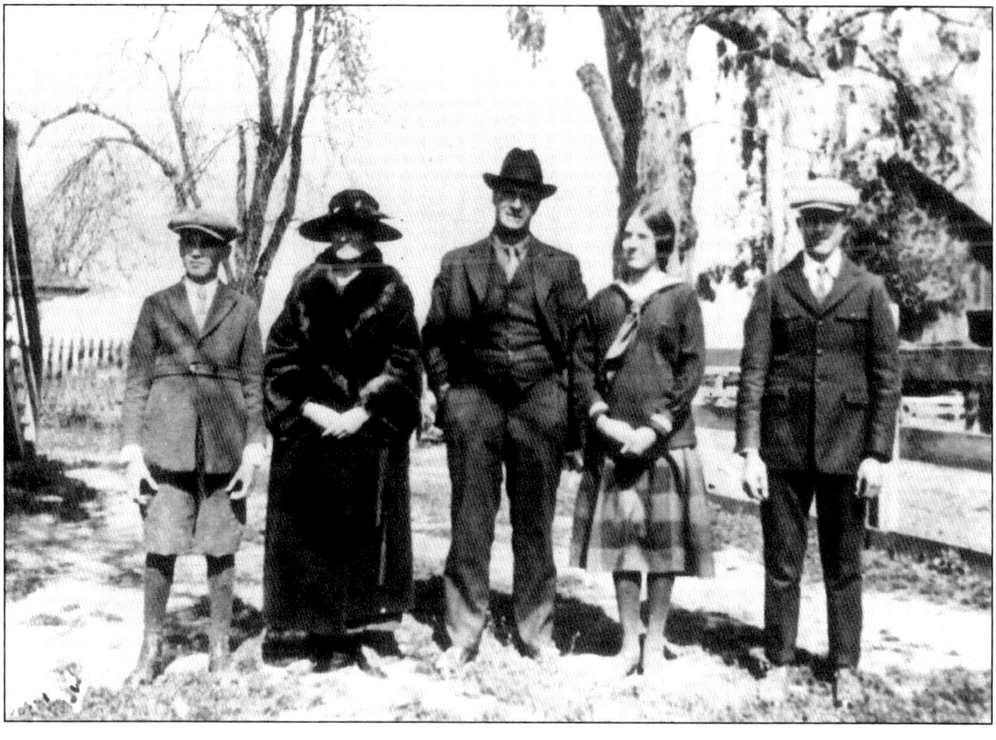

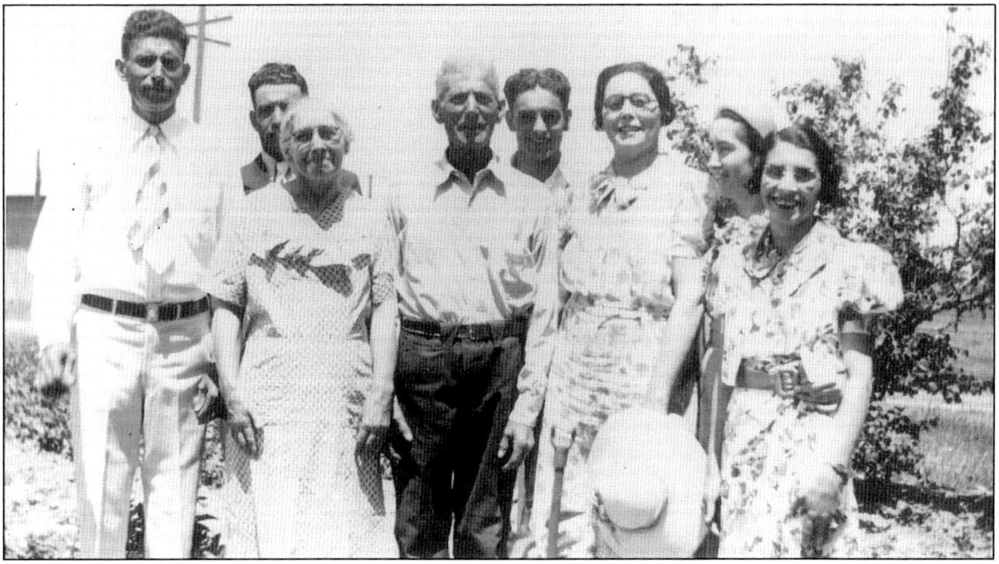

THE PERRY FAMILY IN THE 1930S. Pictured here, from left to right, are Bill, Alfred, Amelia and Tony Perry (Rodrigues), Lawrence, Minnie, Madeline, and Olivia. (Courtesy of P.H.C.S.)

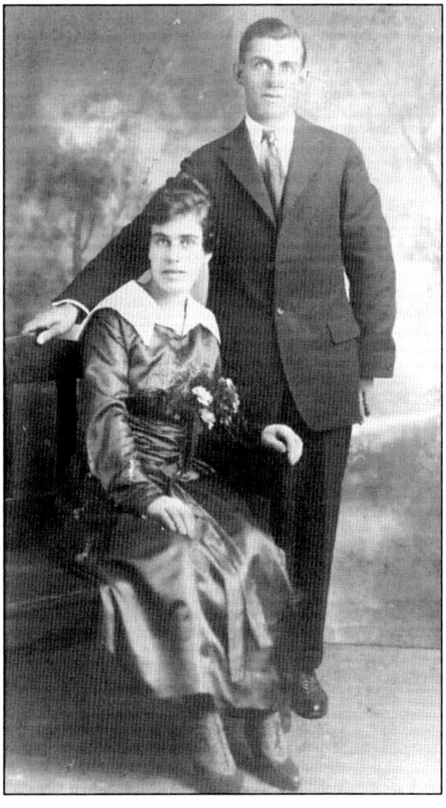

FRANK ROGERS AND MARY SILVA IN 1917. Frank Rogers was the son of Albert and Rose Gear. He had a twin brother named George and both were born on their parents' Pocket area ranch in 1896. The brothers operated a trucking business and Frank later bought a 43-acre ranch in the Pocket area. Mary Agnes Silva was the daughter of Antone L. and Maria Silva from the Pocket. (Courtesy of P.H.C.S., donated by Lorraine Valine)

JOHN GONSALVES RICO WITH HIS WIFE DELFINA SIMONS RICO AND BROTHER JOHN GONSALVES RICO ON HIS WEDDING DAY IN GUSTINE, CALIFORNIA IN 1920. Mr. Rico arrived in the Riverside/Pocket community in 1886 and farmed in the area. His brother John Gonsalves Rico married Alzora Lopes. (Courtesy of P.H.C.S.)

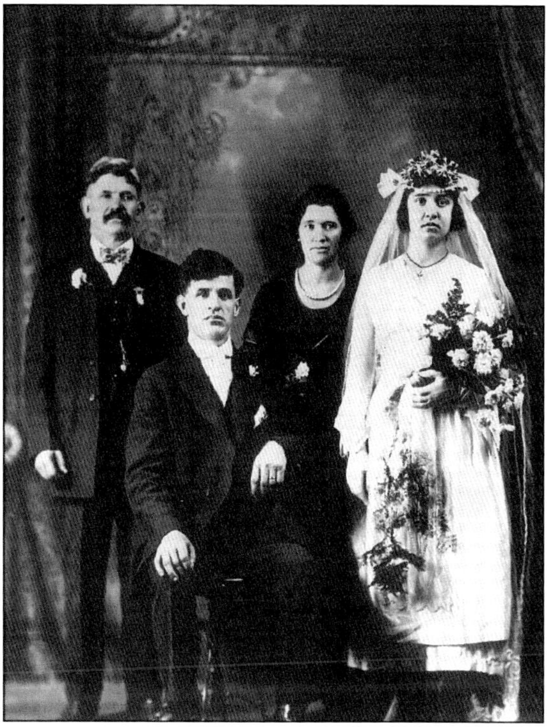

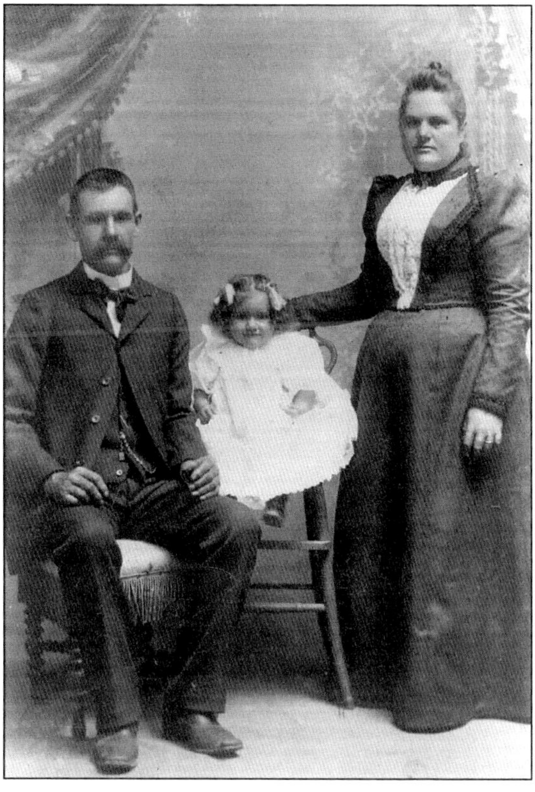

JOSE SILVEIRA WITH WIFE EMELIA LEAL SILVEIRA AND THEIR OLDEST CHILD, DAUGHTER MAMIE SILVEIRA ABOUT 1899 OR 1900. Jose and Emelia had a 40-acre farm in the North Pocket area adjoining the Nevis family ranch. (Courtesy of P.H.C.S.)

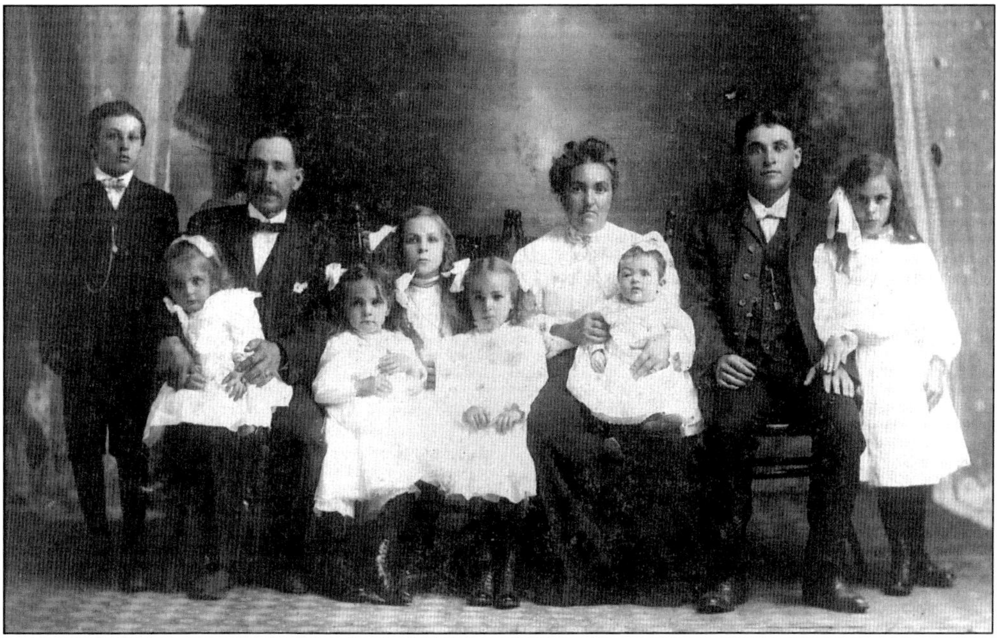

The Joseph F. Silva "Milhomens" Family in 1908. Joe and Mary Terra Vargas came to the Pocket from Faial, one of the nine Azores Islands, in 1896 with their 10-year-old son, Joe F. Silva Jr. In 1903, they bought a 75-acre ranch in the South Pocket area, where they lived for 48 years. (Courtesy of P.H.C.S., donated by Marie Dutra Gambrel)

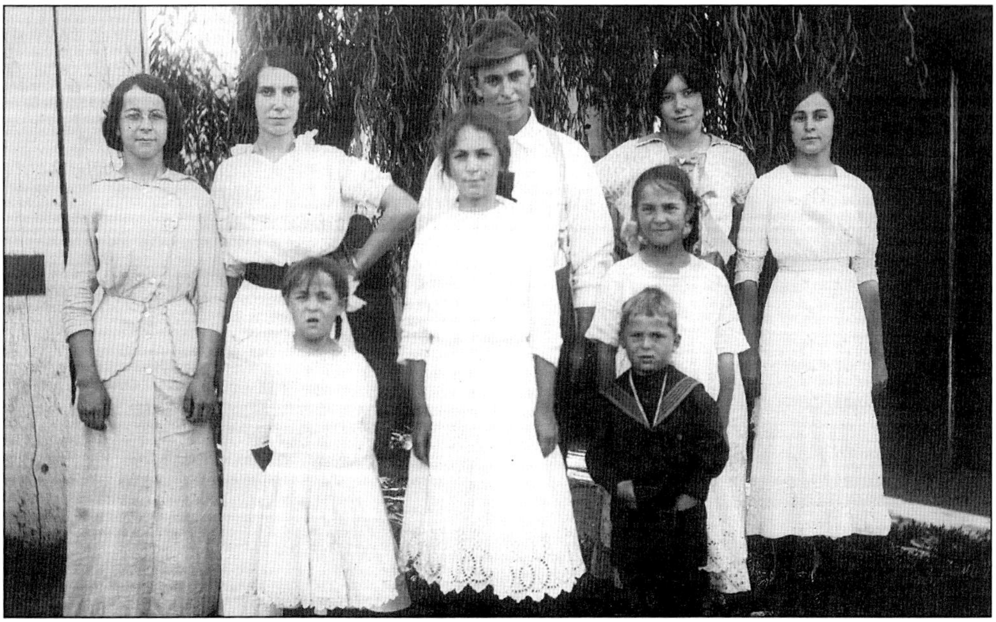

The Silva "Milhomens" Family Children and the Fernandes Children on the Fernandes Farm About 1915. Pictured here, from left to right, are as follows: (back row) Mary L. Silva, Mary Fernandes, Joe F. Silva Jr., Louise Fernandes, and Anna Silva; (second row) Minnie Silva, Eleanora Silva, and Angelina Silva. The boy in the front is Manuel Silva. (Courtesy of P.H.C.S., donated by Marie Dutra Gambrel)

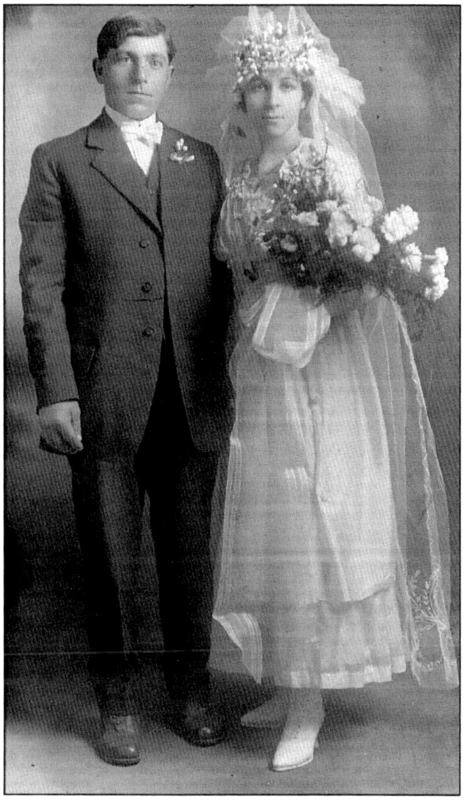

MANUEL DUTRA AND MARY SILVA DUTRA ON THEIR WEDDING DAY ON JANUARY 15, 1917. Mary was the daughter of Joseph F. Silva and Mary Terra Vargas. Manuel Dutra came to the Pocket area on May 24, 1909, and worked for Joe Lewis from 1909 to 1912, milking 30 cows for $1 a day. (Courtesy of P.H.C.S., donated by Marie Dutra Gambrel)

THE WEDDING PICTURE OF ANTHONY LUIS SILVA AND MARIA NEVES IN APRIL 1899. Mr. Silva bought 102 acres of swampland in the Pocket in an area full of tulies and brush around 1906. Before marriage, Maria Neves immigrated to the Pocket area in the early 1880s with her cousin and lived with the Costa family. (Courtesy of P.H.C.S., donated by Tony Silva)

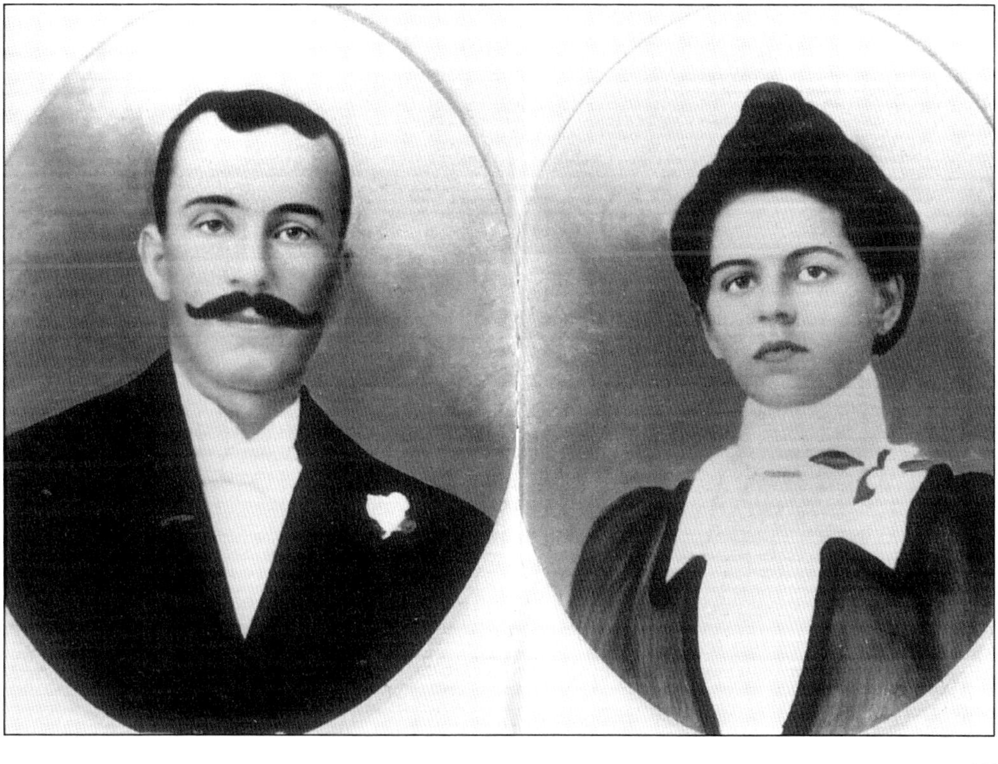

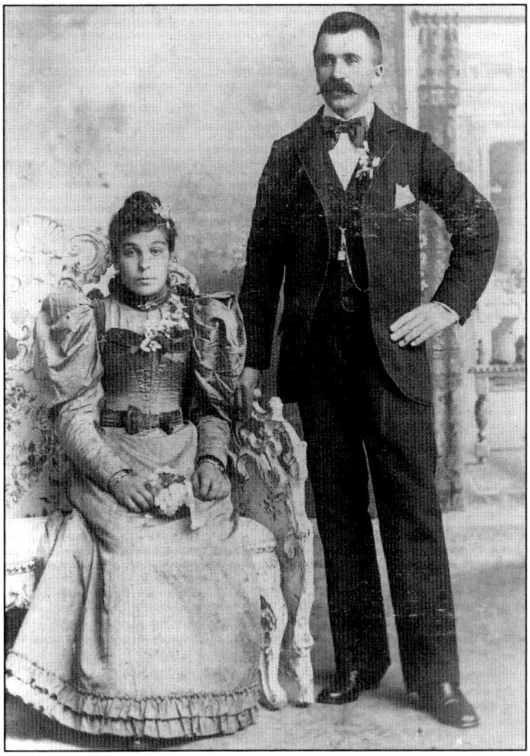

Manuel R. Vargas and Mary Garcia in About 1896. Mary Garcia was the daughter of Manuel da Roza Garcia and Anna Leonora Silveria. (Courtesy of P.H.C.S., donated by Iva Womble)

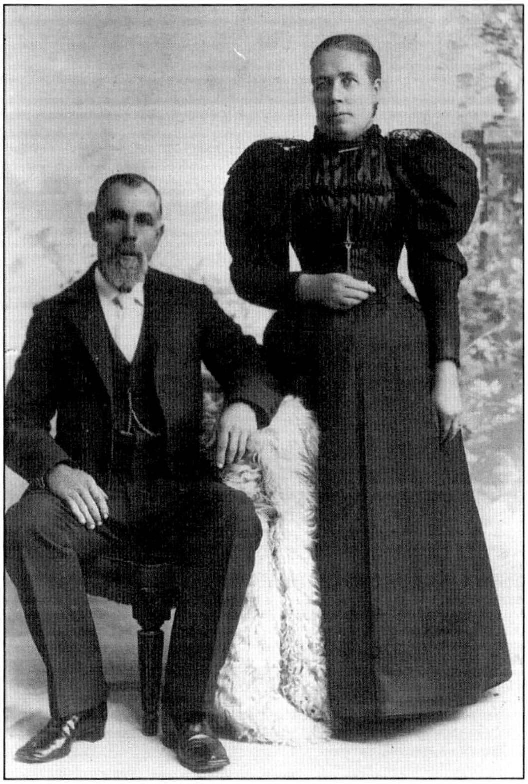

Jose and Maria Isabelle Souza. They may have been among the first settlers in the Pocket in the mid 1800s. They were farmers and owned a number of acres in the Pocket area during its initial settlement. Dolores Silva Greenslate also remembers the Souzas had big surreys, in which they got dressed up to go to church and were transported by carriages and horses. (Courtesy of P.H.C.S., information provided by Dolores Silva Greenslate)

THE LOPES AND VIEIRA FAMILY IN 1917. Pictured here, from left to right, are as follows: (back row) Manuel Vieira Pedro, John Vieira Pedro, Joe T. Lopes, and Anna Paulino Lopes; (front row) Gloria Vieira Pedro, Manuel T. Lopes, and Joe T. Lopes Jr. The Lopes family home still stands today just before the Sacramento River begins to meander on Riverside Blvd. near the Trap. (Courtesy of P.H.C.S.)

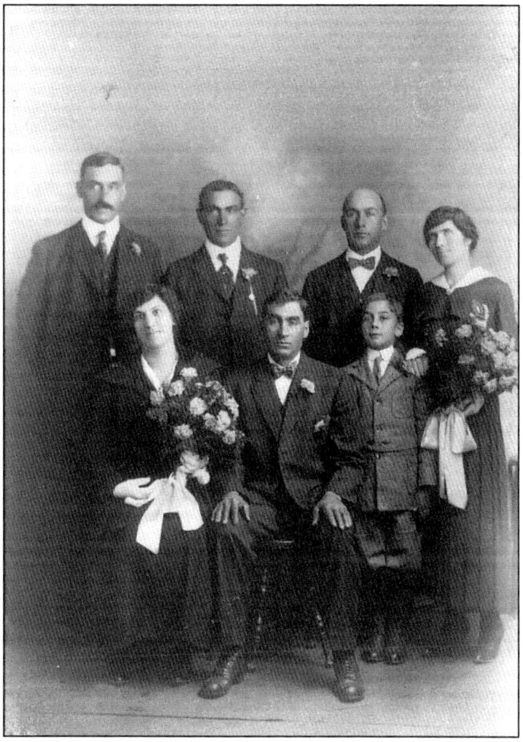

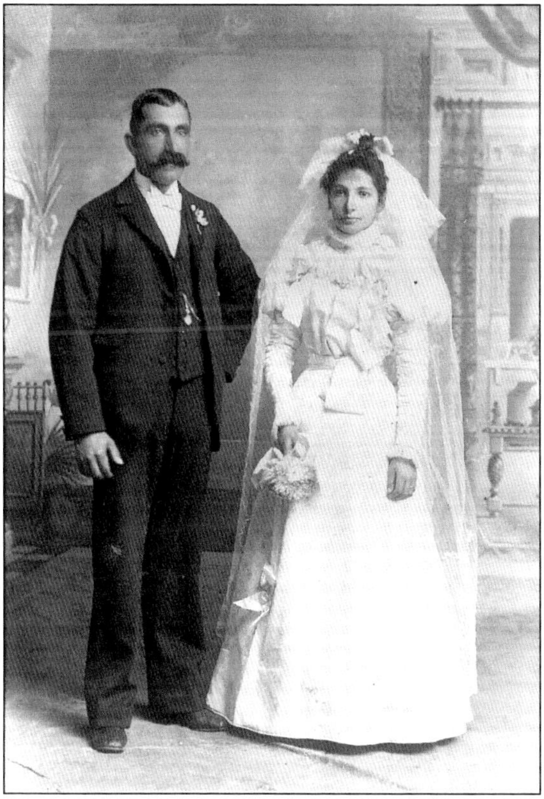

VITAL SILVA FORTADO AND MARY AGNES SILVA ON THEIR WEDDING DAY IN NOVEMBER 1897. Mr. Fortado was employed at the Brickyard and they lived in a small house provided by the Sacramento Brick Company. They later moved to a 40 acre farm in 1900 on Riverside Blvd. where the Trap stands now. (Courtesy of P.H.C.S., donated by Emma Fortado James Buckley)

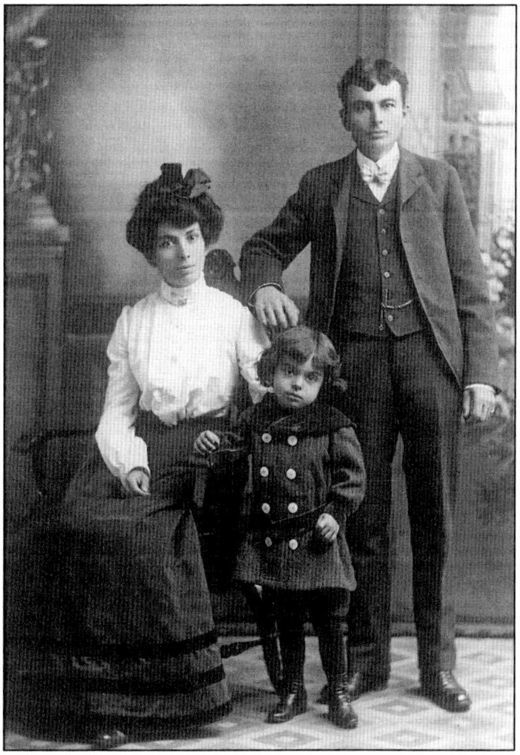

FRANK AND MINNIE (BROWN) ENOS WITH SON ALFRED IN 1901. Mr. Enos started a service station about 1921 and had three gas pumps. It was the only service station in the Riverside/Pocket area. (Courtesy of P.H.C.S., donated by George Enos)

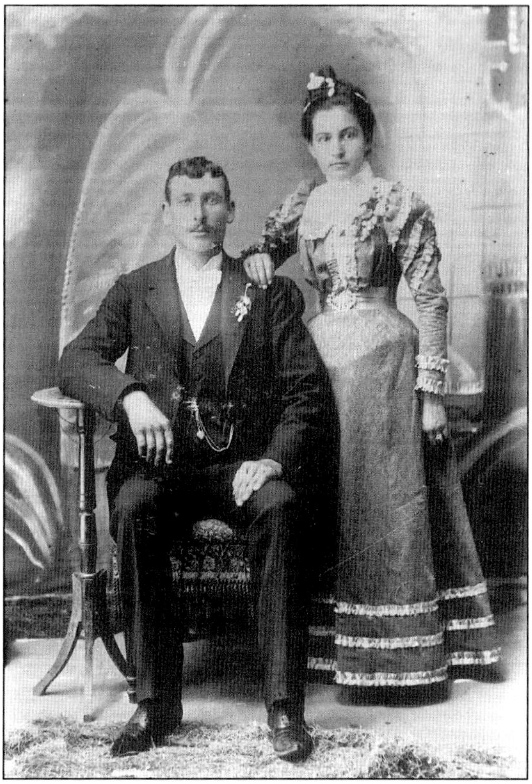

MANUEL FOSTER AND MARY VALINE ABOUT 1900. In 1916, they bought the Gosling Farm in the Pocket area, now the site of Hellenic Place, a Greek retirement home in the South Pocket area. They were known to live at the very end of the Pocket, near the Dutras. Mary Valine was the sister of Maggie Pimentel of the Pimentel family who lived next to the Trap. (Courtesy of P.H.C.S., donated by Grace Rose Freitas)

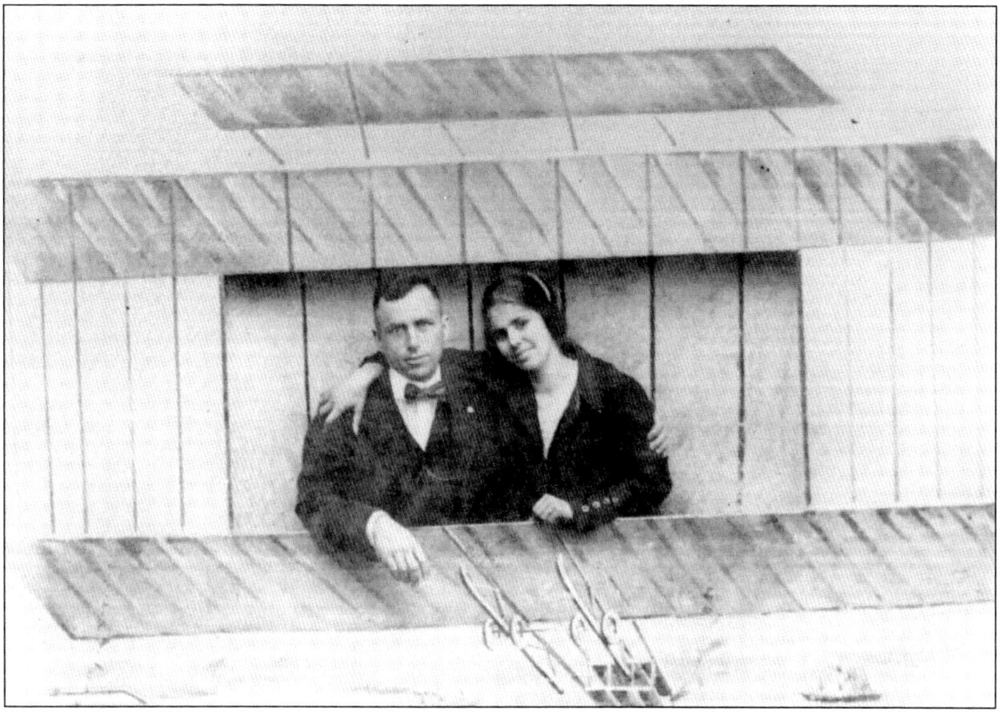

Tony and Mary Facha Frates on Their Honeymoon in Newcastle, California. Mary was the daughter of Frank Lewis Sr. After marrying, they lived and farmed on his 36-acre ranch located in the North Pocket area. Mr. Frates later acquired the land after his father-in-law's death. (Courtesy of P.H.C.S.)

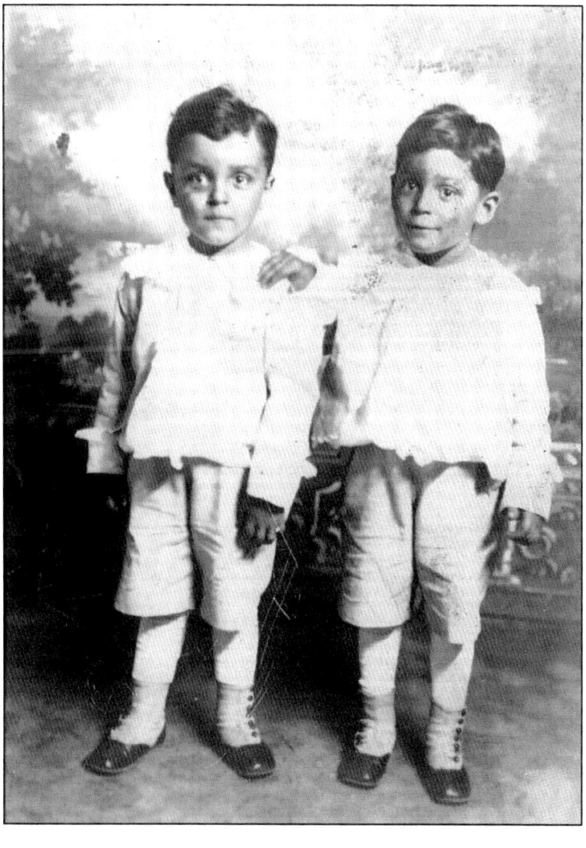

The Twin Sons of Antone Facha Frates and Mary Florence Lewis, Jessie and Joe Frates in 1919 or 1920. Both sons continued to farm their father's land until 1962 when the property was sold for subdivision. (Courtesy of P.H.C.S.)

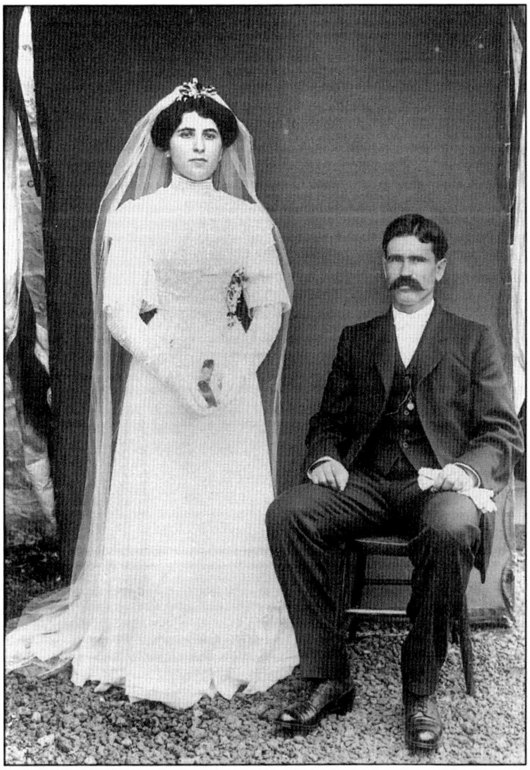

ANTONIO G. DA ROSA AND MARIA FILOMENA SIMAS ON THEIR WEDDING DAY IN JULY 1910. Mr. Da Rosa purchased land in 1915 on the levee side a mile south of the Conley station in Riverside. A store named Riverside Grocery and a house were subsequently built on the property. (Courtesy of P.H.C.S., donated by Alice Rose Powell)

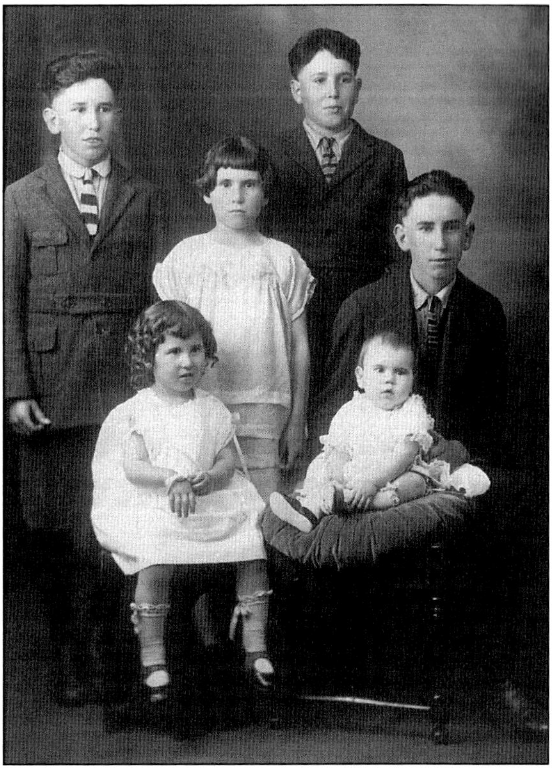

THE CHILDREN OF ANTONIO G. DA ROSA AND MARIA FILOMENA SIMAS IN 1925. Pictured here, from left to right, are as follows: (back) Francis and Irvin; (center) Alice and Elmer; and (front) Elvira and Marie. The eldest son Elmer was killed in 1952 in Iwo Jima, Japan, during a flight in an F 84G Thunderjet when refueling in the air was being experimented. (Courtesy of P.H.C.S, Alice Da Rosa Powell collection)

MANUEL AND MARY NEVIS OF THE RIVERSIDE/POCKET AREA IN 1894. Manuel was the son of Joseph C. Nevis who purchased the 95-acre Reed ranch in the North Pocket area for $2,000 in federal gold coins. Manuel continued to farm his father's property until 1939 or 1940. (Courtesy of P.H.C.S., donated by Tony Dutra)

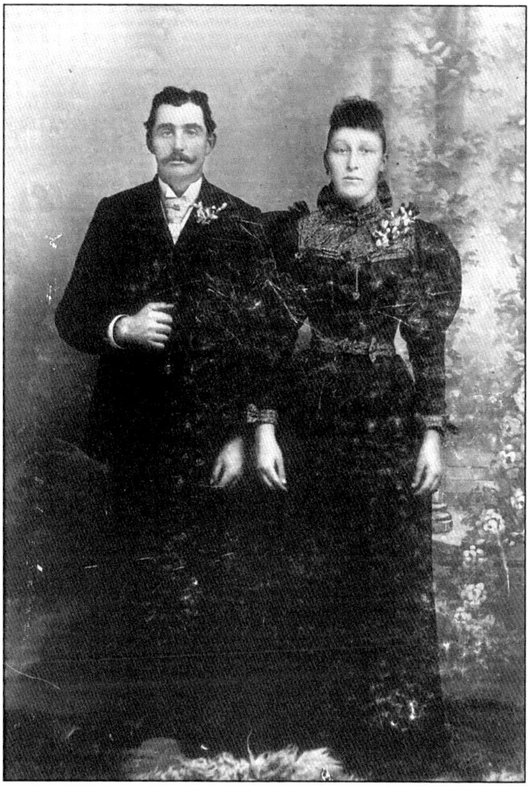

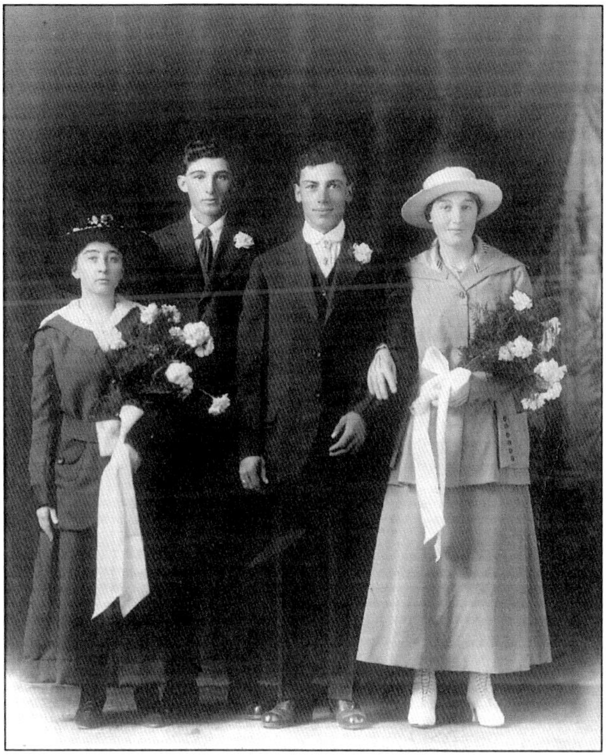

A FAMILY WEDDING. From left to right are Mary Curry, Manuel Nevis, Manuel Maurico, and Carrie Nevis Maurico. (Courtesy of P.H.C.S.)

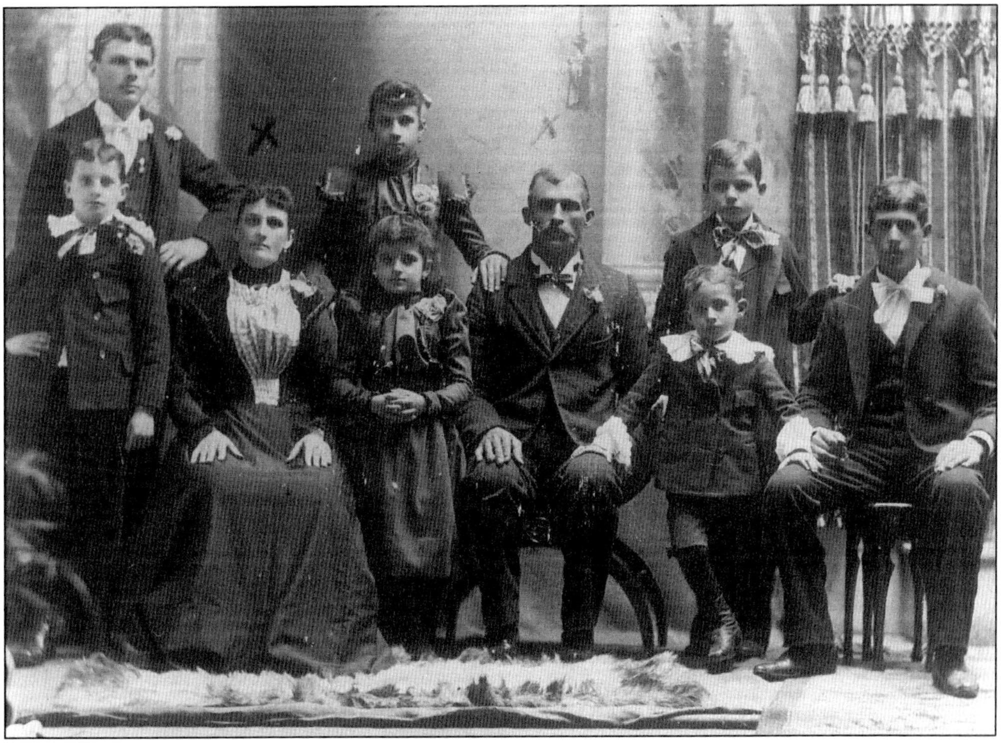

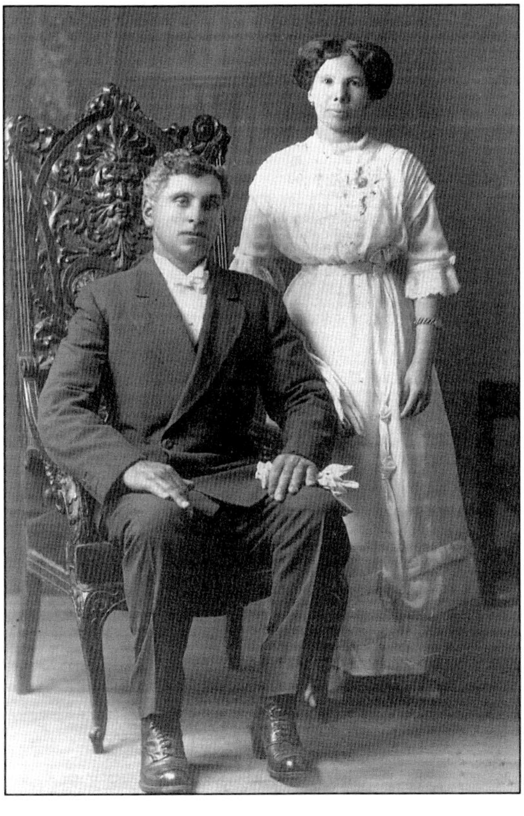

THE ANTONE MACHADO COREY FAMILY OF RIVERSIDE ABOUT 1895. Pictured here, from left to right, are as follows: (front row) Frank, mother Mary (Enos) Corey, Lucille, father Antone Machado Corey, George, and Tony; (back row) Manuel, Mary, and Jim. The Corey family settled in a home across the road from the Frank Enos home and gas station. (Courtesy of P.H.C.S.)

MANUEL SILVEIRA ALVERNAZ JR. AND MARIE DO ROZARIO SEAMAS ON THEIR WEDDING DAY IN FEBRUARY 1912. Mr. Alvernaz first lived with the Manuel Rosa family in their home on the levee just south of the Da Rosa Grocery Store in Riverside. Marie Seamas ultimately settled in the Manuel Rosa family house as well, taking care of Manuel Rosa Jr. before her marriage to Mr. Alvernaz. (Courtesy of P.H.C.S., donated by Manuel Rosa Jr.)

JOHN M. SILVA (NICKNAMED "JOAO MARIA") AND LOUISE (FERNANDES) SILVA OF THE POCKET AREA, MARRIED IN JANUARY 1923. Mr. Silva worked on the Frank Lewis haypress before later owning a dairy in the Pocket about 1939 or 1940. Louise Silva's parents, Joaquim and Maria Fernandes, lived and farmed in the Pocket area as well. Mr. Silva later purchased her parents ranch of 75 acres in 1946. The same property was still farmed by other interests as late as 1983. (Courtesy of P.H.C.S.)

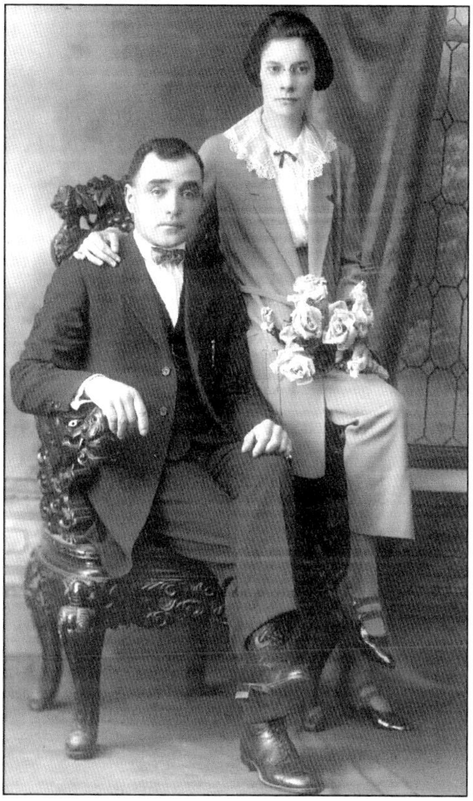

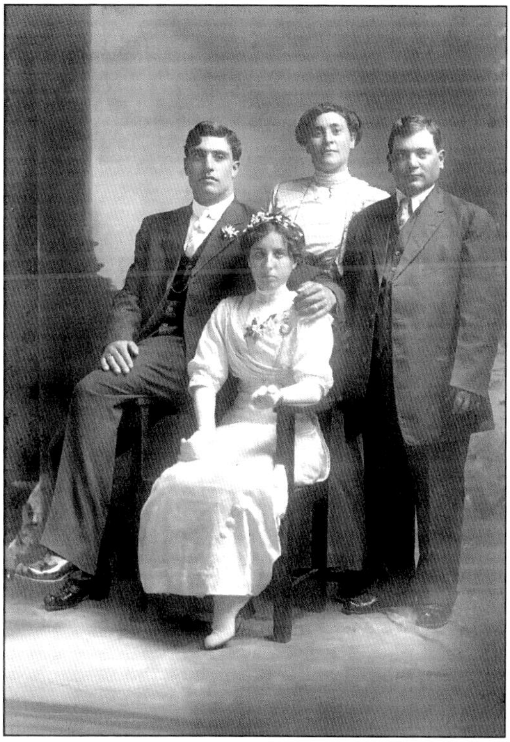

WEDDING PORTRAIT OF FRANK MELLO AND LOUISE ELENA ROSE IN 1913 OF THE RIVERSIDE/POCKET AREA. Standing in the back are brother and sister Mary and Joe Lewis. (Courtesy of P.H.C.S.)

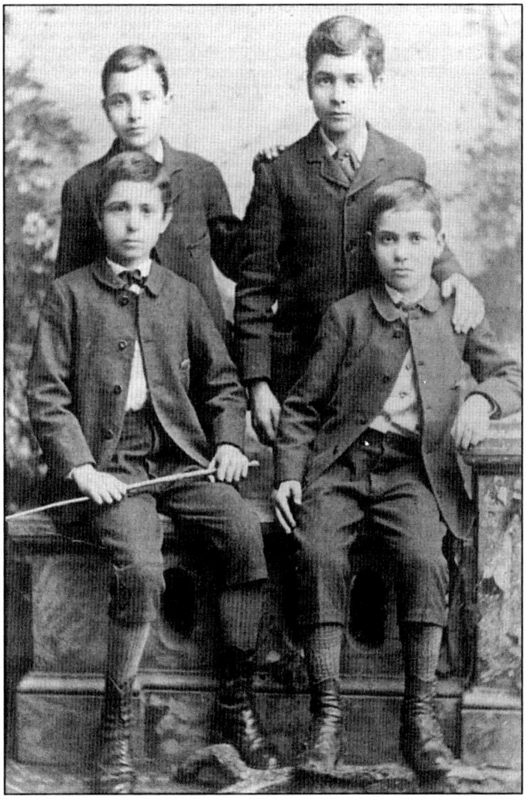

THE CHILDREN OF FRANK DE COSTA AND MARY ROMANA, ABOUT 1888, ONE OF THE EARLIEST DAY FAMILIES THAT SETTLED IN THE POCKET AREA. Pictured here, from left to right, are as follows: (back row) Joseph and Arthur, (front row) Frank and Manuel. (Courtesy of P.H.C.S., from the Romana Viera collection)

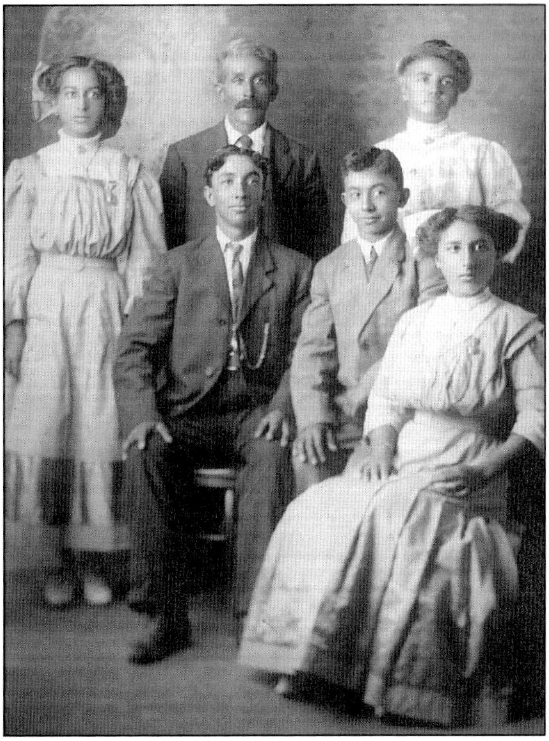

THE ROSE FAMILY OF THE RIVERSIDE/ POCKET AREA IN 1900. Pictured here, from left to right, are as follows: (standing) Amelia Rose, Joaquin (Da Rosa) Rose, and Mary Rose Silveira; (seated) Dan Rose, Frank Rose, and Louisa Rosa Mello. (Courtesy of P.H.C.S.)

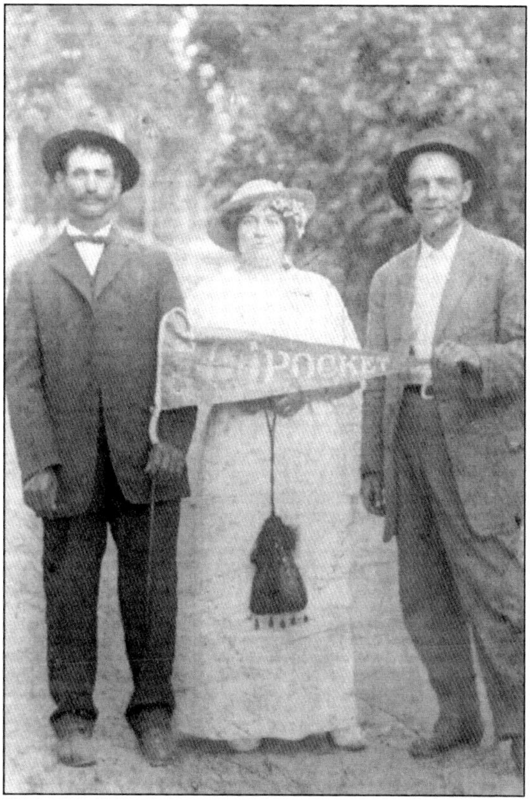

MANUEL AVILA WITH WIFE DOLORES SILVA AVILA AND JOE RAMOS. This picture was taken at Pocket's Holy Ghost Picnic c. 1916. Notice the banner that Mrs. Avila is holding with the word "Pocket" on it. (Courtesy of P.H.C.S., Ellen Silva Loaerde and Grace Rose Freitas)

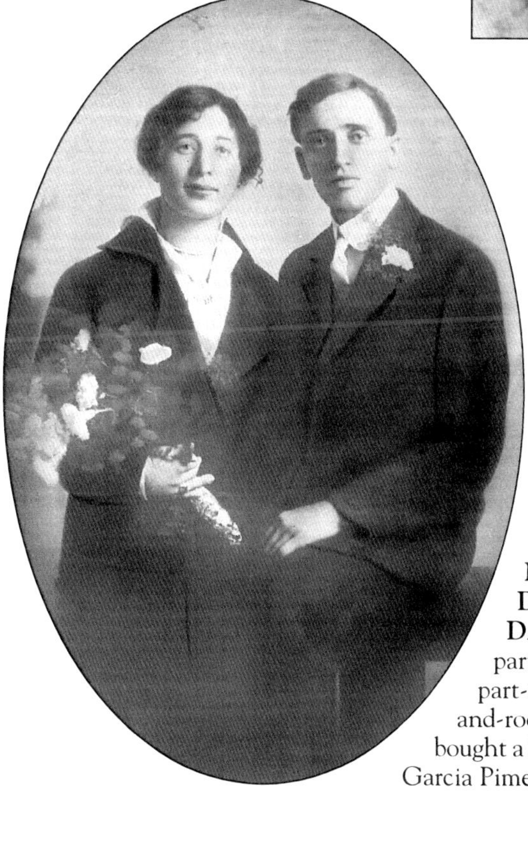

MANUEL BENTO SIMAS AND HIS WIFE DEOLINDA ISABELLA SILVA ON THEIR WEDDING DAY IN NOVEMBER 1914. Mr. Simas worked part-time for Manuel Rosa of Riverside and part-time at the Brickyard, living at the board-and-room house for single men. Earlier in 1914, he bought a 20-acre ranch for $7,000 from Anna Leonora Garcia Pimentel. (Courtesy of P.H.C.S.)

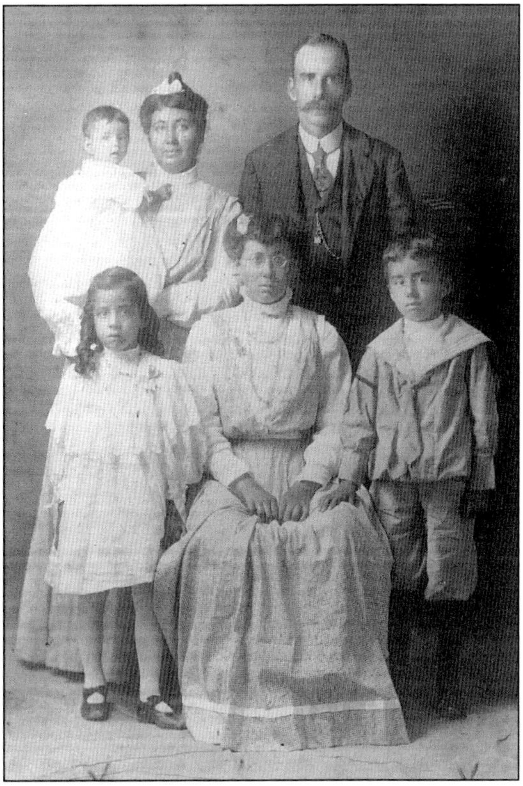

The Souza Family of the Pocket Area. Pictured here, from left to right, are as follows: (back row) Flora (Curry) Souza holding baby Helen, and her husband Antone Souza; (front row) daughter Mary Souza, Rose (sister of Flora), and son Antone (Tony) Souza. (Courtesy of P.H.C.S., Mary Souza Lewis collection)

Manuel Simas Sebastiao, Who Changed His Name to Seamas, and Roselina (Rosalinna) Silveira on Manuel's 90th Birthday in October 1937. Mr. Seamas was the owner of the Pocket area's Grangers Dairy. This picture was taken at a yard in the dairy. (Courtesy of P.H.C.S.)

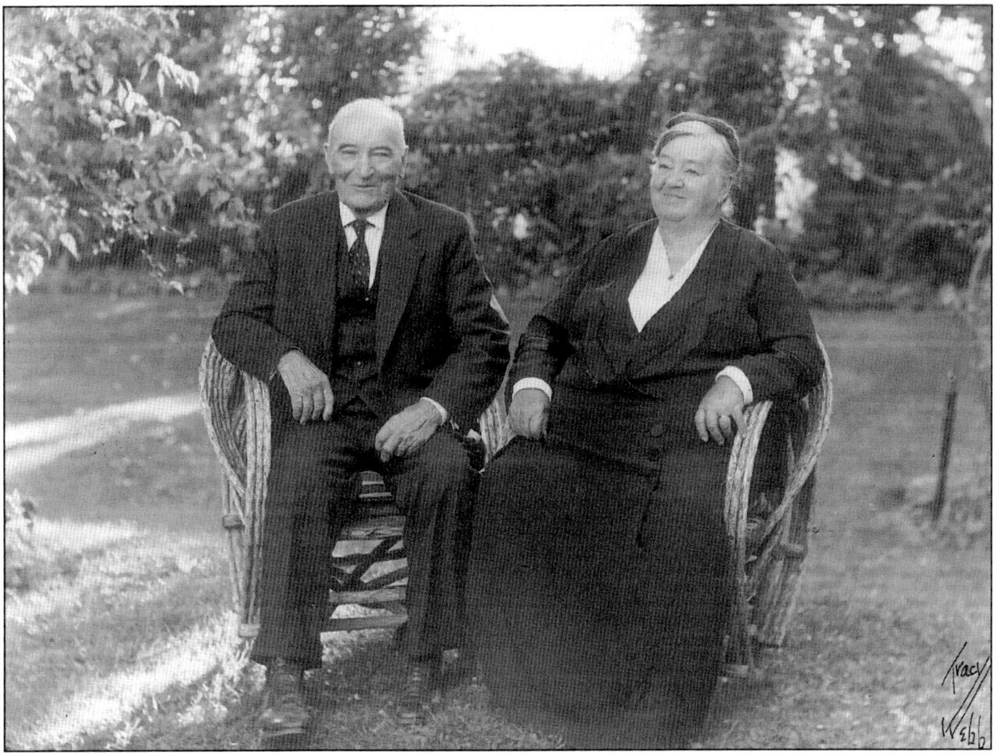

Two

Work Life

Before suburban development, the Pocket area provided many economic opportunities for settlers and their families. Most settlers farmed on land they owned or leased to raise crops for their family or for sale. Farmers raised a variety of crops including tomatoes, asparagus, lettuce, gyp corn, milo, cabbage, onions, spinach, sugar beets, alfalfa, potatoes, beans, grain, barley, oats, and hay. They also had cows, chickens, rabbits, geese, and pigs for dairy and meat purposes. Most farms had tree groves producing oranges, pears, figs, cherries, apples, apricots, peaches, lemons, and walnuts. The food harvests would often be used to feed the farmer's family, but produce, eggs, and cream would also be sold to businesses and grocers in downtown Sacramento. A few early day Pocket settlers sold produce to miners during the Comstock Lode. Hay would be pressed for sale, and some families operated businesses from this type of farming activity. In later years, truck farming in the Pocket area was common, especially among Japanese farmers. The Brickyard, Sacramento River levee construction, a few dairies, a slaughterhouse, and grocery and service stations also provided the economic base and, in most cases, seasonal employment opportunities for Pocket area farmers and families.

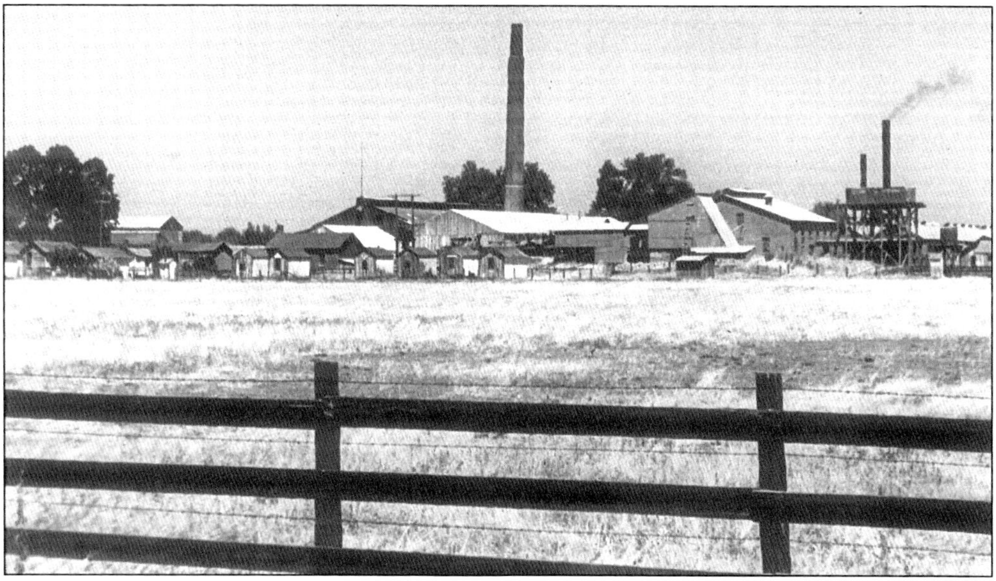

The Sacramento Brick Company. Located off of Riverside Road in the northern Pocket area, the company began operation in 1854 and was the first brickyard in Northern California. The principal market for the brickyard was San Francisco, but several important early brick buildings in the Sacramento area were built with material from this brickyard. These buildings include the Cathedral of the Blessed Sacrament, the Memorial Auditorium, the foundation of the State Capitol, and St. Joseph's Church in Clarksburg. The brickyard closed its operations on January 3, 1971, due to encroaching suburban development.

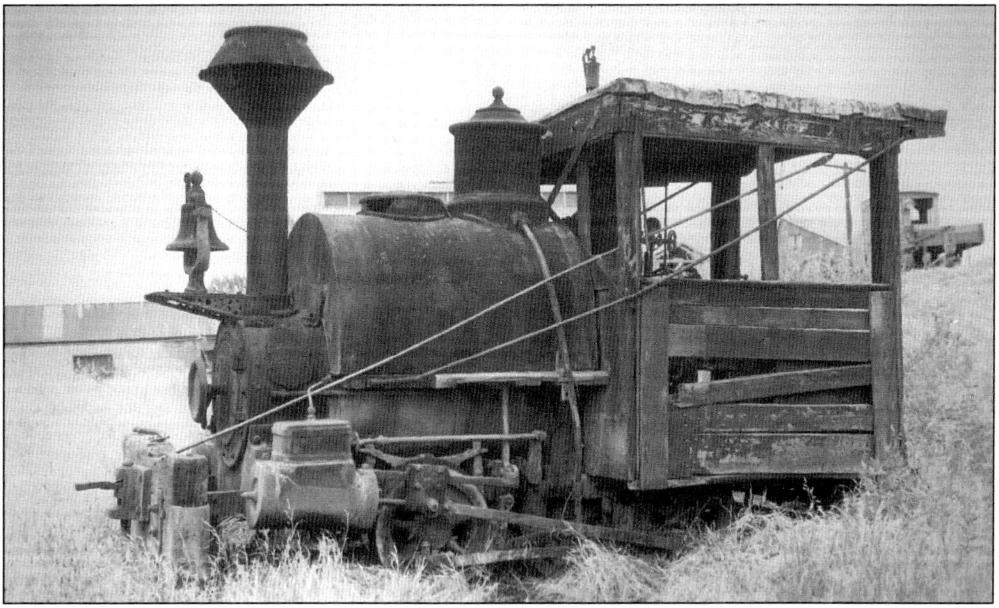

Brick Company Train. The small train pictured pulled ore-type cars that transported clay from the clay pit to the factory at the Sacramento Brick Company on Riverside Road. The clay pit was strategically located across from the brickyard and provided the source material for the making of the bricks. Today, the clay pit is Greenhaven Lake. Earlier on, the clay from the pit was dug by Chinese laborers and hauled to the plant by mule carts. (Courtesy of P.H.C.S.)

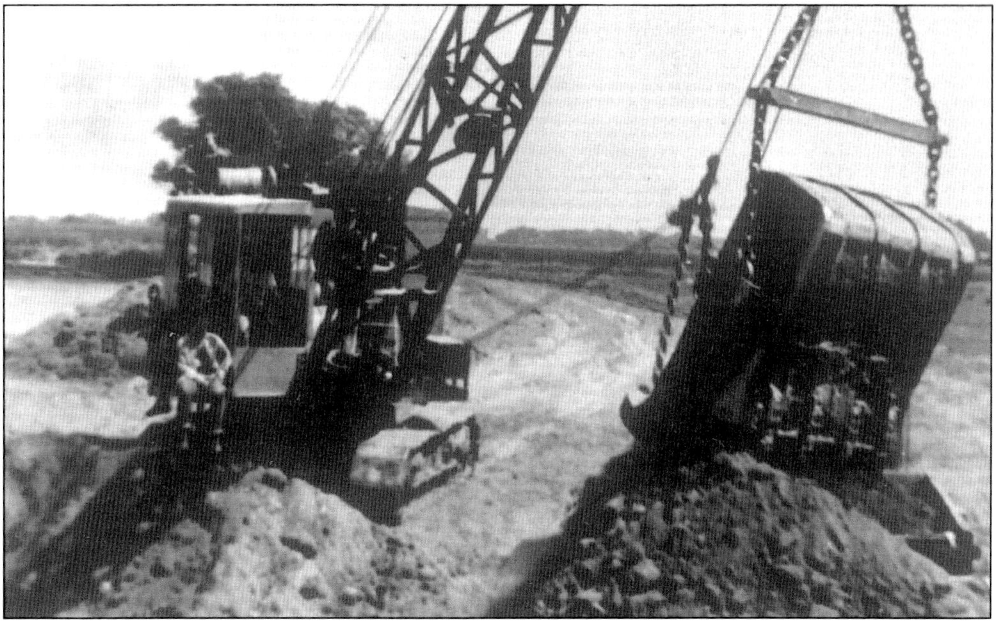

John Azevedo Loading Brickyard Rail Cars at the Clay Pit (Present Day Greenhaven Lake). The clay was loaded in a small locomotive that would take it from the clay pit to the brick making machines near the river. As technology improved into the 1950s, the clay was pumped to the plant by a hydraulic-type dredge at the rate of 200 cubic yards per hour. (Courtesy of P.H.C.S.)

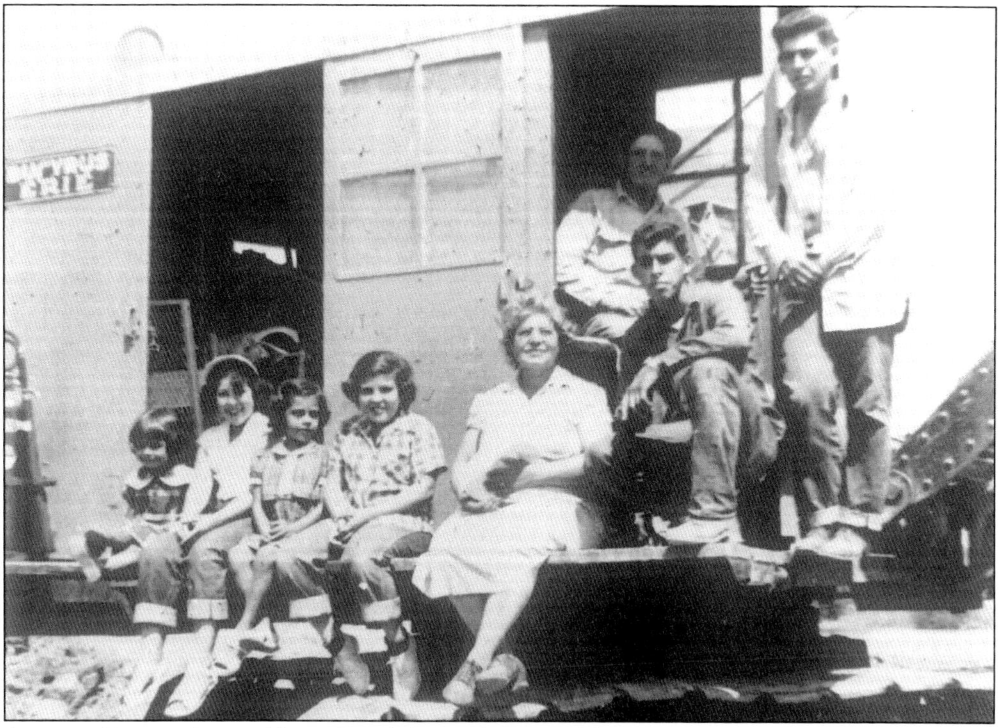

AZEVEDO FAMILY. Pictured here, from left to right, are as follows: Linda Azevedo, Carolyn Azevedo Peters, Patsy Azevedo, Rosie Azevedo de Oliveira, Carrie Azevedo, John Azevedo Jr., Richard Azevedo, and inside the dragline is John Azevedo (father). John Azevedo was the operator of the dragline that dug three-fourths of present day Greenhaven Lake, the clay pit of the brickyard. Mr. Azevedo would make a levee with the clay and then in the spring he would load it onto a small railroad that would take it to the brickyard. (Courtesy of P.H.C.S, donated by Ernie Azevedo)

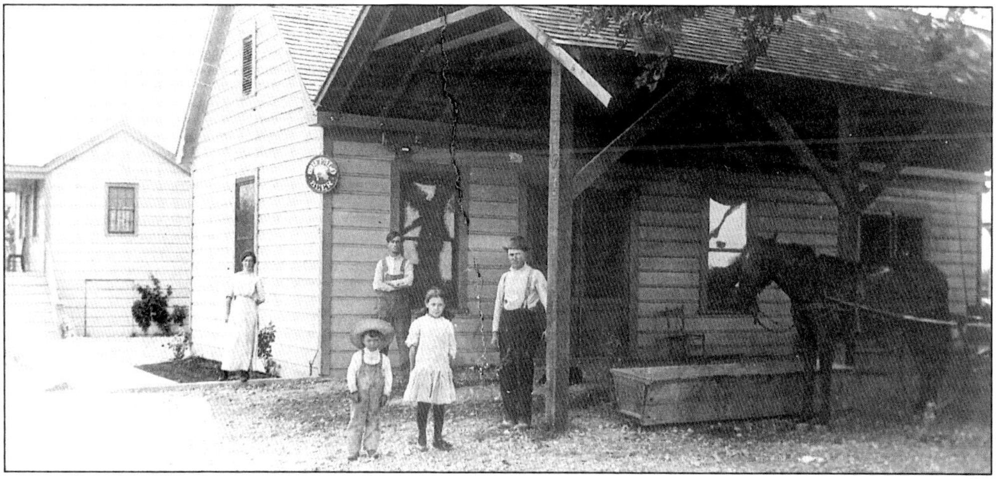

PIMENTEL'S INGLESIDE CAFÉ C. 1910, LOCATED ON RIVERSIDE BLVD. AT FOURTY-THIRD AVENUE. Today it is presently know as the Trap. Pictured here, from left to right, are Anna Seamas Savoie, Joe Prady, and Alvin Savoie. The children in front are Ernest Garcia and Mamie Koch. The original Pimentel home is shown at the left rear of the picture. (Courtesy of P.H.C.S, donated by Maggie Pimentel)

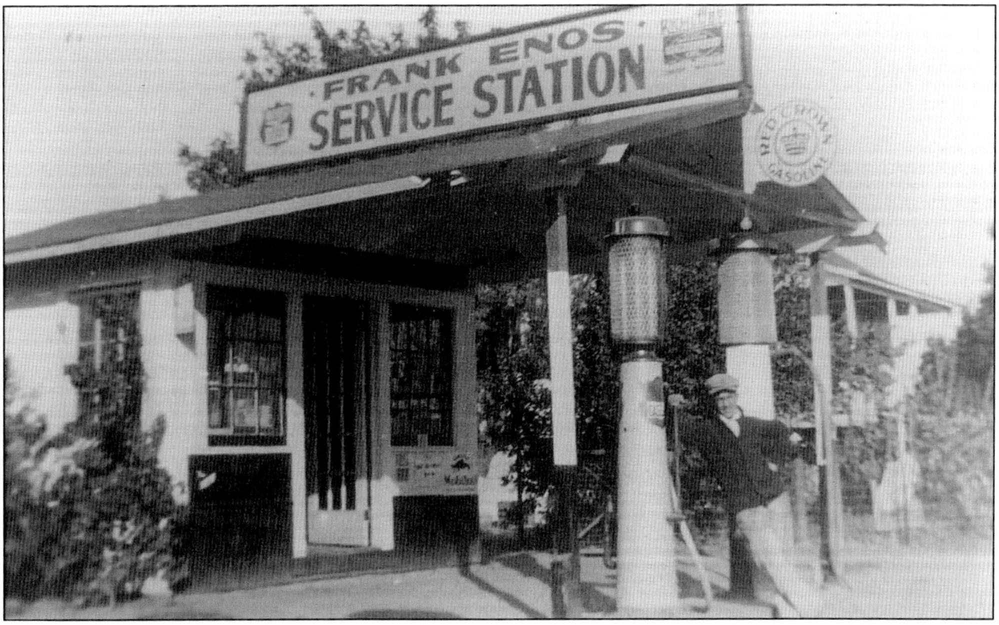

The Frank Enos Service Station in the Riverside Area During the Late 1920s. It was the only service station in the Riverside/Pocket area between Y Street (now Broadway) and Freeport Blvd. It was also just north of the Da Rosa Grocery store and Thirty-fifth Avenue. Louie Enos, son of Frank, is leaning at the pump. (Courtesy of P.H.C.S., George Enos collection)

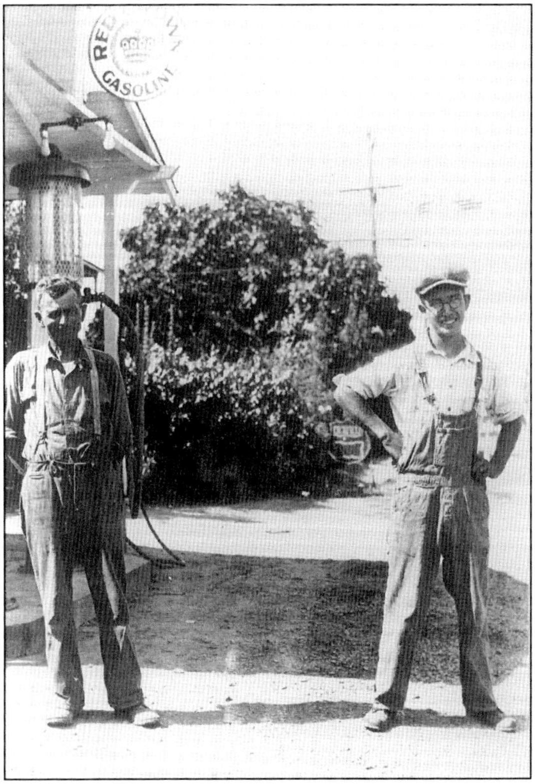

Frank Enos at Left With His Son Ernie in Front of the Enos Service Station. (Courtesy of P.H.C.S., George Enos collection)

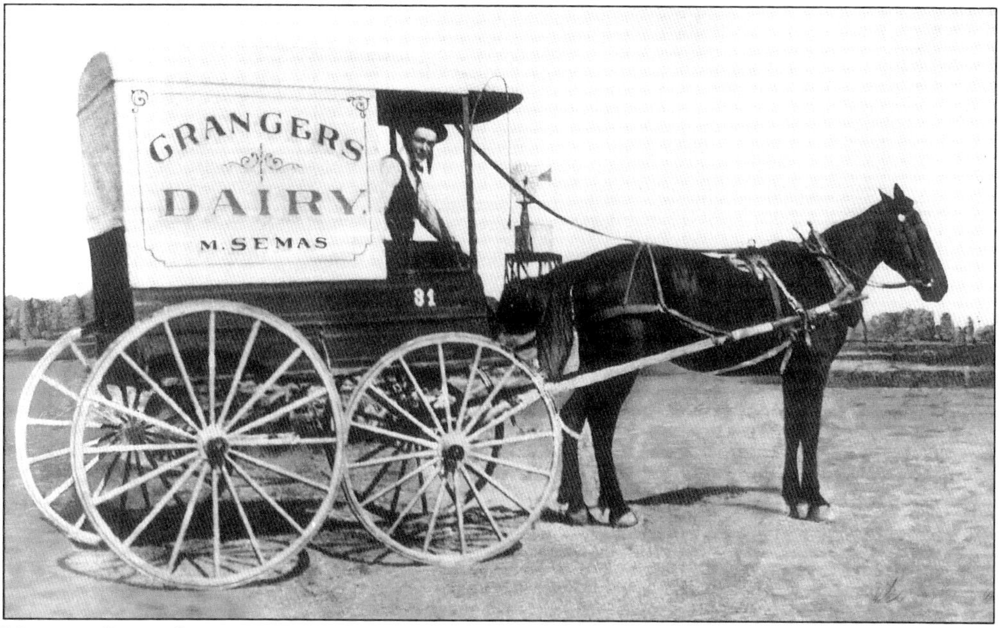

MANUEL SIMAS SEBASTIAO, WHO LATER CHANGED HIS NAME TO SEAMAS, ON HIS GRANGERS DAIRY DELIVERY WAGON IN 1910. He owned Grangers Dairy, one of the larger dairies in the Pocket area. He and his wife Roselina (Rosalinna), bought 100 acres in 1883 about one-half mile south of the Brickyard and established Grangers Dairy. Grangers Dairy wagons made deliveries, twice daily, to Sacramento doorsteps at the turn of the century. (Courtesy of P.H.C.S.)

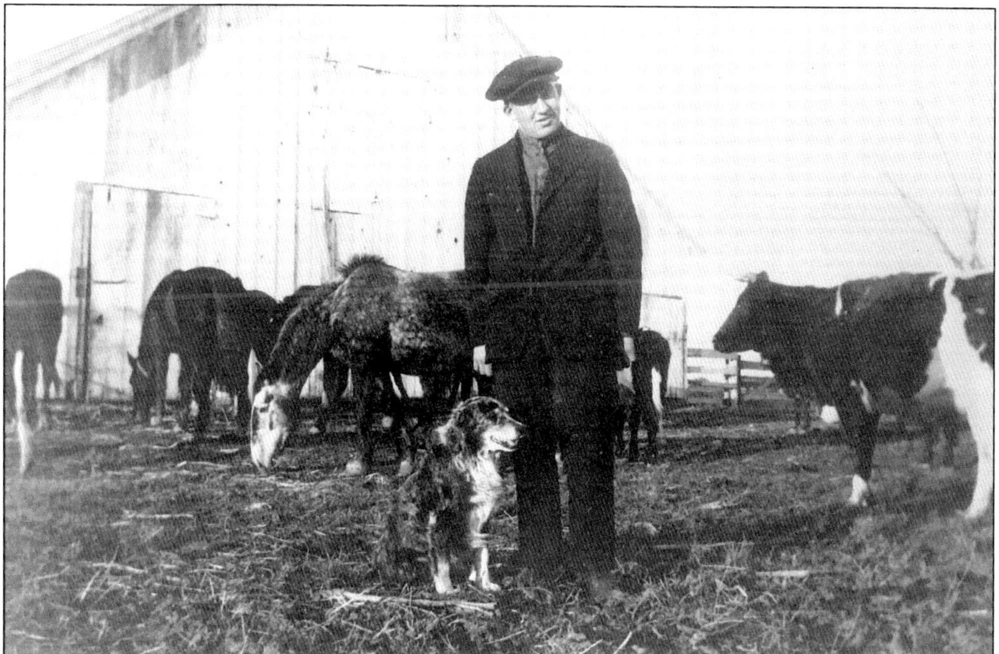

EMANUEL "BABE" SEAMAS, SON OF MANUEL SEAMAS, TAKEN AT THE GRANGERS DAIRY HOME. After his father retired in 1917, Babe Semas took over the operation of the dairy until 1940, when it was sold to Crystal Creamery. (Courtesy of P.H.C.S.)

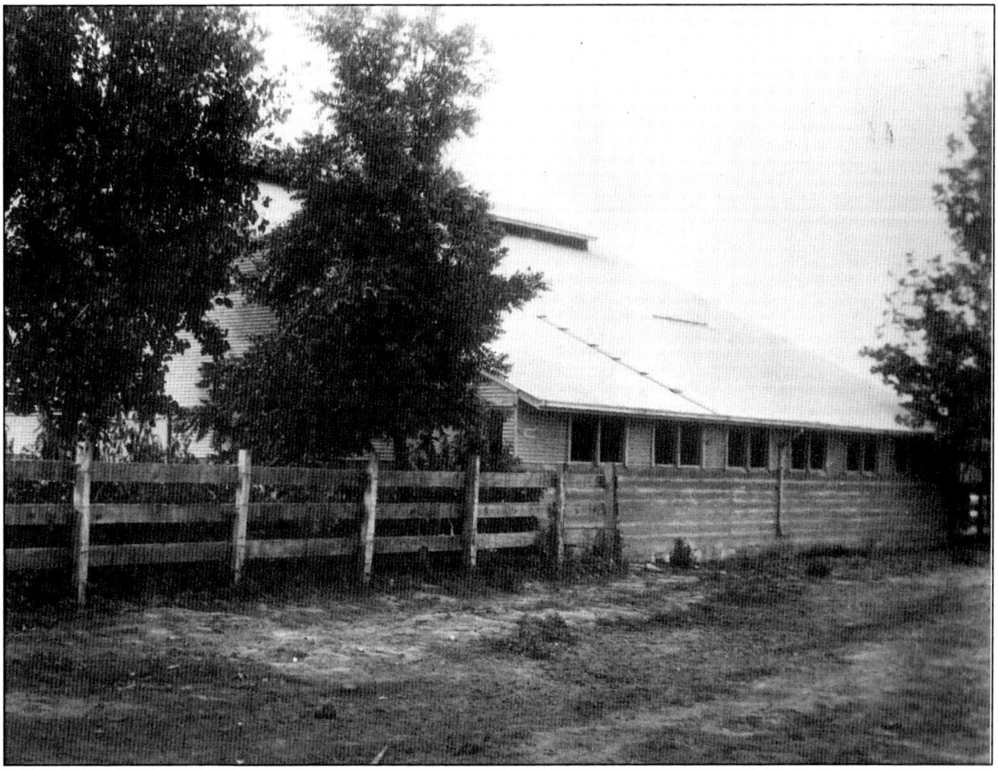

SIDE VIEW OF GRANGERS DAIRY. (Courtesy of P.H.C.S, Manuel Seamas collection)

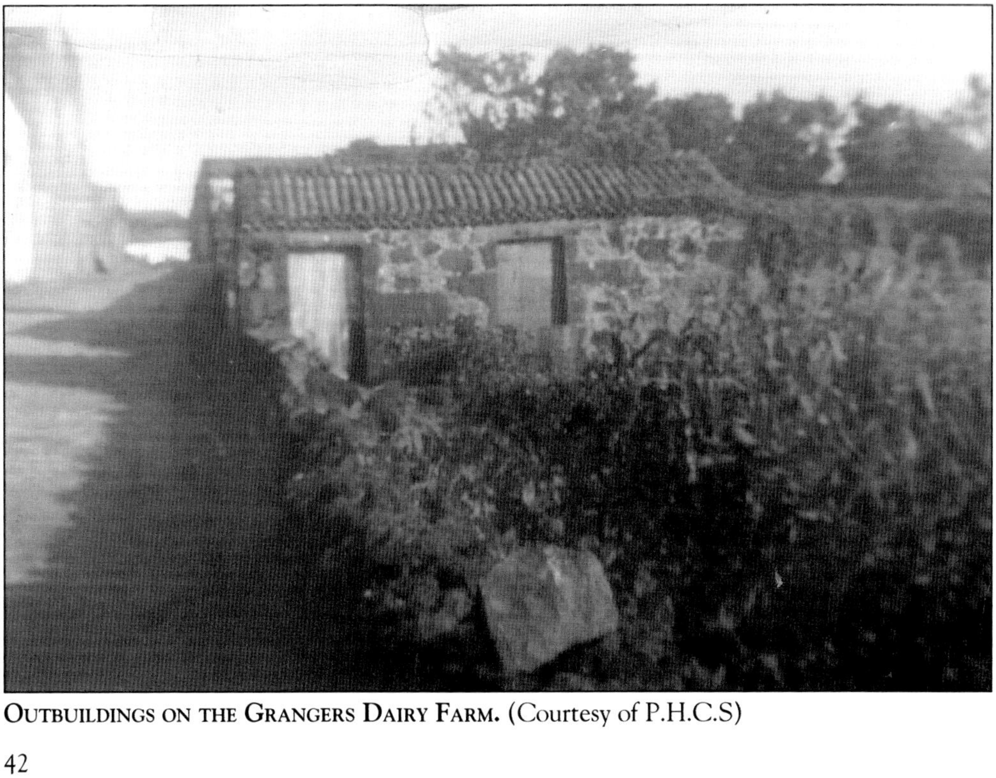

OUTBUILDINGS ON THE GRANGERS DAIRY FARM. (Courtesy of P.H.C.S)

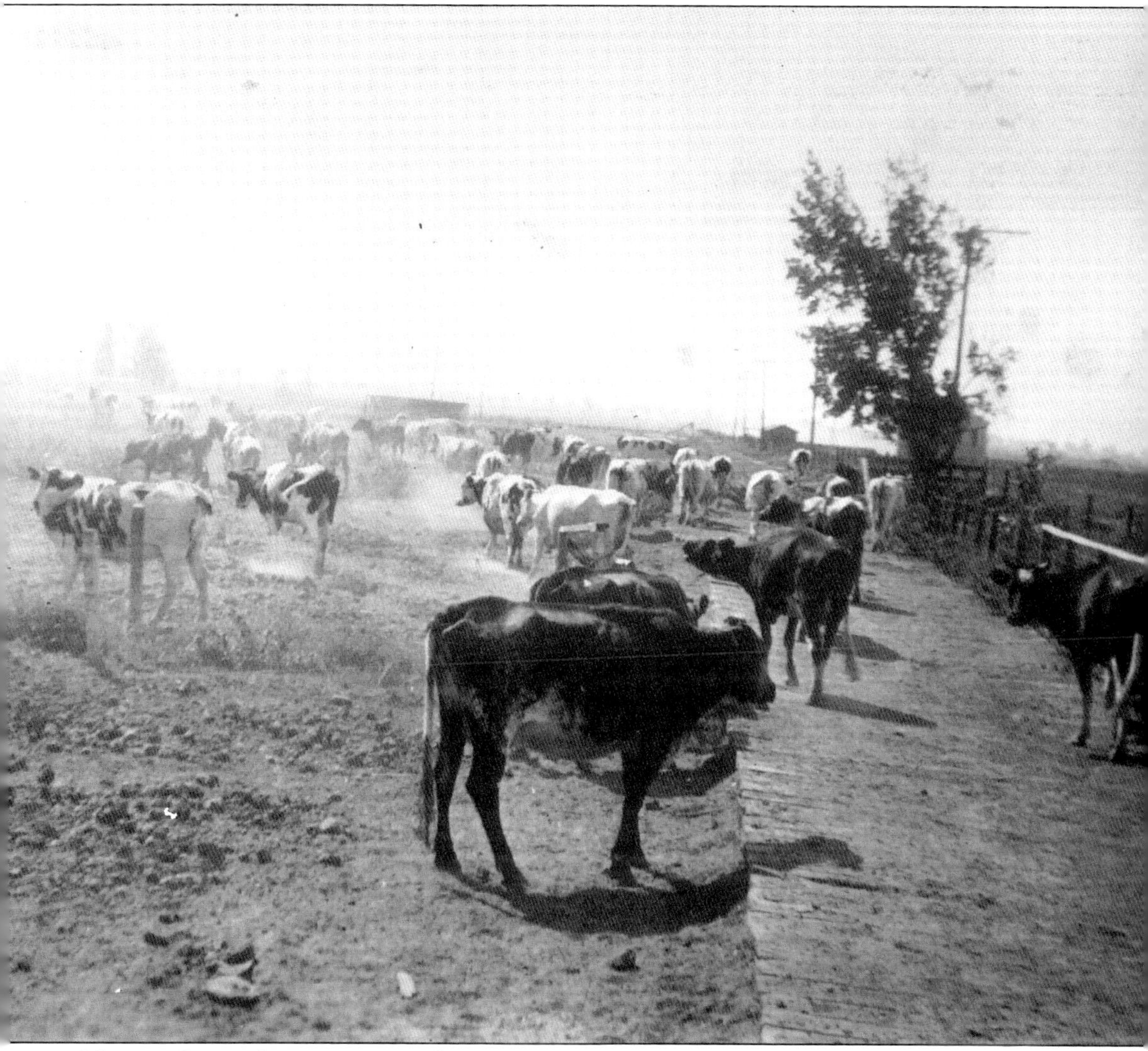

View of Dairy Cattle on the Grangers Dairy Land Owned by Manuel Seamas in the Pocket Area. Picture was taken in the 1920s or 1930s. (Courtesy of P.H.C.S.)

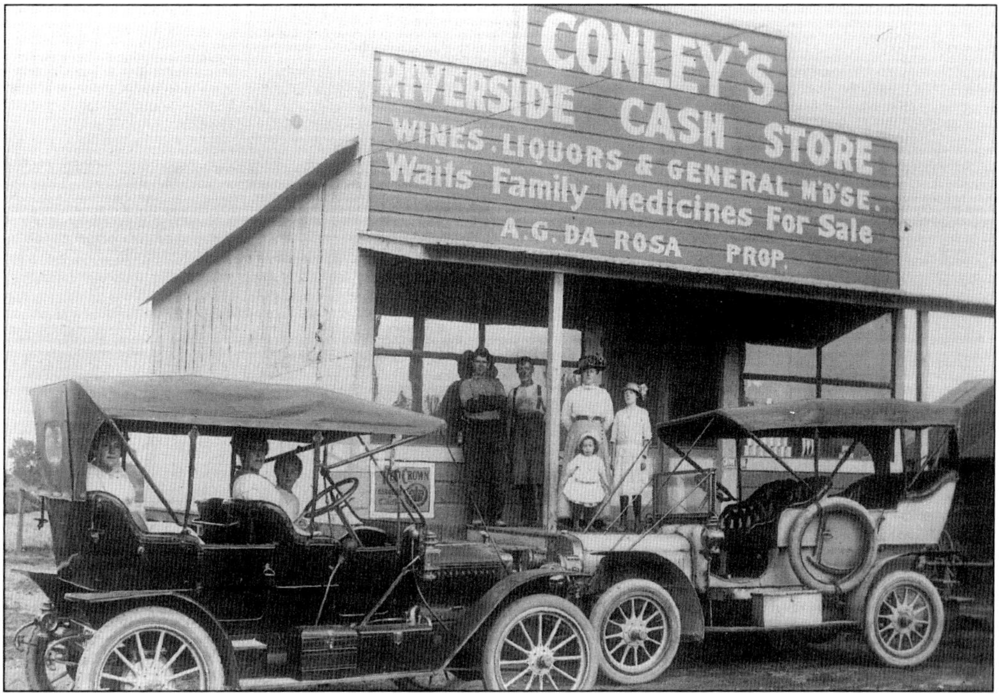

Antonio G. Da Rosa (Far Left With Arms Crossed on Porch) in 1912. He was the proprietor of the Conley Cash Store, just south of the Sutter School on Riverside Road. In 1915, he built a new store known as the Riverside Grocery about a half-mile south. The business was owned and operated by Mr. Da Rosa and his wife Maria until their retirement in 1948. (Courtesy of P.H.C.S.)

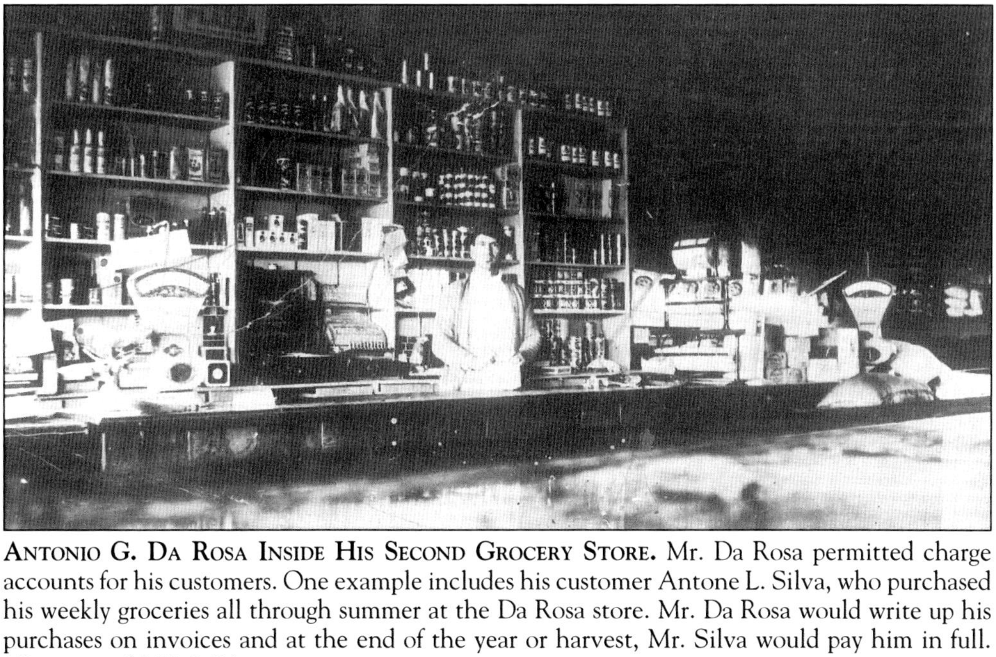

Antonio G. Da Rosa Inside His Second Grocery Store. Mr. Da Rosa permitted charge accounts for his customers. One example includes his customer Antone L. Silva, who purchased his weekly groceries all through summer at the Da Rosa store. Mr. Da Rosa would write up his purchases on invoices and at the end of the year or harvest, Mr. Silva would pay him in full. (Courtesy of P.H.C.S.)

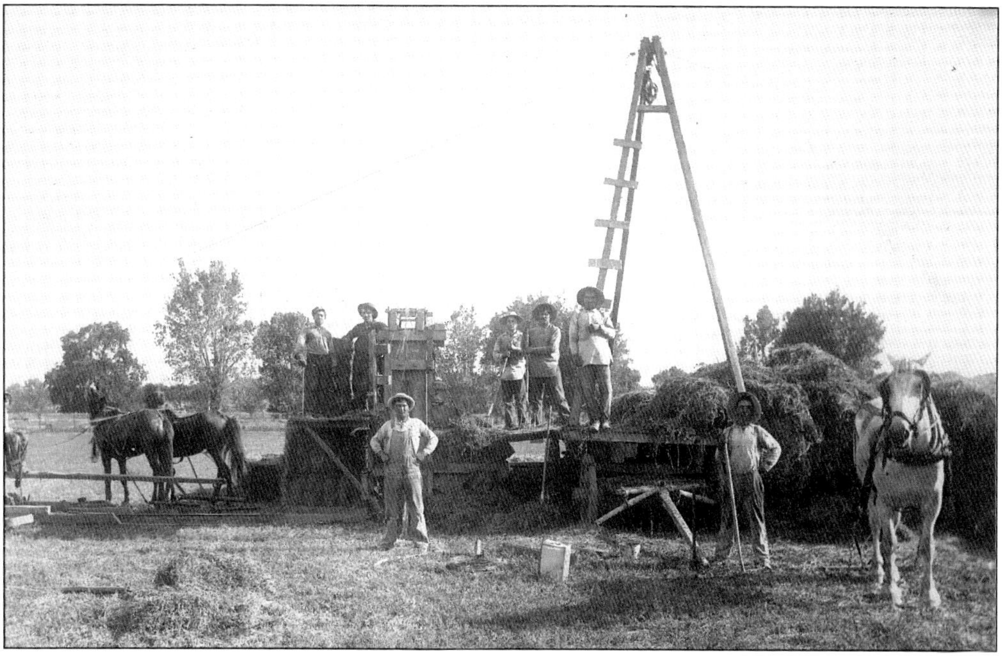

The Frank Lewis Haypress About 1911. This was called a "Petaluma Press" and in its early days it was horse mechanized. Pictured at left in the foreground is Frank "Capp" Perry with the horses. Pictured at center is John Vierra, and pictured at right is Joe Cabral. The men in the upper background are unidentified. (Courtesy of P.H.C.S., donated by Herman Mello)

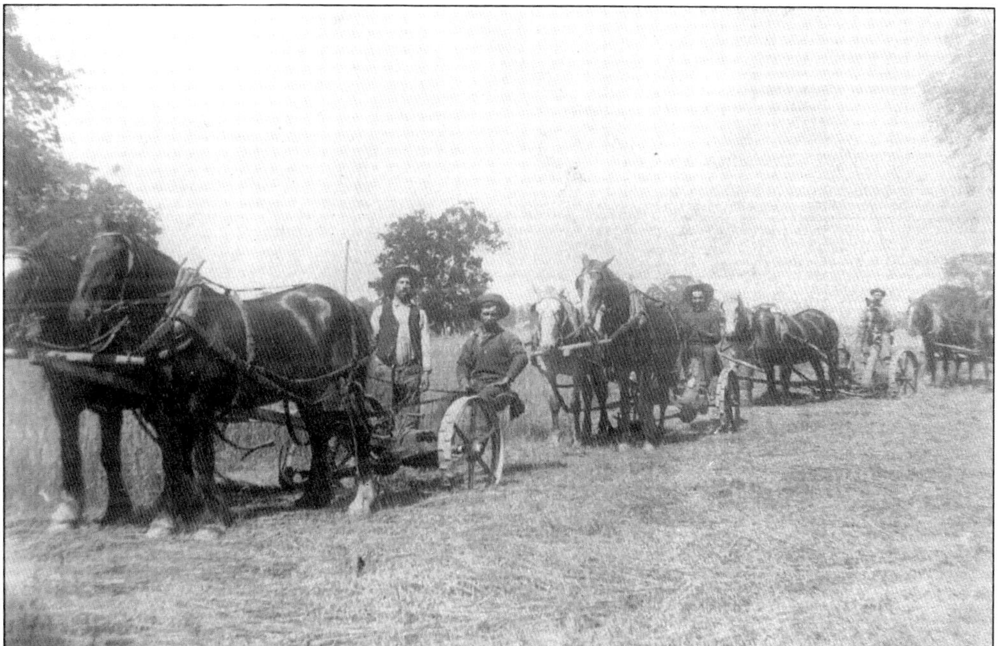

Manuel Rosa "Magun" Sr. (At Far Left Wearing the Vest), Who Lived in the Riverside Area. Here he is working as a Haymower on the Antone Silva Ranch in the Grant Area. The picture was taken about 1900. (Courtesy of P.H.C.S., Manuel Rosa, Jr. collection)

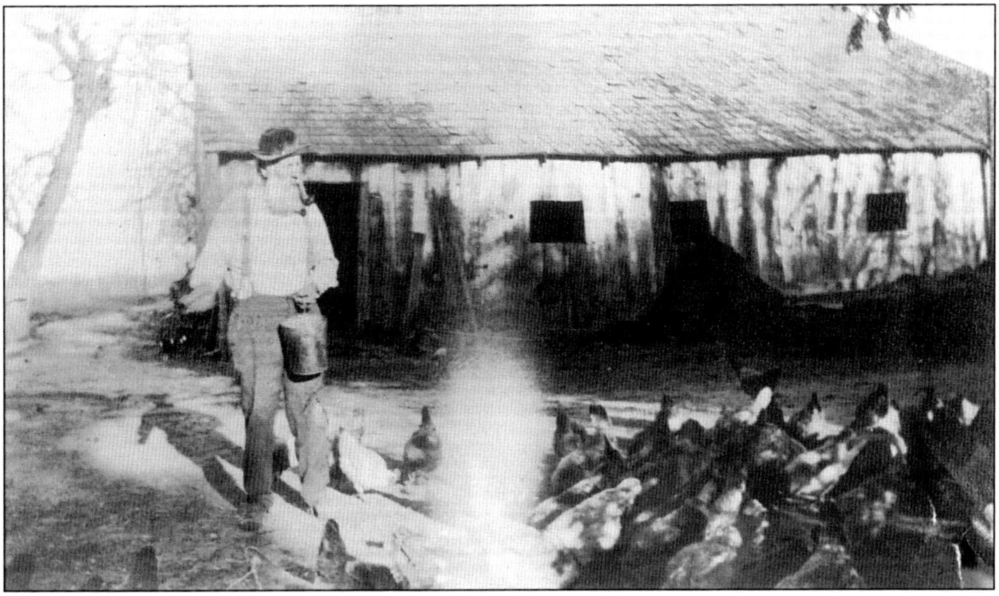

Joseph Tash, a Pioneer Pocket Farmer, at His Pocket Area Farm Feeding Chickens at Age 81 in 1926. He first worked as a farmhand in the Pocket area and later purchased a 37-acre tule-filled ranch located to the east of the Garcia (Gracia) ranch that he drained, cleared, and farmed one section at a time. He raised fruit and vegetables and at one time had a small dairy. Tash Court in the South Pocket area is named after the family. (Courtesy of P.H.C.S.)

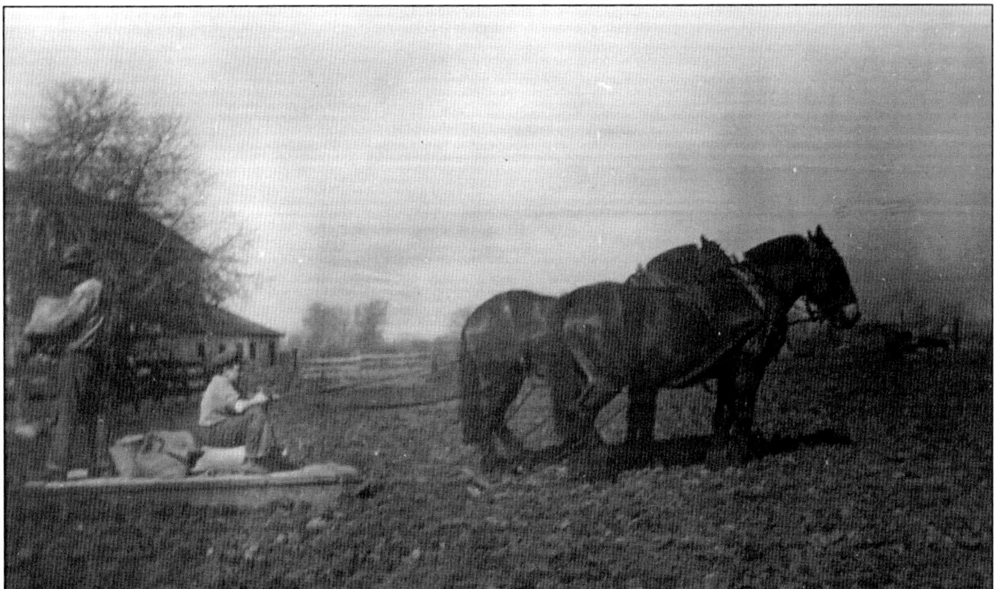

The Joe Tash Family Ranch in the Pocket Area About 1935 During the Planting of Alfalfa. Frank Tash, Joe's son, is seeding at left, with his son Albert driving the team of horses. (Courtesy of P.H.C.S., Mary Tash collection)

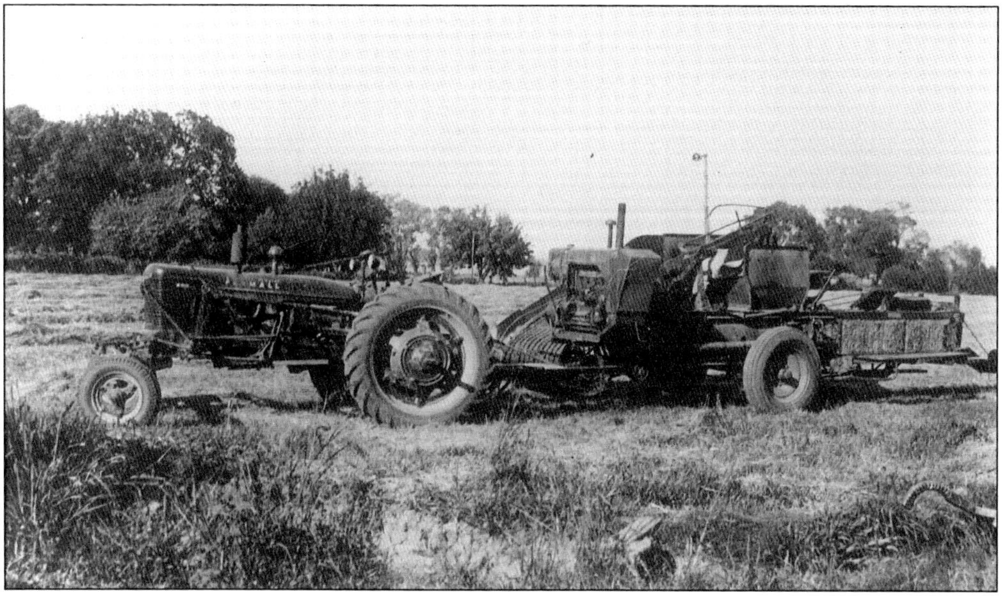

THE JOE TASH FAMILY RANCH IN THE POCKET AREA ABOUT 1947. Pictured is a case 3-wire baler pulled by a farmall tractor, used for the baling of hay. (Courtesy of P.H.C.S., Mary Tash collection)

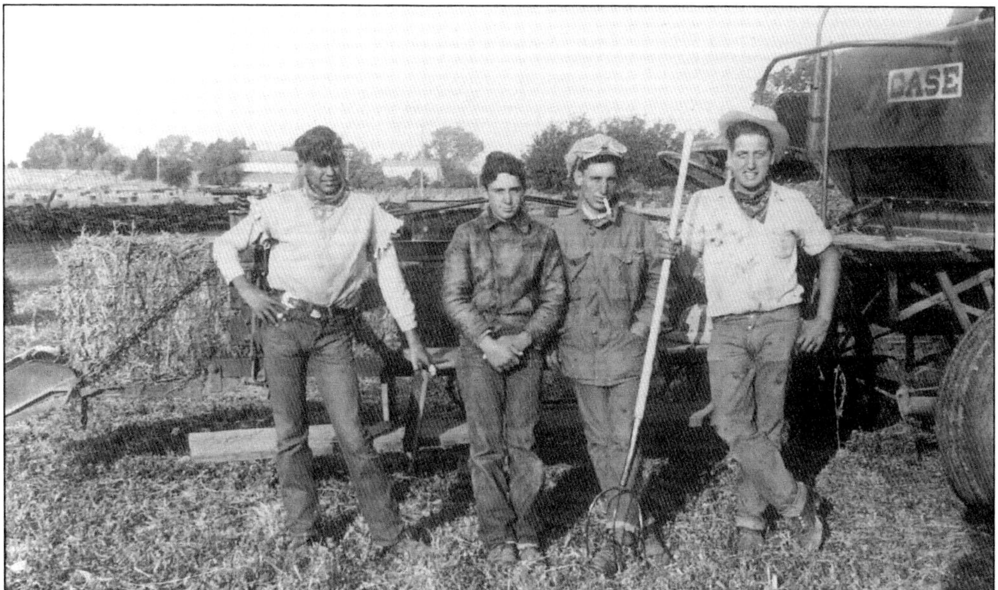

THE JOE TASH FAMILY RANCH IN THE POCKET AREA ABOUT 1947. Shown is the baling crew next to the case 3-wire baler. Pictured here, from left to right, are Bob Garcia, Bob Silva (son of Faustino Silva), Joe Alves Jr., and Edward Tash (grandson of Joe Tash). (Courtesy of P.H.C.S., Mary Tash collection)

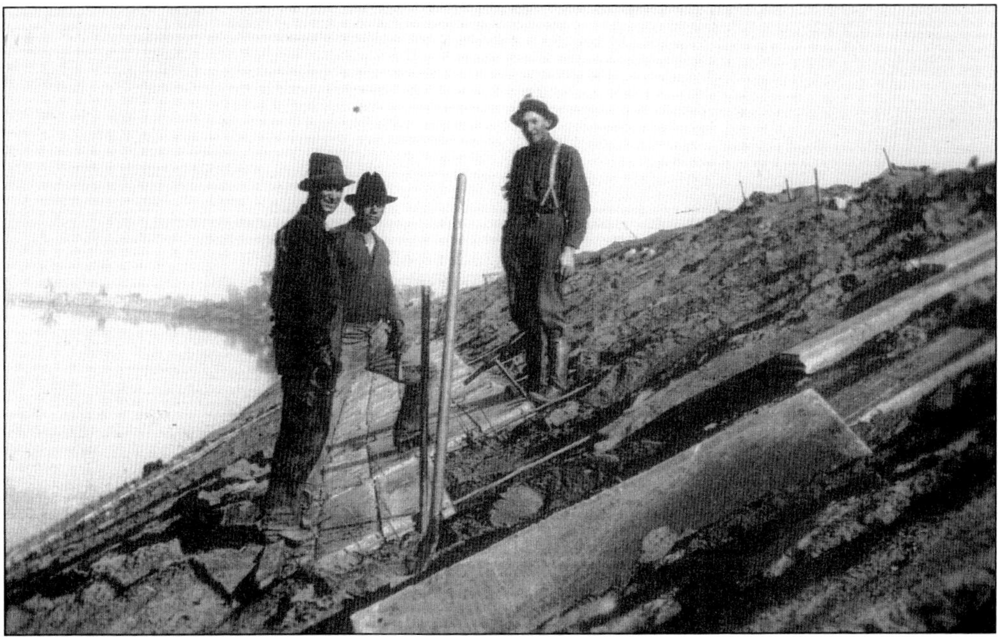

Workers Reinforcing the Levee on the Sacramento River along Riverside Road in the Riverside/Pocket Area. This picture was taken in the early 1920s around the Sacramento River bend. (Courtesy of P.H.C.S.)

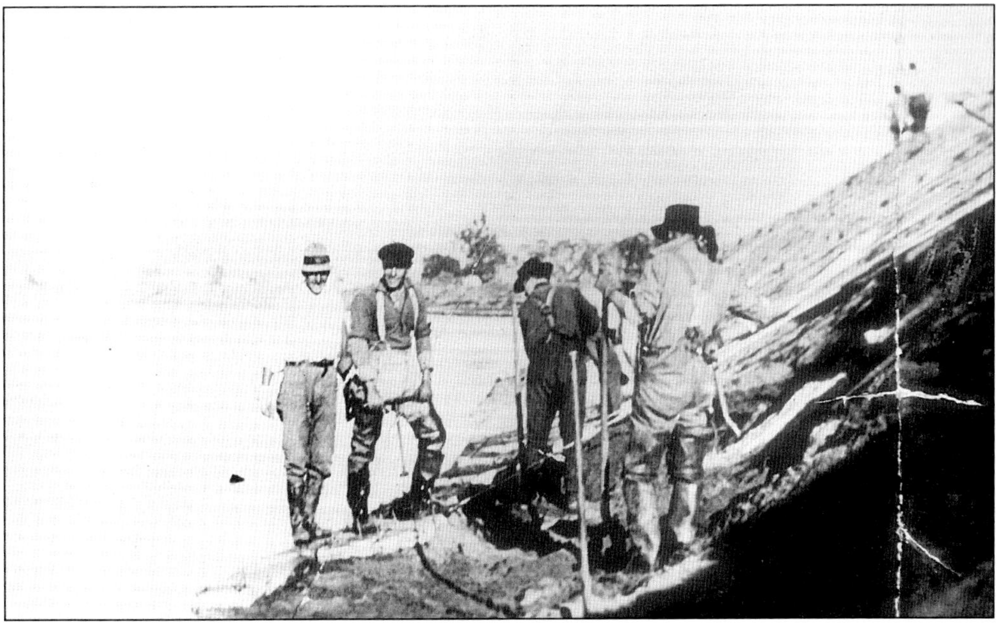

Another View of Workers Reinforcing the Levee on the Sacramento River in the Riverside/Pocket Area Near Where the Trap is Located Today. The Argyle Dredger was used for reinforcing the levees and employed hundreds of crewmen. Minnie Perry Corey, daughter of Antone and Amelia Perry from the Pocket area, worked as a cook for the Argyle crewmen, serving 28 men at one time. She made $80 a month, getting up at 4 a.m. to prepare three full meals and snacks for the crew. (Courtesy of P.H.C.S).

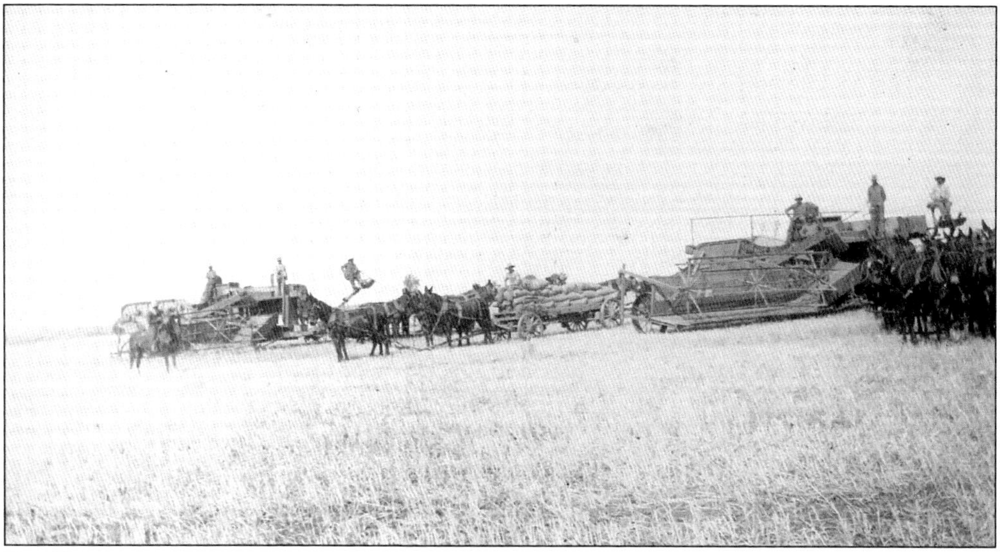

THE FRANK LEWIS HAYPRESS IN THE POCKET AREA, LOADING GRAIN ON THE OVERLAND WAGON WHERE GRAIN IS COMBINED AND THRASHED. This was done in the in the 1920s and before. (Courtesy of P.H.C.S., Herman Mello collection)

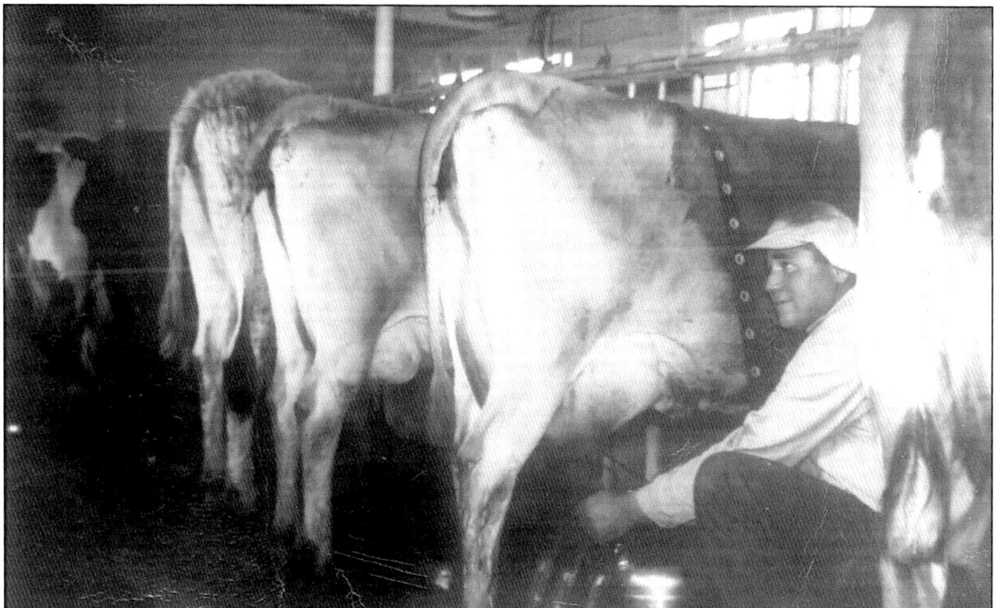

MANUEL "MILHOMENS" SILVA, SON OF JOE F. "MILHOMENS" SILVA, MILKING COWS IN THE SILVA FAMILY DAIRY LOCATED IN THE SOUTH POCKET AREA. (Courtesy of P.H.C.S., donated by Marie Dutra Gambrel)

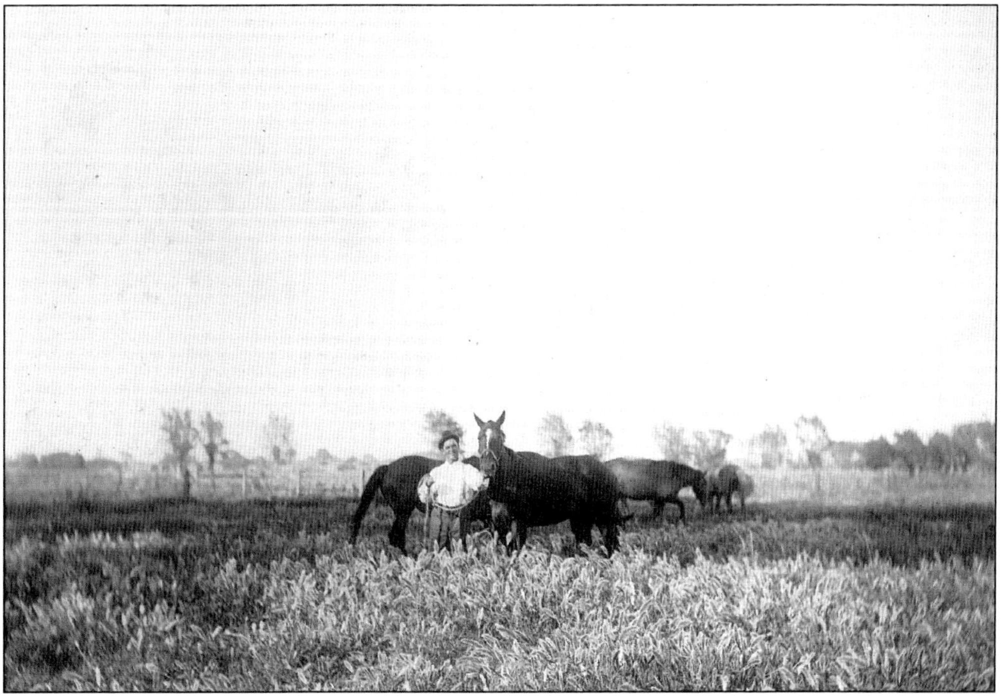

Joe F. Silva Jr., Son of Joe F. "Milhomens" Silva Sr. on the Family Ranch with Their Horses About 1915. (Courtesy of P.H.C.S, donated by Mary L. (Silva) Dutra)

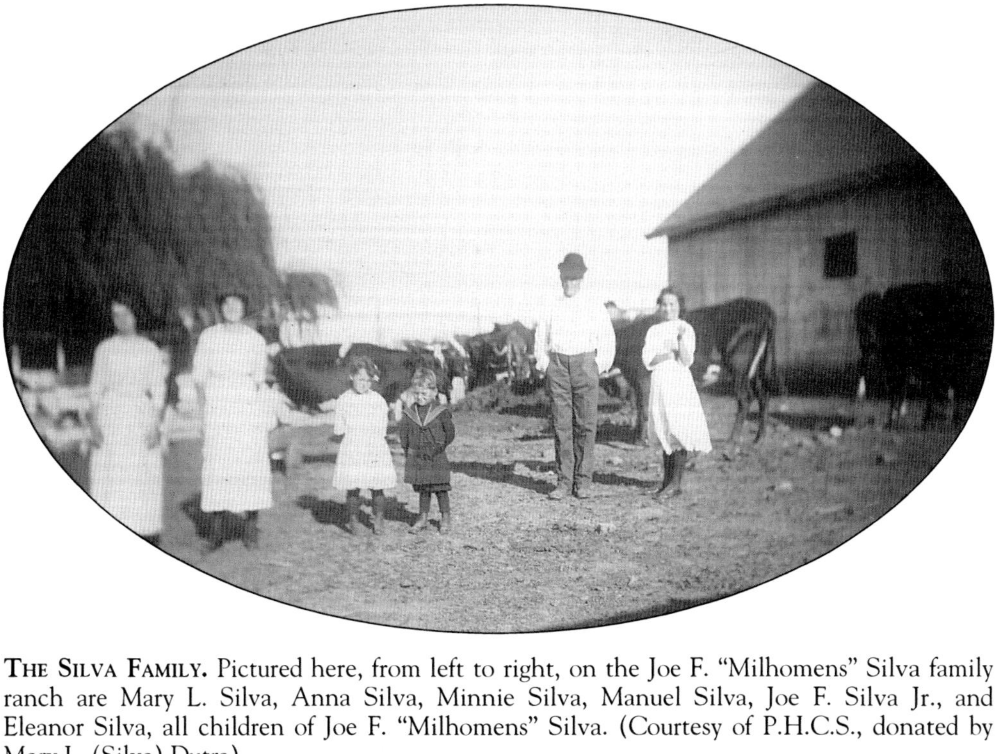

The Silva Family. Pictured here, from left to right, on the Joe F. "Milhomens" Silva family ranch are Mary L. Silva, Anna Silva, Minnie Silva, Manuel Silva, Joe F. Silva Jr., and Eleanor Silva, all children of Joe F. "Milhomens" Silva. (Courtesy of P.H.C.S., donated by Mary L. (Silva) Dutra)

Three

FAMILY HOMES AND RANCHES

Houses found in the Pocket area before suburban development were mainly two story, with bedrooms on the second story and a kitchen and pantry on the first story. A stairwell at the front of the house and sometimes at the back as well would be found leading up to the bedrooms. Usually a rowboat would be tied to the stairwell so the family could leave the house safely when it flooded. Along with a house, farmers generally had a water pump used for irrigation, a barn, several ranch hands, work horses, a wagon, and in later years, an automobile. Although a majority of the homes found in the Pocket area before development are no longer in the area, a few older homes are still in the community, clustered on certain street blocks. Notably, across the street and in the vicinity of Lewis Park on Park Riviera Way, there is a cluster of older homes (pictures provided in Chapter 6). There are also older homes along Pocket Road about one half-mile north of Garcia Bend Park, clustered near the levee next to vacant lots set for construction.

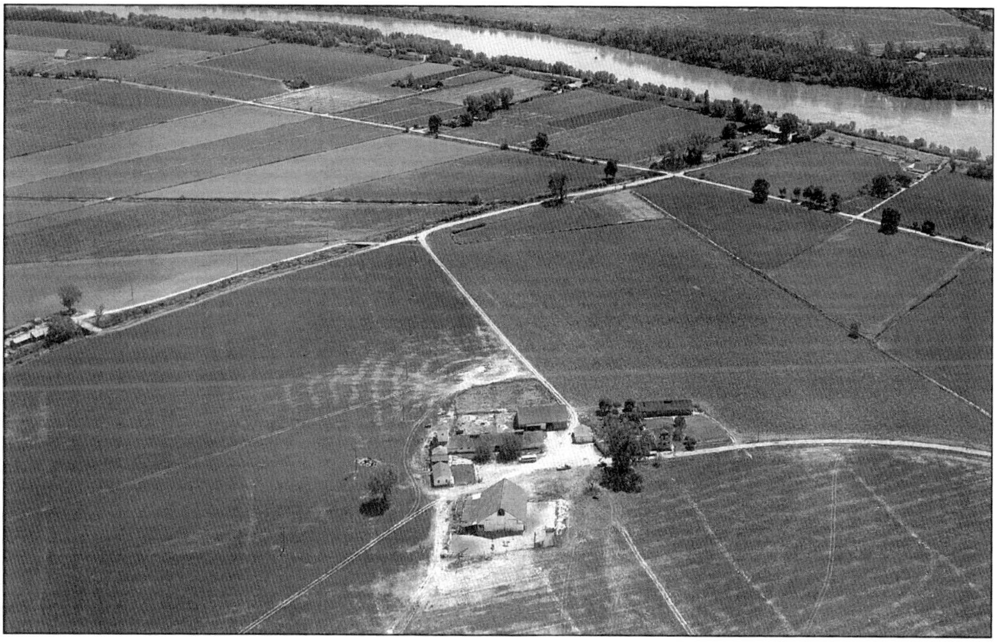

AERIAL PHOTO VIEW OF THE FRANK AND CLARA LEWIS RANCH IN THE SOUTH POCKET AREA ABOUT 1946. The 350-acre ranch was purchased in 1918 by Frank Lewis, son of Francisco (Luiz) Lewis Sr., a pioneer Pocket farmer. The Sacramento River is at the far right of the picture, with Riverside Road, present day Pocket Road, running parallel to it. Farms and ranches in the Pocket area before suburbanization were divided according to the long-lot system, a diagonal dividing system common along river settlements. (Courtesy of P.H.C.S., photo taken by Americo D'Alessandro, Gabriella Lewis collection)

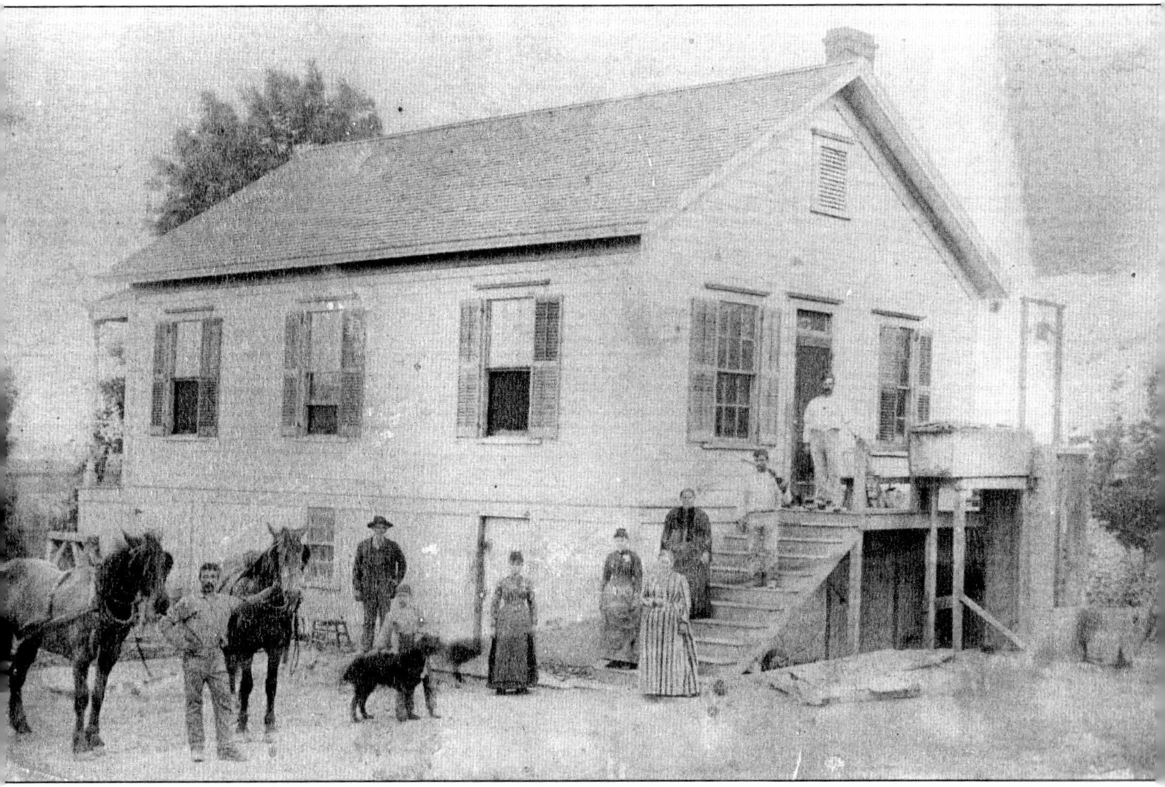

The Jose and Maria Da Neves Family Farm and Home. This picture was taken in the early 1870s and includes the Da Neves family and friends, early settlers in the Pocket area. (Courtesy of P.H.C.S.)

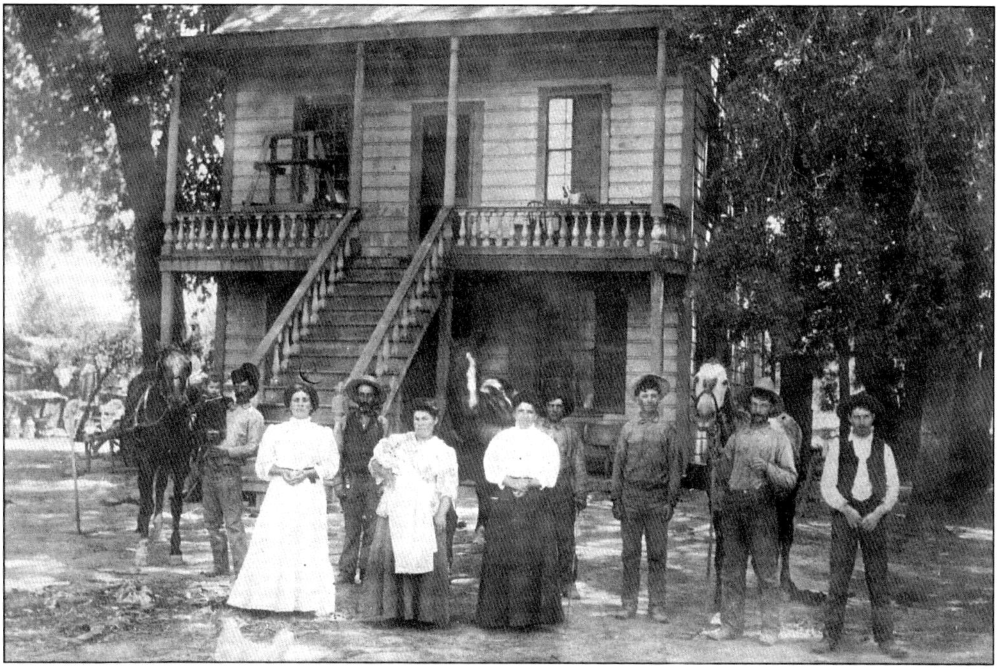

THE FRANK J. LUIZ (LEWIS) HOME IN THE LATE 1800S. Pictured is his family and ranch hands. (Courtesy of P.H.C.S.)

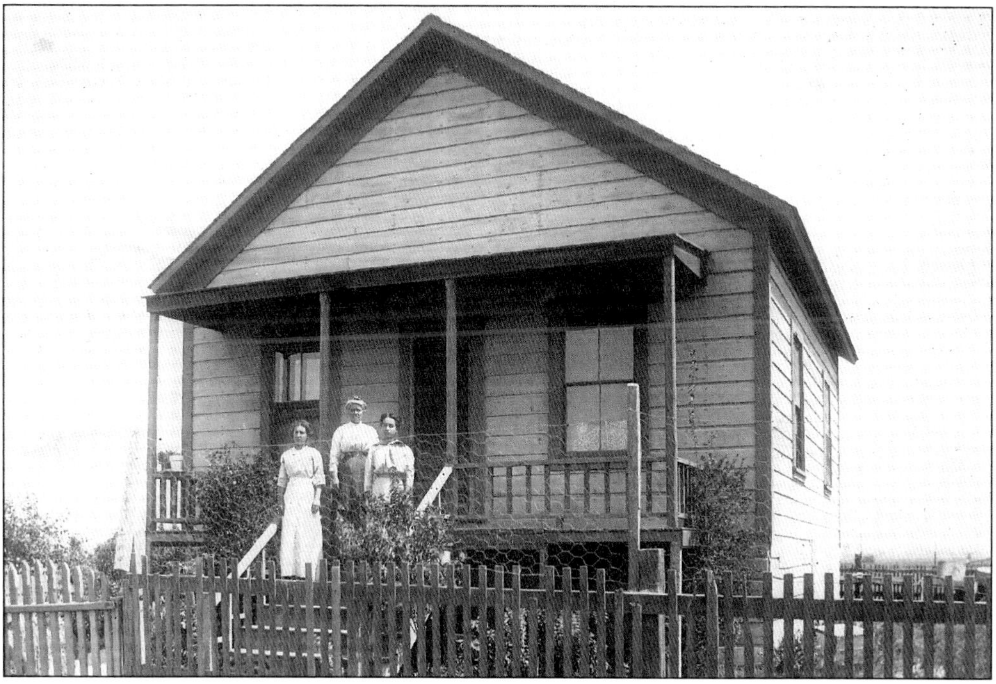

THE JOAQUIM AND AMELIA ROSE HOME IN 1904. Pictured here, from left to right, are Louisa Rose Mello, Amelia Rose, and Mary Rose Silveira. This home has the same architectural style as the original cluster of homes that housed families at the brickyard and were later moved to private properties. (Courtesy of P.H.C.S.)

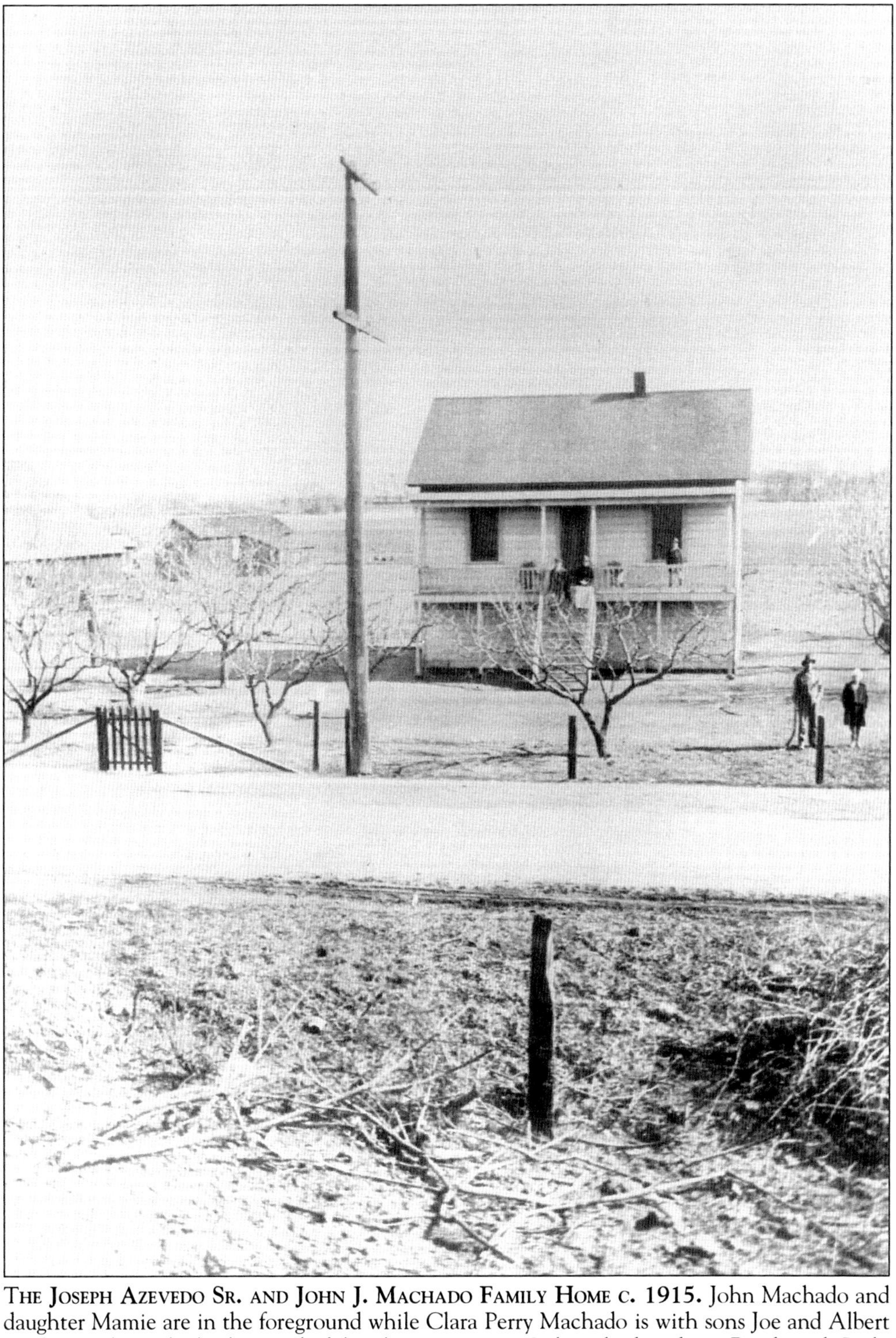

THE JOSEPH AZEVEDO SR. AND JOHN J. MACHADO FAMILY HOME c. 1915. John Machado and daughter Mamie are in the foreground while Clara Perry Machado is with sons Joe and Albert on the porch. In the background of the photo is Munger Lake, which today is Reichmuth Park. (Courtesy of P.H.C.S.)

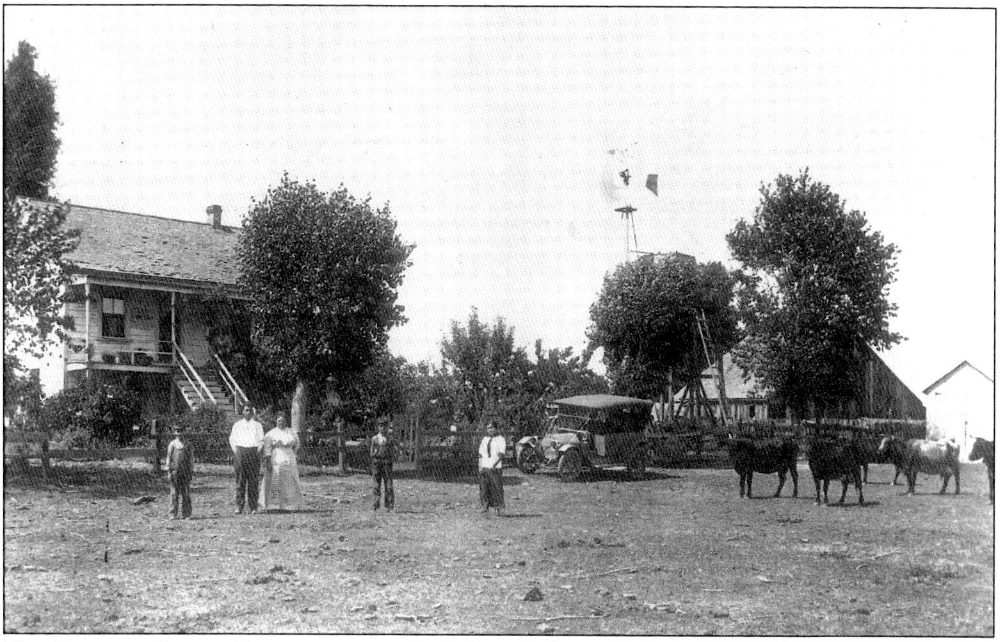

THE SILVEIRA FAMILY RANCH ABOUT 1912. From left to right is Manuel Silveira, Manuel Enos, Emelia Silveira, Tony Silveira, and Mary Agnes Silveira (Holmes). The ranch was located in the North Pocket area and the house was located just south and slightly west of today's intersection of Driftwood and Harmon Way. The front of the house faced Riverside Road. The home was demolished in January 1963 after being sold to Harmon Reality. Today, nearby Silveira Way is named after the family. (Courtesy of P.H.C.S.)

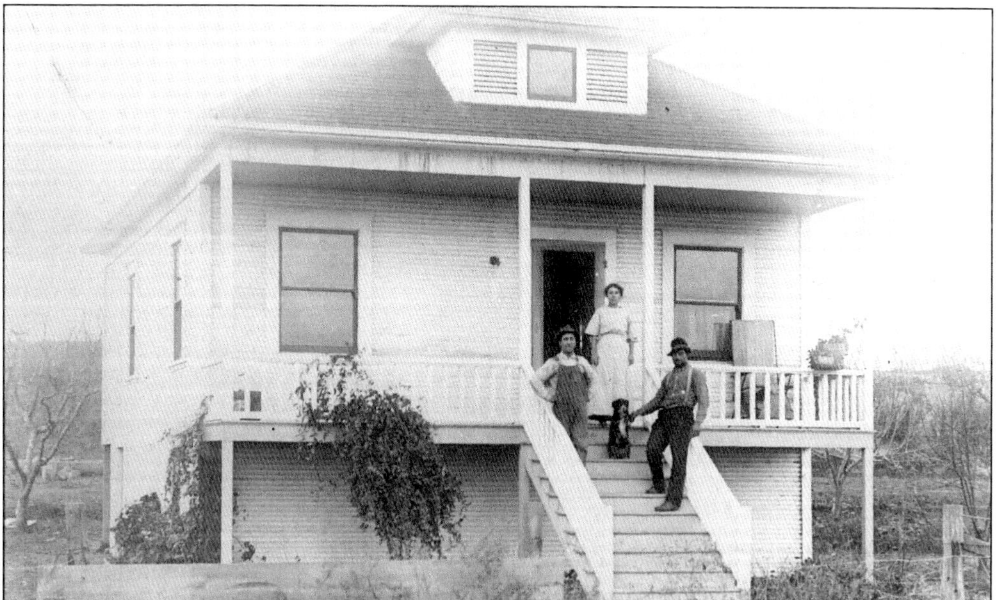

THE JOHN L. SILVA HOME IN THE POCKET AREA. Pictured here, from left to right, are Dan Rose, Luisa Rose Mello, and Frank Mello. The home was rented to the Mello family and is no longer standing today. (Courtesy of P.H.C.S.)

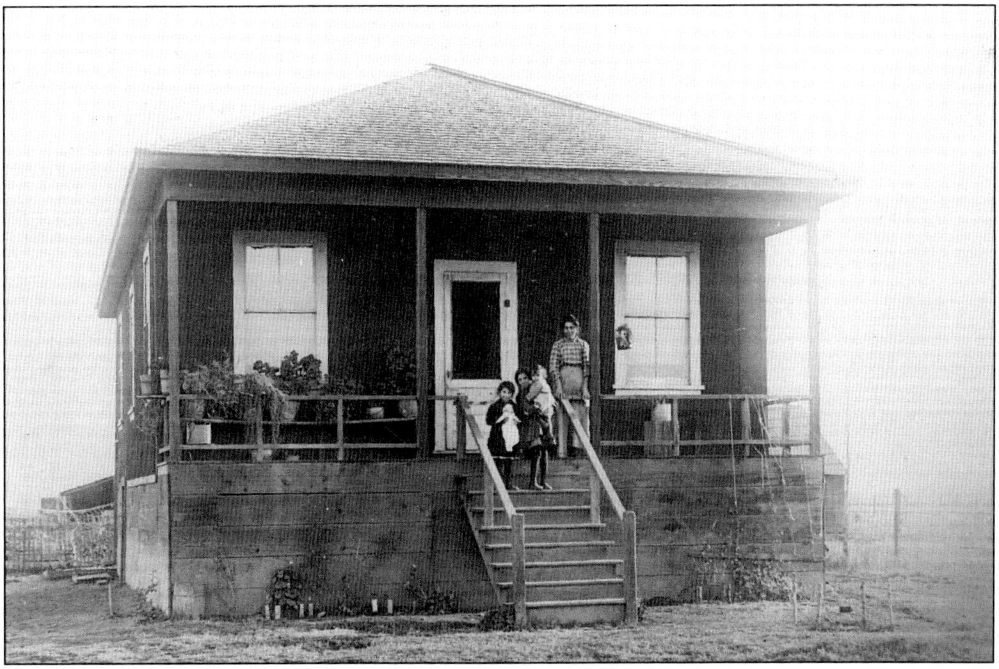

The Antone and Amelia Perry Family Home in the North Pocket Area. This picture was taken in 1914. At top right is Amelia, with Olivia at left holding a doll, and Madeline at right holding baby Lawrence. Lawrence Perry's family still lives in this home today. (Courtesy of P.H.C.S.)

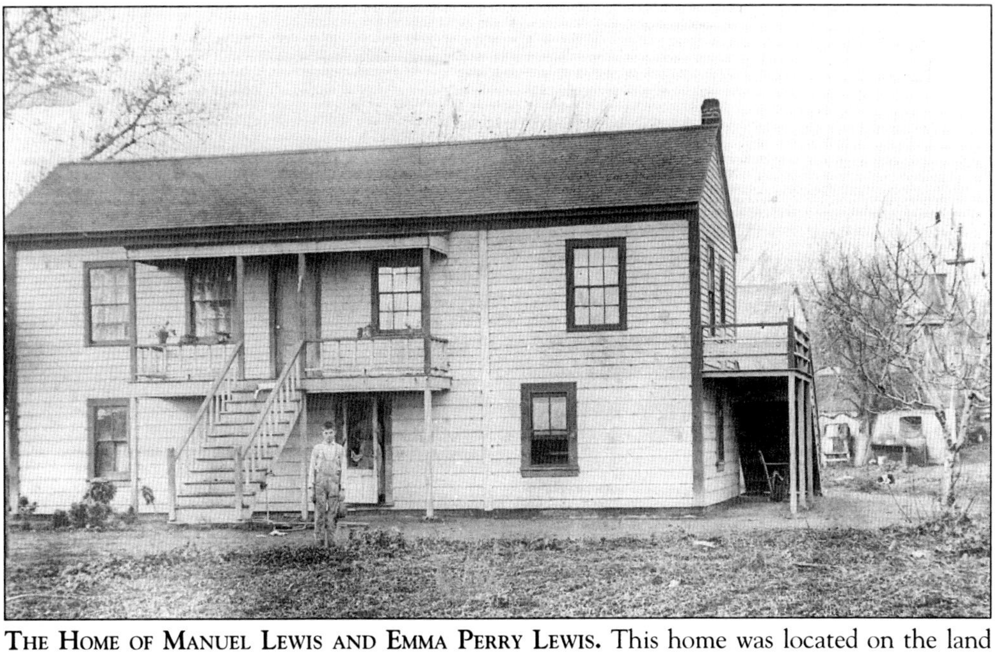

The Home of Manuel Lewis and Emma Perry Lewis. This home was located on the land where Lewis Park in the North Pocket area is today, thus named after the family. The ranch was owned by Antone Pereira Rodrigues (Perry) and a small parcel was deeded to daughter Emma when she married Manuel Lewis. (Courtesy of P.H.C.S.)

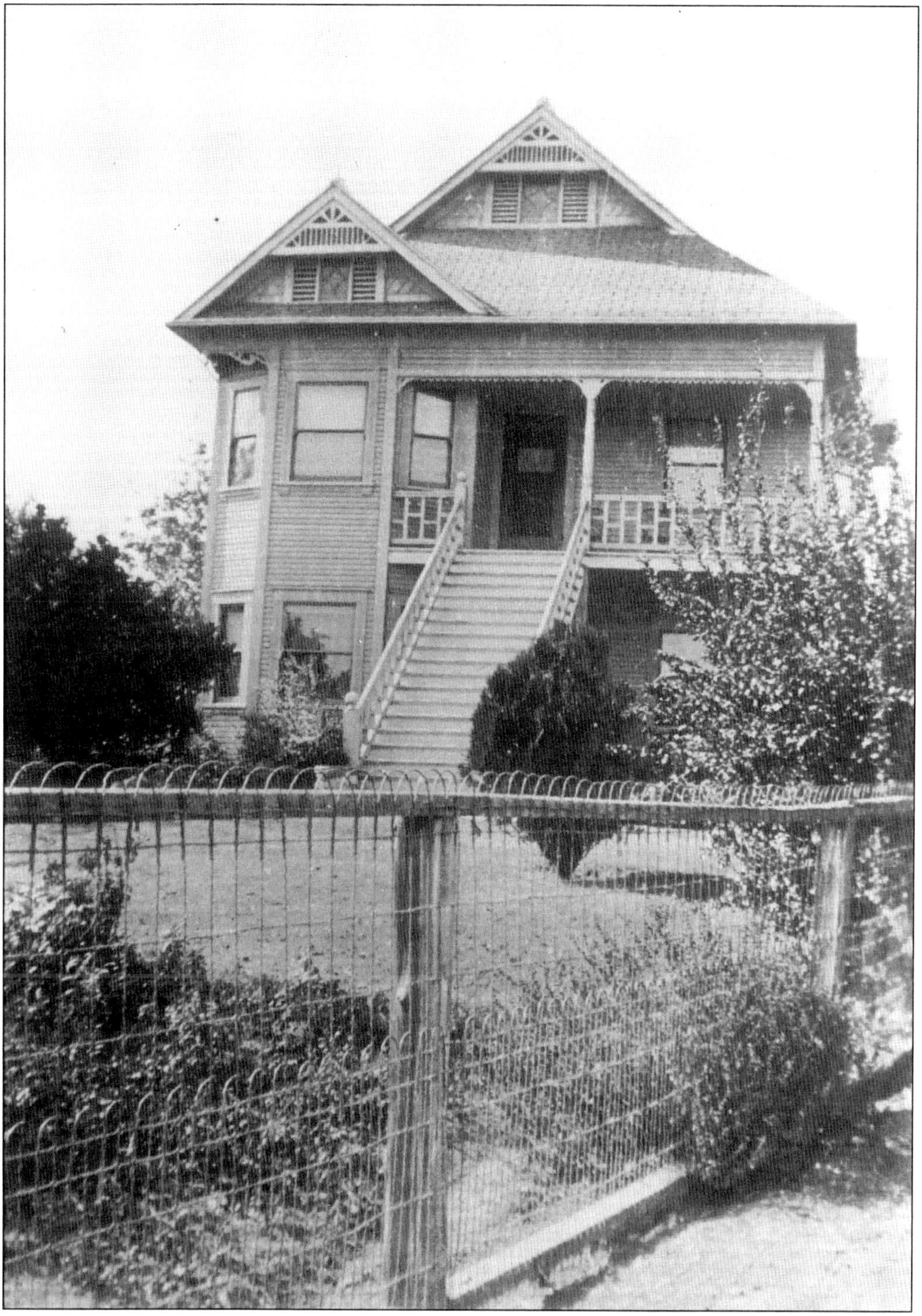

The Antone Luiz Silva Home in the South Pocket Area about 1910. The Victorian home was built by Christopher Valine, known as "Caliste," in 1909. The house was built on a knoll to avoid flooding. The Victorian family home was sold in 1986. (Courtesy of P.H.C.S., Tony Silva collection)

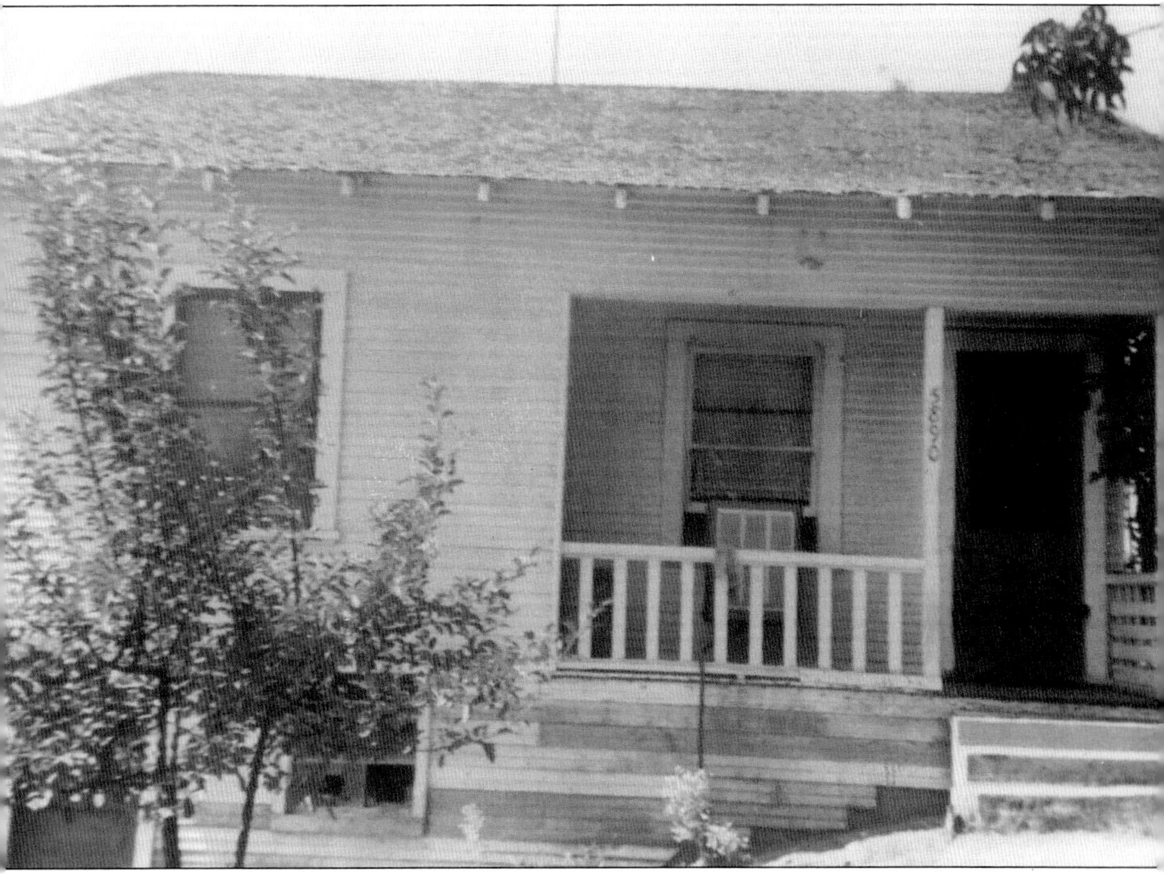

THE HOME OF MANUEL MAURICIO AND CARRIE NEVIS MAURICIO IN THE RIVERSIDE/POCKET AREA. (Courtesy of P.H.C.S.)

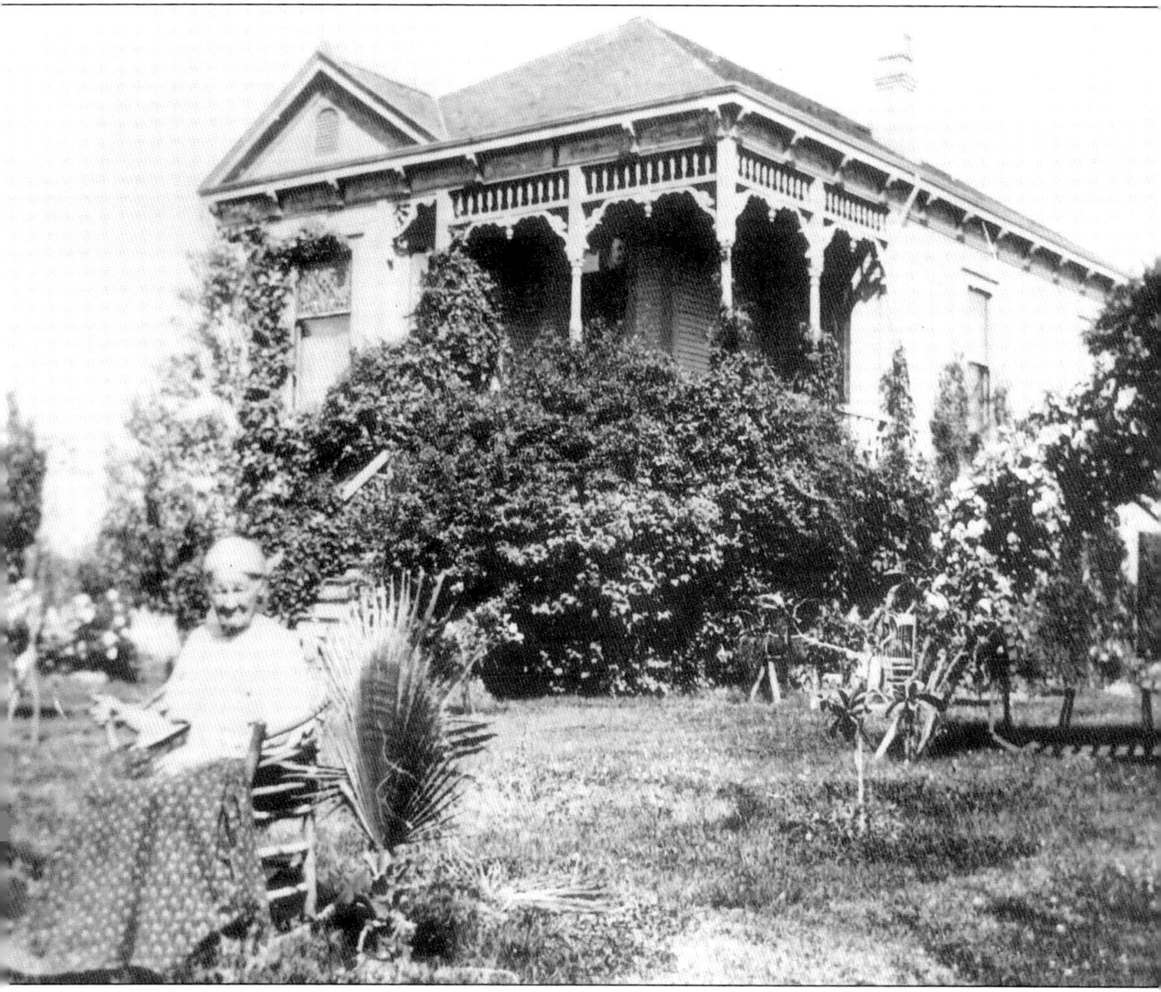

THE HOME OF MANUEL AND ROSELINA (ROSALINNA) SEAMAS C. 1920, OWNERS OF GRANGERS DAIRY. Seated at the front of the house is Leonora Silveira, mother of Roselina (Rosalinna) Seamas. (Photo Courtesy of P.H.C.S.)

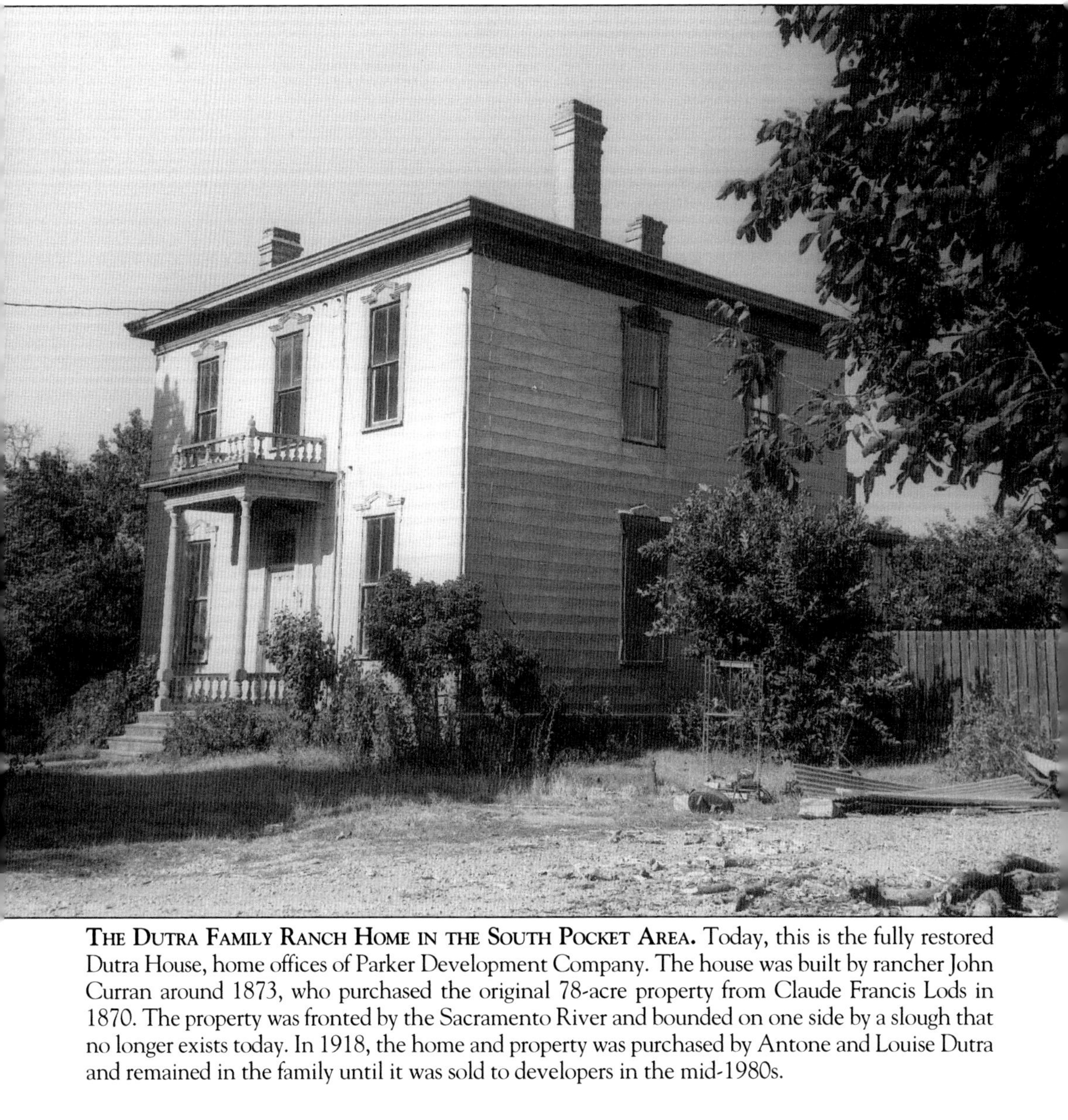

THE DUTRA FAMILY RANCH HOME IN THE SOUTH POCKET AREA. Today, this is the fully restored Dutra House, home offices of Parker Development Company. The house was built by rancher John Curran around 1873, who purchased the original 78-acre property from Claude Francis Lods in 1870. The property was fronted by the Sacramento River and bounded on one side by a slough that no longer exists today. In 1918, the home and property was purchased by Antone and Louise Dutra and remained in the family until it was sold to developers in the mid-1980s.

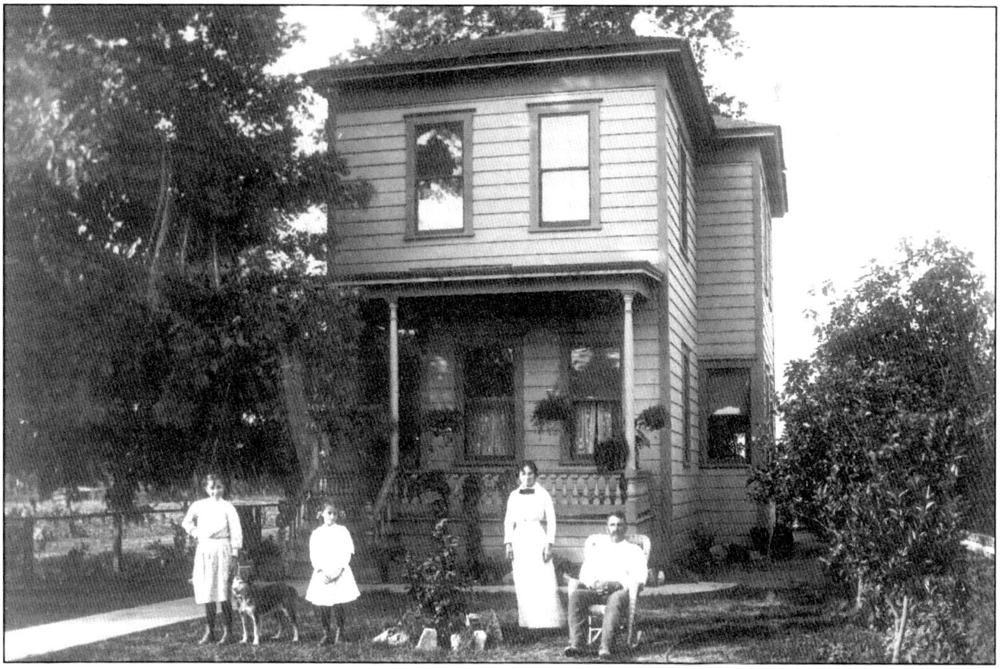

The Vital S. Fortado Home in the Riverside/Pocket Area c. 1912. Pictured here, from left to right, are Vital S. Fortado (seated), wife Mary (Silva) Fortado, daughter Emma (later a schoolteacher at Sutter Union School), the Fortados' dog "Guy," and daughter Minnie. (Courtesy of P.H.C.S.)

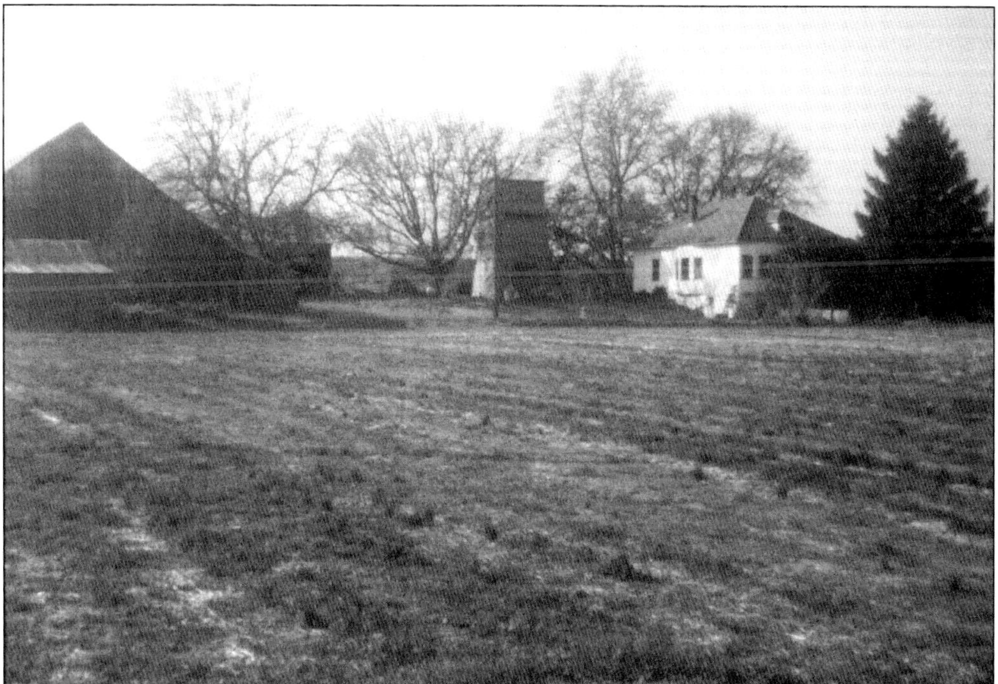

The John L. Silva Farm Located on Pocket Road in 1979. (Courtesy of P.H.C.S.)

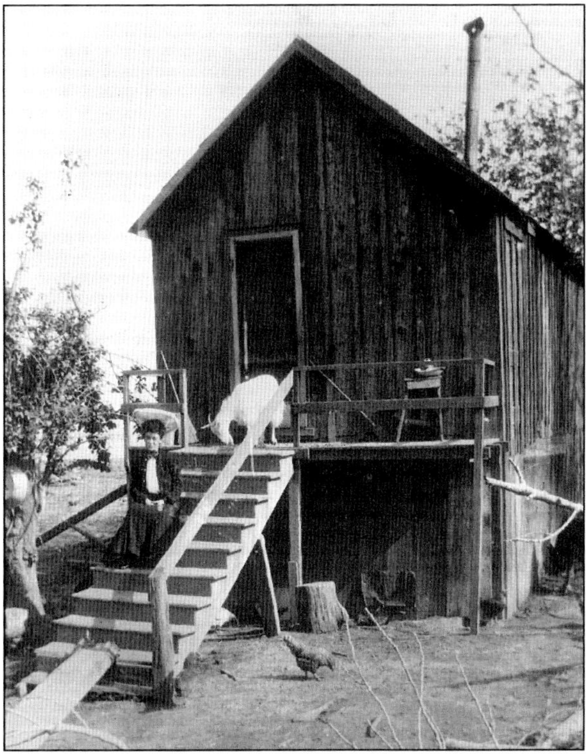

An Old Home Near the Sacramento River Levee on Manuel Seamas' Grangers Dairy Property. Later on an electric pump to pump water from the river was in the basement of the house. The woman in the picture is unidentified, but she did occupy the house before it became the home of Tony Seamas, brother of Manuel, perhaps in the early 1900s. (Courtesy of P.H.C.S., Manuel Seamas Grangers Dairy collection)

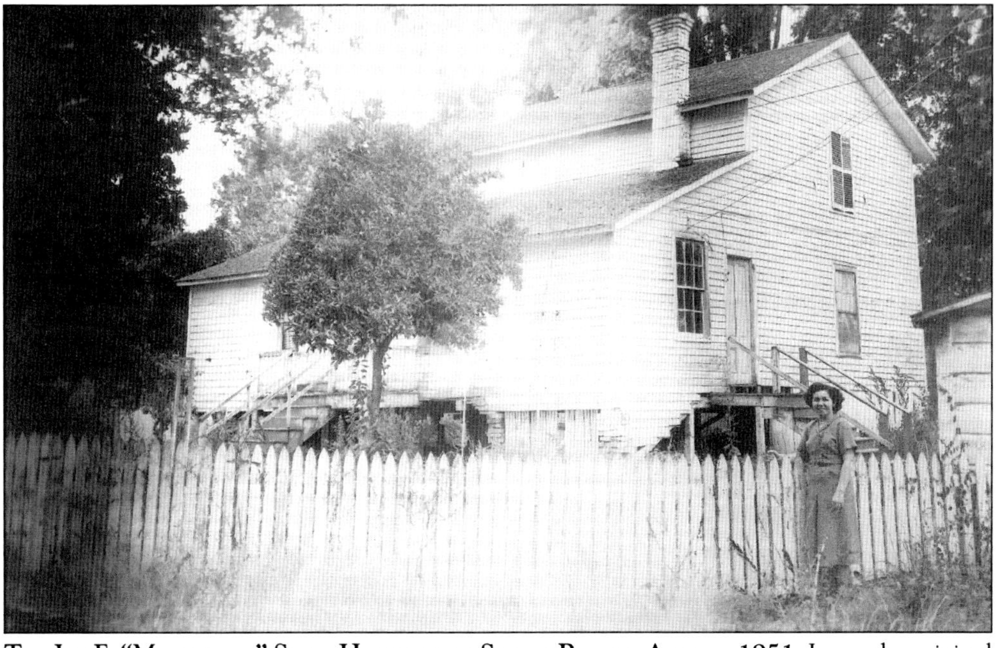

The Joe F. "Milhomens" Silva Home in the South Pocket Area in 1951. It was the original home of Joseph and Mary Waxon, Pocket pioneer settlers in 1865. The house of 10 rooms was moved back from the levee and remodeled. In the front of the house is Marie Dutra Gambrel, granddaughter of Joe F. "Milhomens" Silva who lived in the house in the early 1950s. (Courtesy of P.H.C.S., donated by Mary L. (Silva) Dutra)

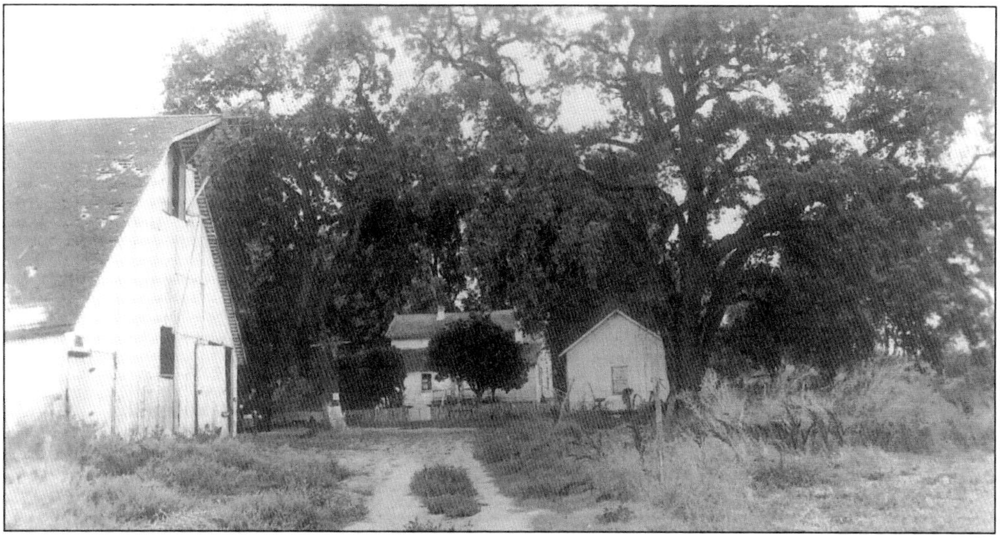

VIEW OF THE HOME AND RANCH OF JOSEPH AND MARIA "MILHOMENS" SILVA FROM 1903–1953. Two large oak trees were at the front of the house. Previously, this was the home and property of Manuel and Mary Waxon. Marie Dutra Gambrel remembered that she could see the lights of the State Capitol in downtown Sacramento from her grandfather's home on the second level when she lived there in the early 1950s. (Courtesy of P.H.C.S., donated by Mary L. (Silva) Dutra and Marie Dutra Gambrel, information provided by Marie Dutra Gambrel)

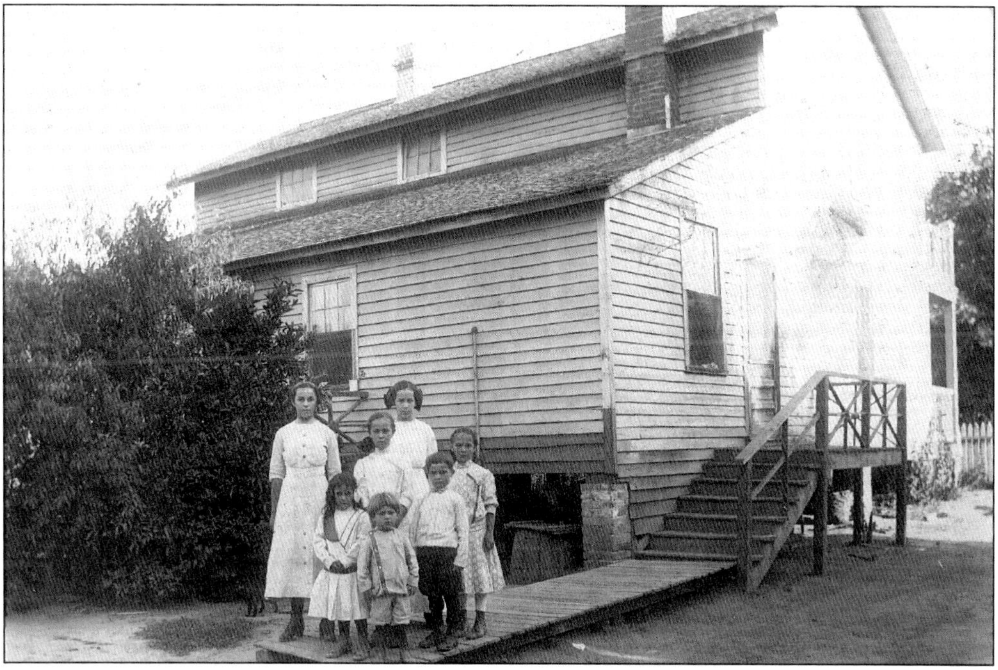

ANOTHER VIEW OF THE JOE F. "MILHOMENS" SILVA FAMILY HOME IN AUGUST 1913. Pictured here, from left to right, are the Silva children: Anna, Eleanor, Mary L., Minnie S., Manuel, Joaquin F., and Angelina Silva. Today, the "Milhomens" Silva family property is part of the Oakshore gated community of the Riverlake development in the South Pocket area. (Courtesy of P.H.C.S., donated by Marie Dutra Gambrel)

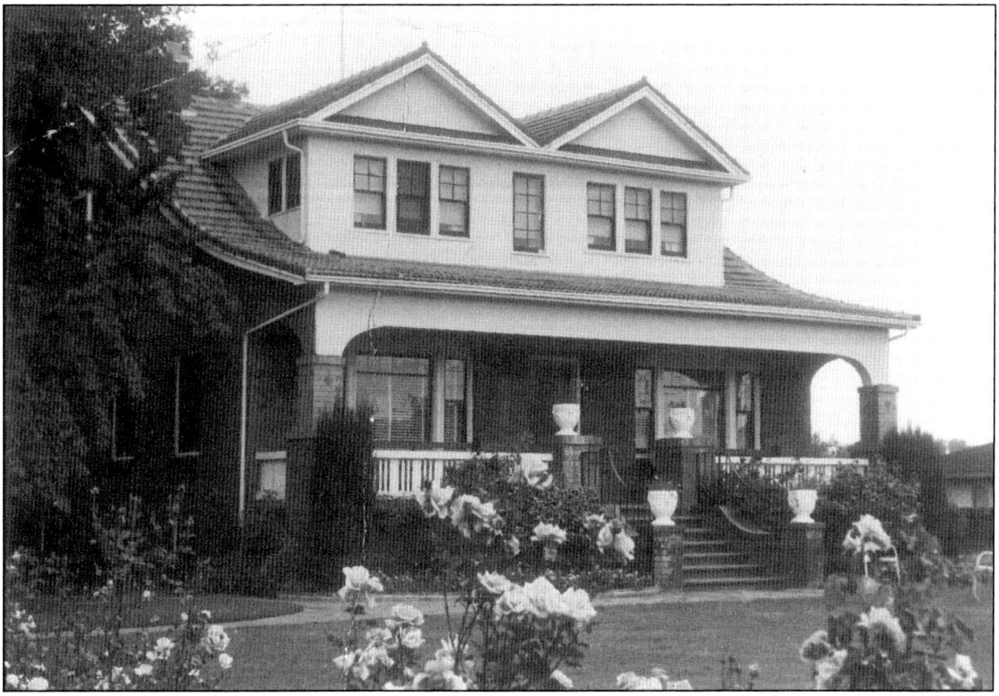

The Alvernaz Home in the Riverside Area, Built About 1928. It was built by Frank and Tony Terra of Terra Brothers Builders, who built a number of Greenhaven custom homes in later years. The home had two bedrooms upstairs along with a sleeping porch. The downstairs also had two bedrooms along with a living room, bathroom, and kitchen with a breakfast nook. (Courtesy of P.H.C.S.)

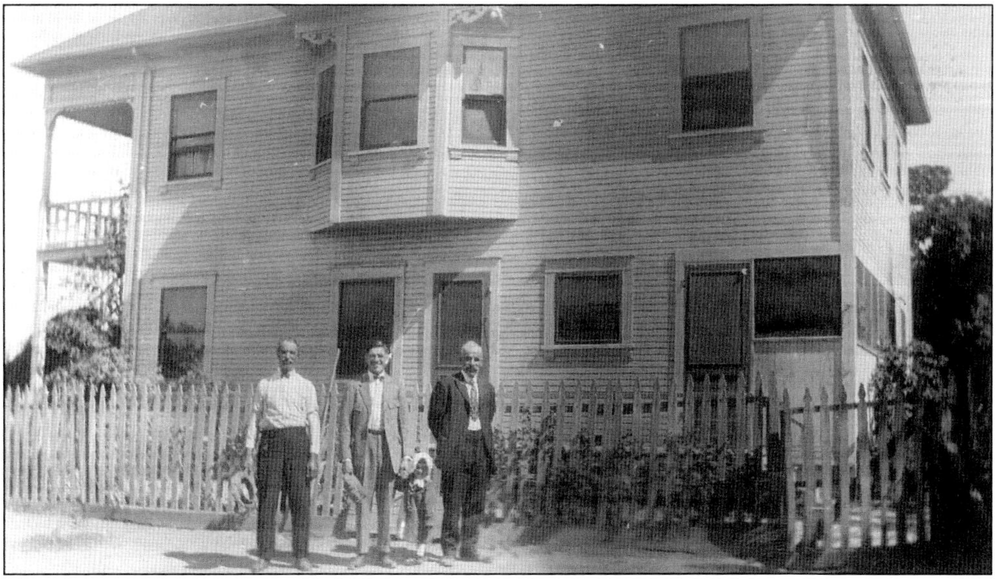

The A.L. Silva Home in the Pocket Area. This picture was taken *c.* 1920. (Courtesy of P.H.C.S.)

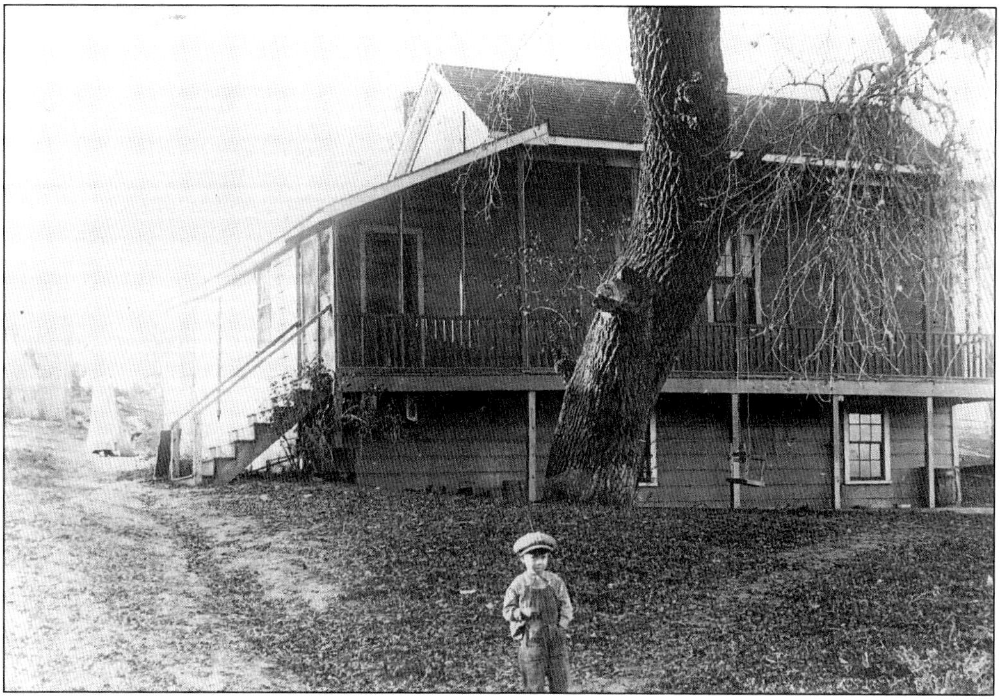

Manuel Rosa Sr. Home in the Riverside/Pocket Area. The young boy in the foreground of the house is Manuel Rosa Jr. (Courtesy of P.H.C.S., donated by Manuel Rosa Jr.)

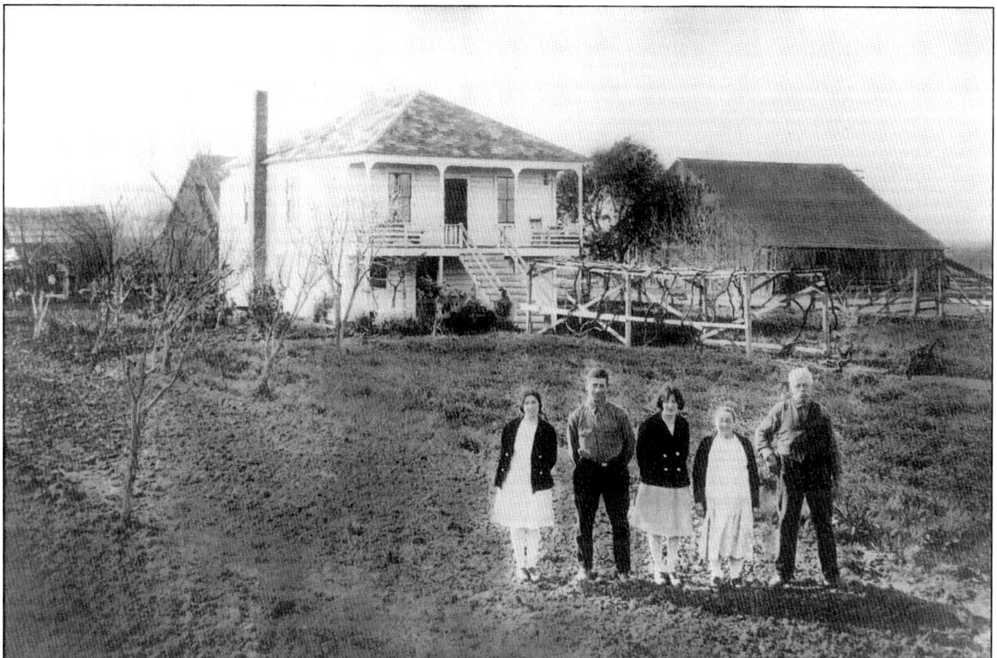

The Antone and Louise Amarel Home c. 1926–1928, Which Was Located on Twenty-Fourth Street Near Florin Road. Their daughter, Mary Amarel, not shown, married Frank Tash, son of pioneer Pocket farmer Joe Tash.

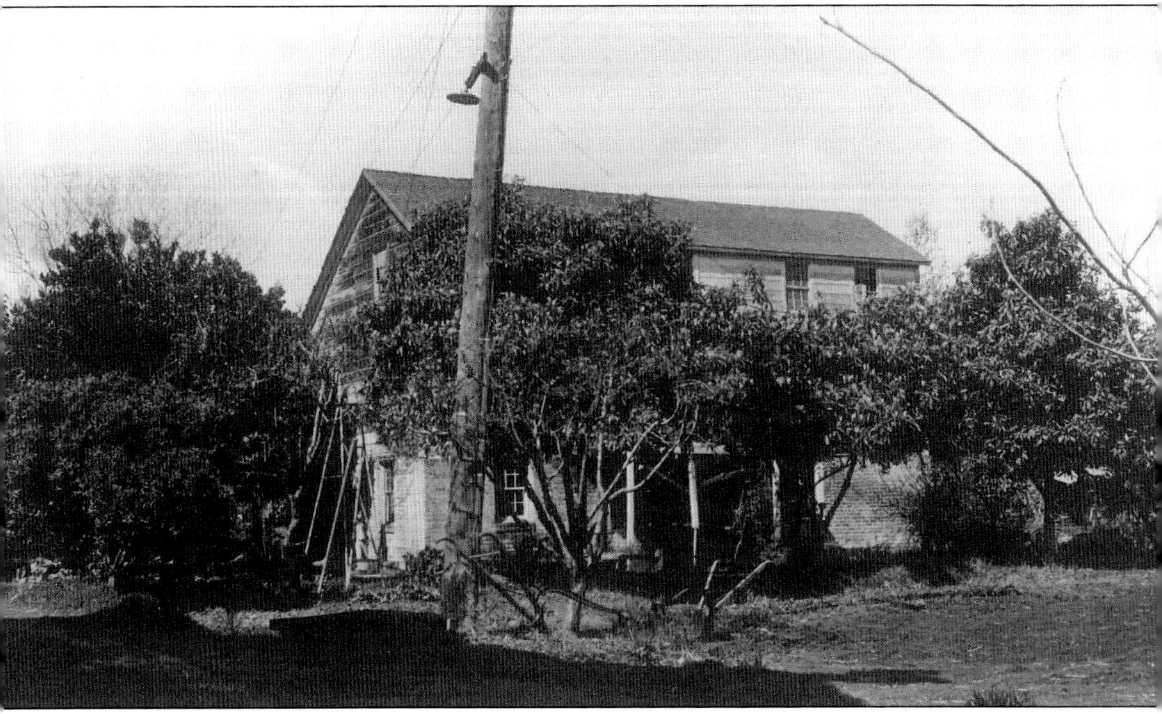

THE JOE TASH FAMILY HOME IN THE POCKET AREA JUST BEFORE IT WAS DEMOLISHED AROUND 1947. It was located in the northern Pocket area next to the Garcia ranch to the east. In later years, the daughter-in-law of Joe Tash, Mary Tash, would let students from nearby Kennedy High School ride horses on the ranch and provided room and board for the horses. She also built an arena on her ranch for the children to ride their horses in. (Courtesy of P.H.C.S., Mary Tash collection, information provided by Lucille Carter, daughter of Mary Tash)

Four

SCHOOLS

The schools found in the Pocket area before suburban development were noted as being the only ethnic public school system found in the Sacramento area from the 1870s to the 1940s. The large settlement of Portuguese families in the Pocket area wanted their children educated but also wanted their children to not lose their cultural heritage by attending American schools and not being able to help at home. As had been done across the Sacramento River in Yolo County a few years before, the Portuguese community established their own public school districts in the Riverside/Pocket area. The Sacramento Lisbon School District was established on January 21, 1873, by a group of Portuguese Americans under the leadership of Manuel E. Da Costa, who petitioned the Sacramento County Board of Supervisors to establish their own district. School-age children residing in the Pocket area of all nationalities attended the Lisbon Schools, learning the major subjects from first through eighth grades. When two schools were established in the Pocket, children in the South Pocket area attended Lower Lisbon School while children in the North Pocket area attended Upper Lisbon School. Sutter Union School, affiliated with the Sutter School District in the Riverside area was attended by school-age children who lived in Riverside, its boundary being where Fourty-Third Avenue and the Trap is located today.

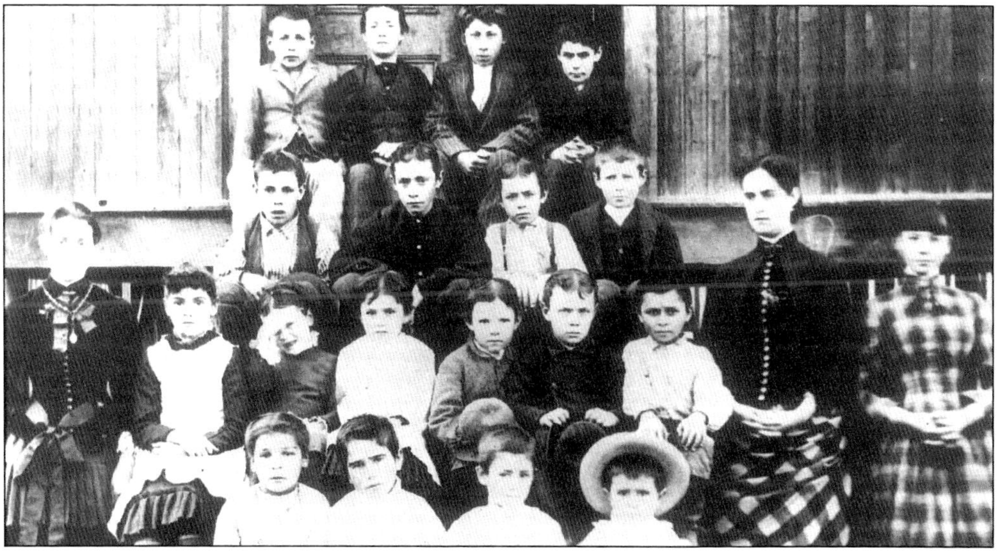

PICTURE OF THE ORIGINAL LISBON SCHOOL C. 1885, A CONVERTED WOODEN BARN. Pictured here, from left to right, are as follows: (front row) Mary Garcia, Joe Perry, Domingas Lucas, and Joe Williams; (second row) Rose De Costa, Emma Perry, Mildred Waxon, "Minnie" Perry, Frank Durch, Peter Waxon, Joe Garcia, teacher Miss Agnes Devine, and Josie Waxon; (third row) Manuel Peters, Manuel Waxon, Frank Waxon, and Will Da Costa; (fourth row) Tony Da Costa, Anthony Waxon, George Da Costa, and Antone "Tony" Perry. (Courtesy of P.H.C.S, identified by Cecilia (Waxon) O'Kane)

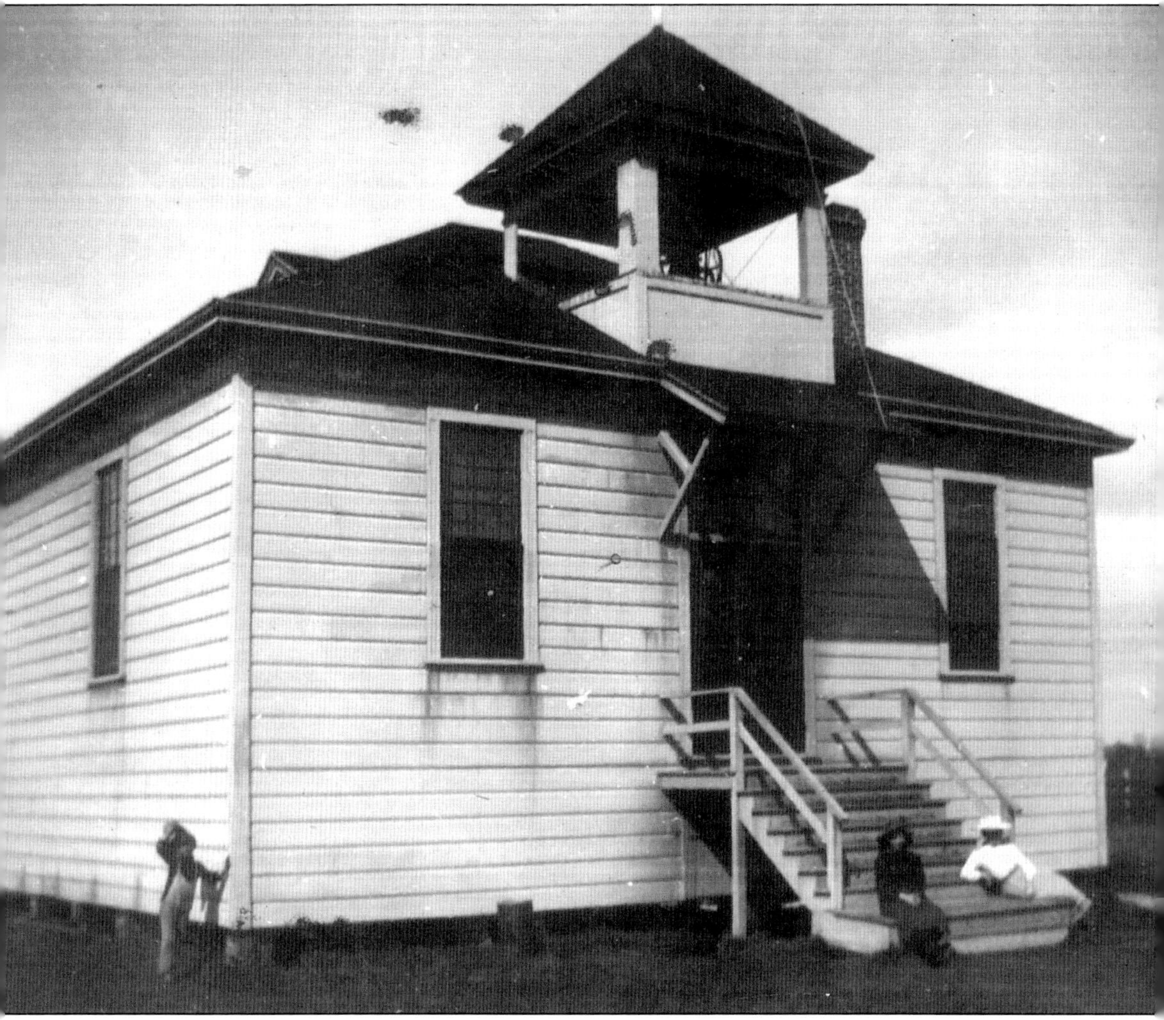

THE UPPER LISBON SCHOOL ON RIVERSIDE ROAD C. 1890. The Portuguese raised money to build the new schoolhouse at that time. It was located on the west side where Park Riviera Way intersects with Riverside Blvd. today. (Courtesy of P.H.C.S)

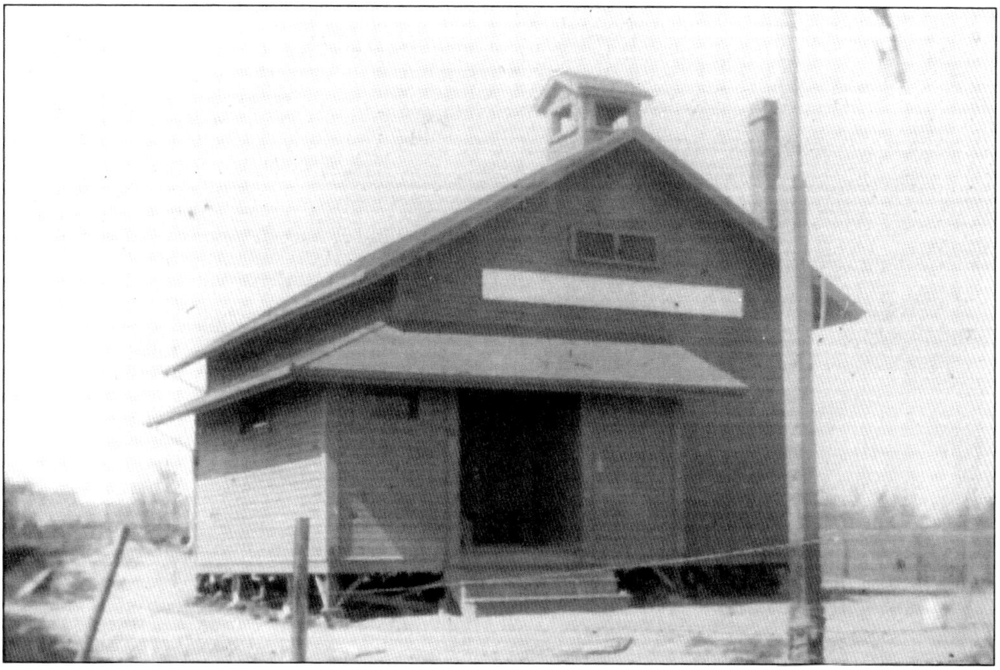

THE LOWER LISBON SCHOOL ON POCKET ROAD WHEN IT WAS NEWLY BUILT AROUND 1909–1910. This building replaced the original Lisbon School destroyed by the 1904 flood (Edwards Break) and money was subsequently raised to build the new schoolhouse. (Courtesy of P.H.C.S.)

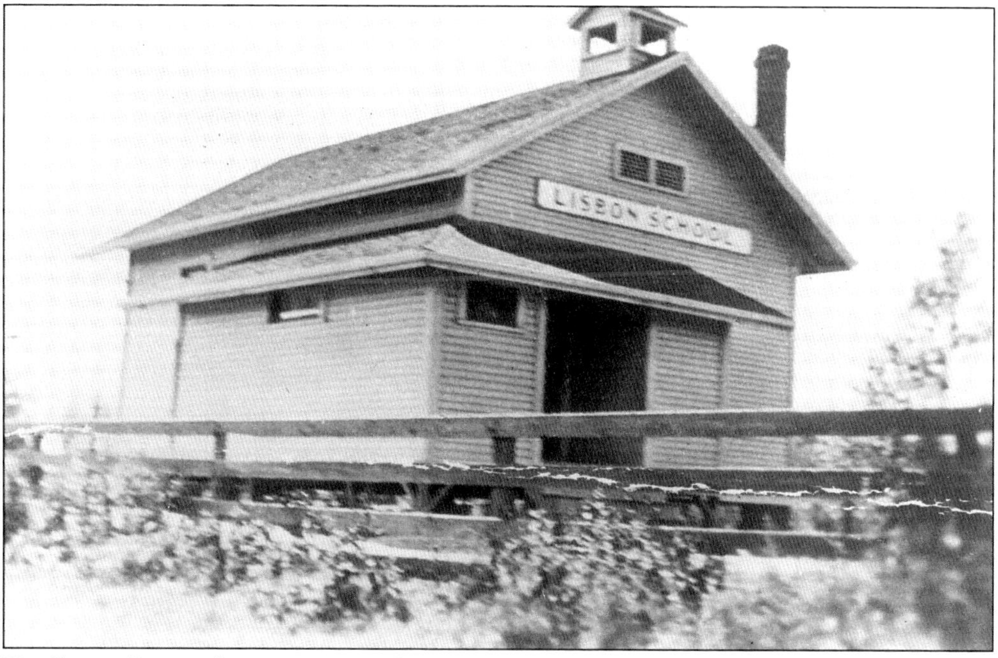

THE LOWER LISBON SCHOOL C. 1912, DISPLAYING THE LISBON SCHOOL SIGN. The Lisbon School building, located next to the drainage canal in the South Pocket area, was condemned and finally demolished in 1940. (Courtesy of P.H.C.S.)

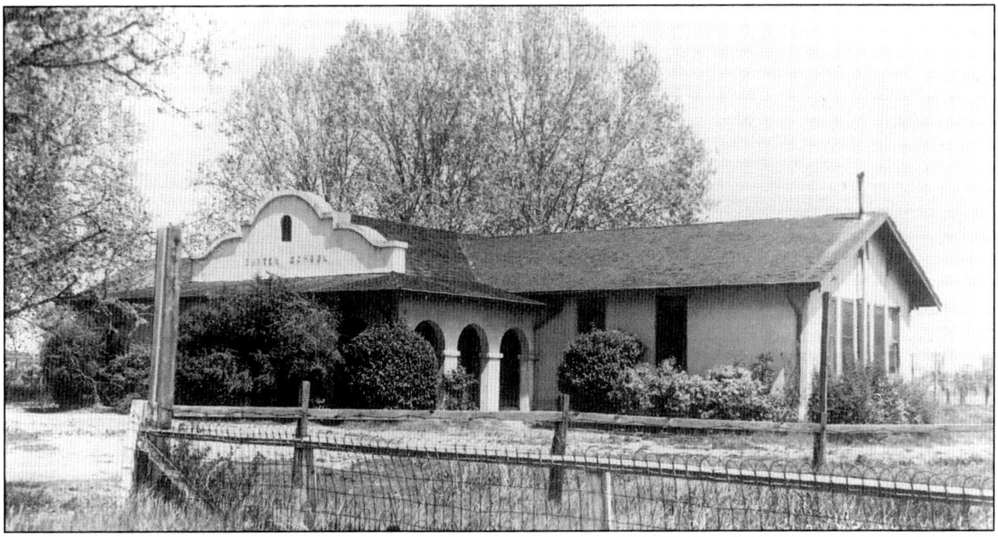

The Sutter Union School in 1953 on Riverside Road. The school building was built about 1915, and the property of the school was owned by J.M. and Katie J. Mason and mother Louisa. The first graduating class of the school was Mamie G. Machado and John "Griff" Mason. The original Sutter Union School building is still located in its exact location on Karbet Way, owned and operated by Cabrillo Civic Club #5, a Portuguese lodge. (Courtesy of P.H.C.S.)

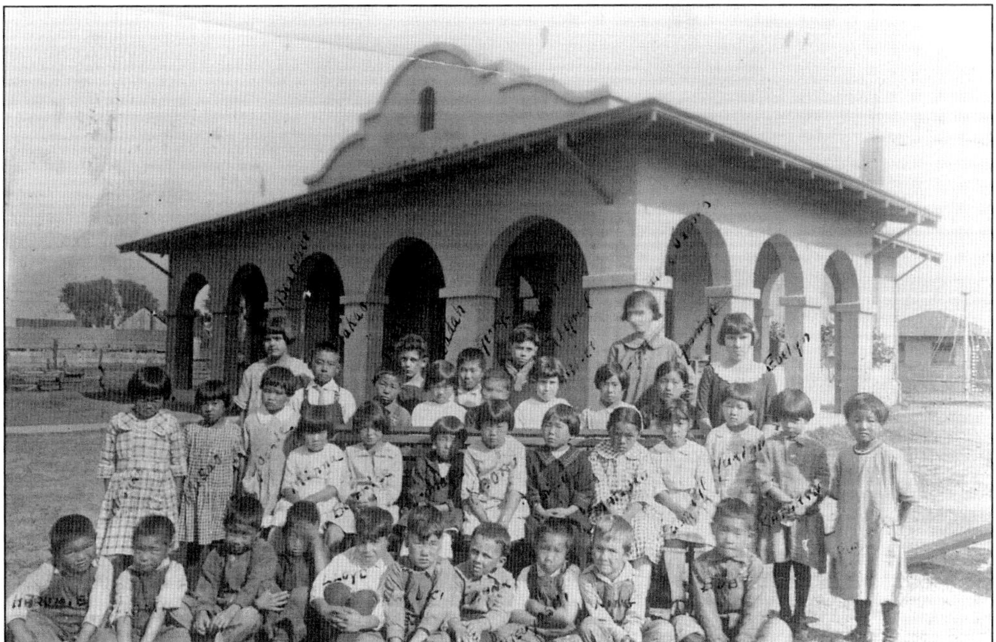

Sutter Union School Class About 1925 With Mrs. Emma Fortado James as the Teacher. Mrs. James was the daughter of Vital Silva Fortado, who farmed in the Pocket area. She received her education from Chico Normal School (later Chico State College) in 1922. Her first teaching job was at Sutter Union School from 1922–1928. (Courtesy of P.H.C.S.)

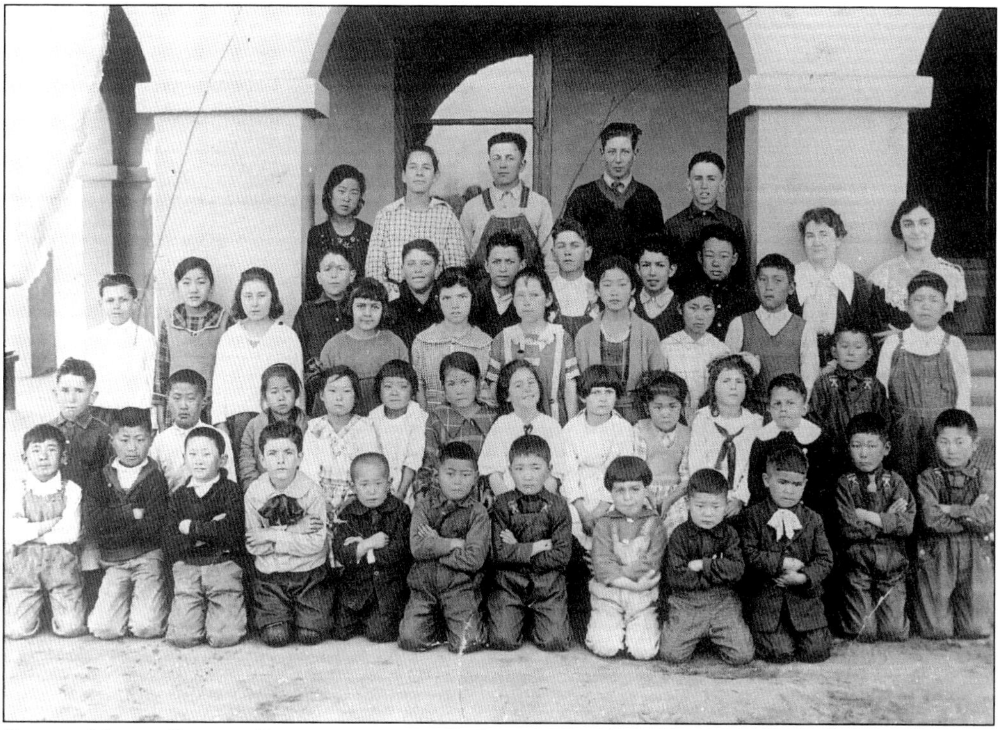

Sutter Union School Class in 1922. Mrs. Emma Fortado James, the teacher, is located to the far right in the fourth row. This was her first year and class of teaching. (Courtesy of P.H.C.S.)

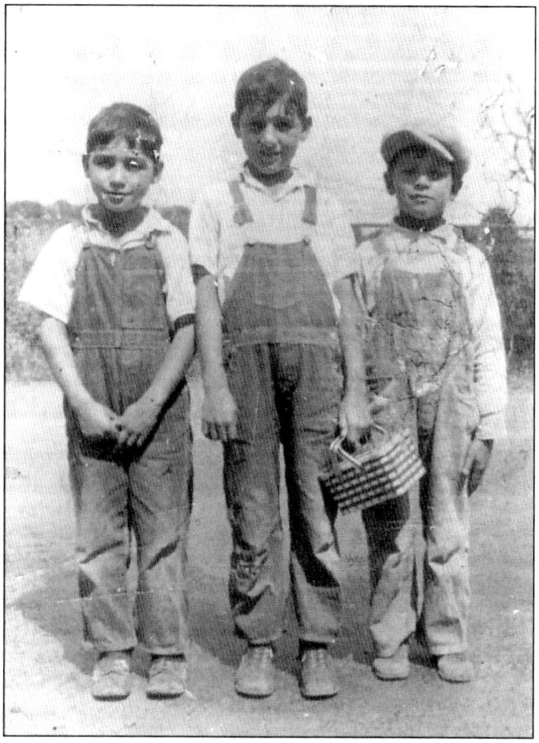

After School. From left to right are Edward Mauricio, Herman Mauricio, and Marvin Silva returning home from Sutter Union School on Riverside Road in 1929 or 1930. (Courtesy of P.H.C.S)

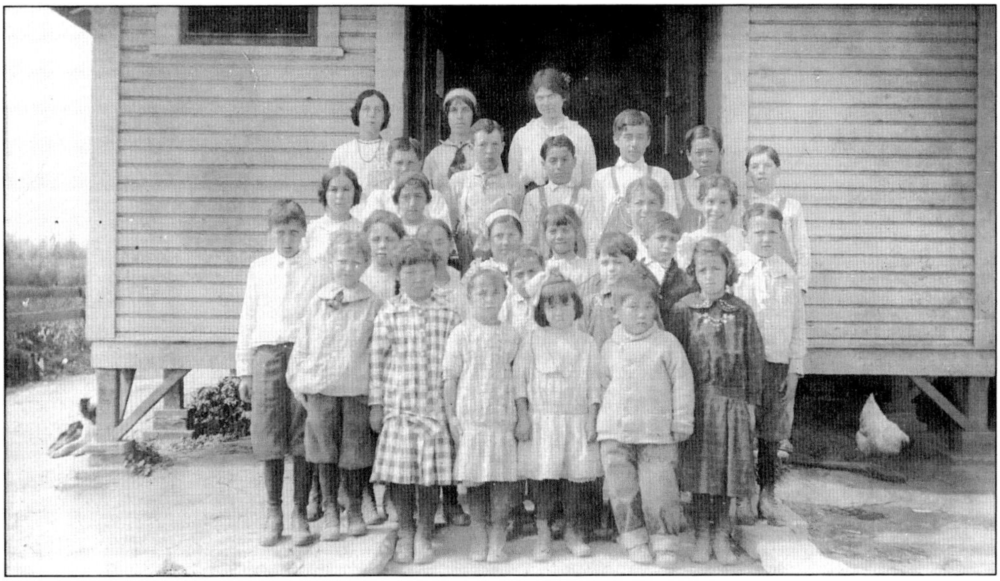

A LOWER LISBON SCHOOL CLASS IN THE EARLY 1900S. (Courtesy of P.H.C.S)

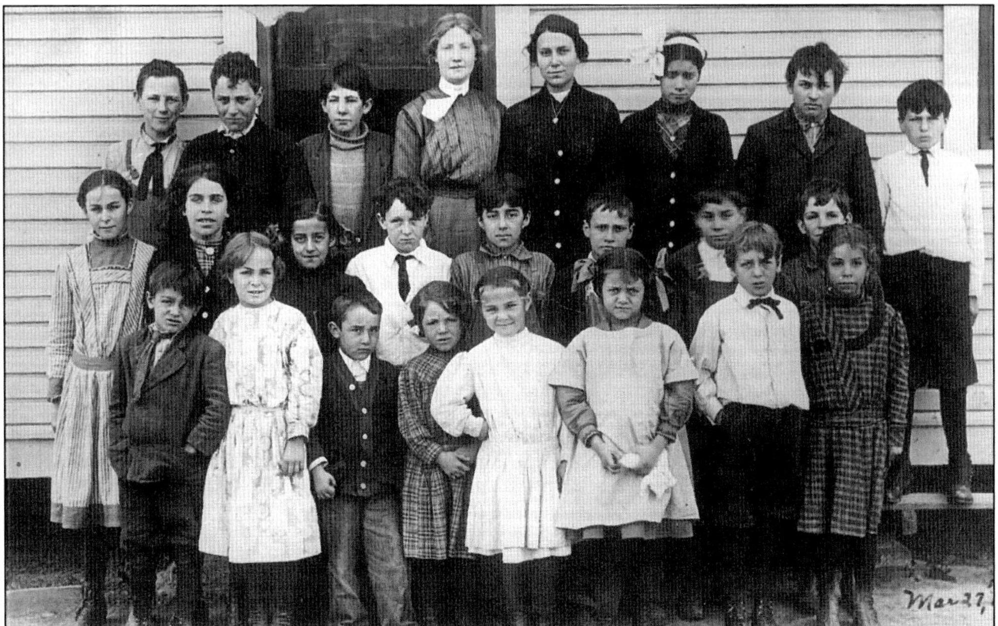

THE CLASS AT THE LOWER LISBON SCHOOL ON POCKET ROAD IN MAY 1912. Miss Lily E. Jones, fourth from the left in the top row, is the teacher. Miss Jones began teaching at the Lisbon School at the age of 18 and was one of the very first teachers at the Lisbon schools. (Courtesy of P.H.C.S.)

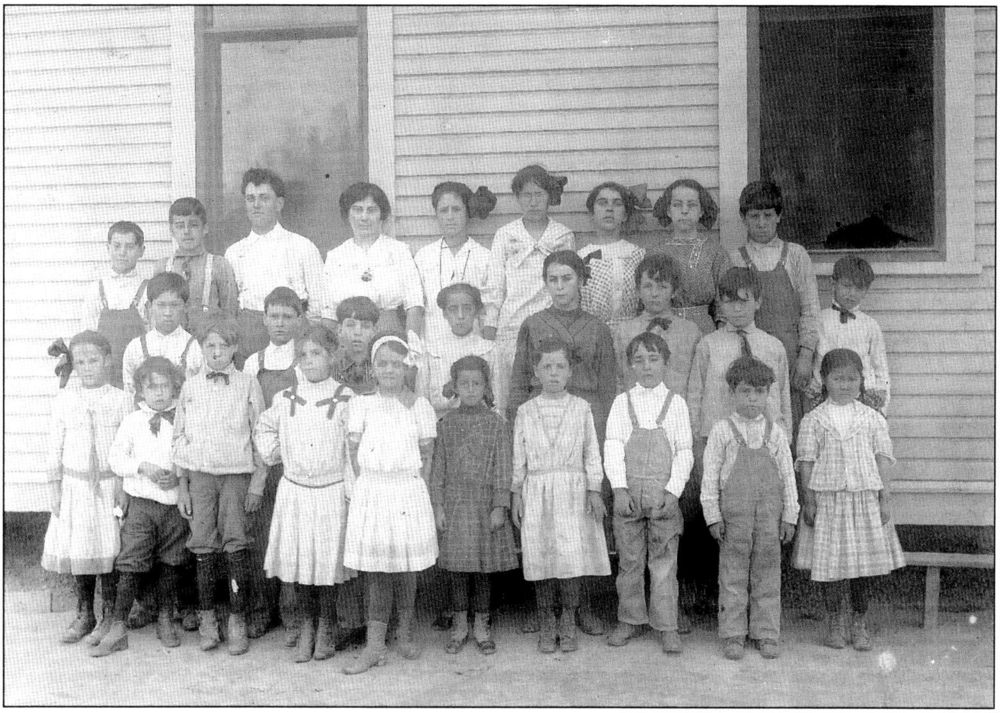

The Lower Lisbon School Class c. 1913. (Courtesy of P.H.C.S., Mary L. "Milhomens" Silva Dutra and Marie Gambrel collection)

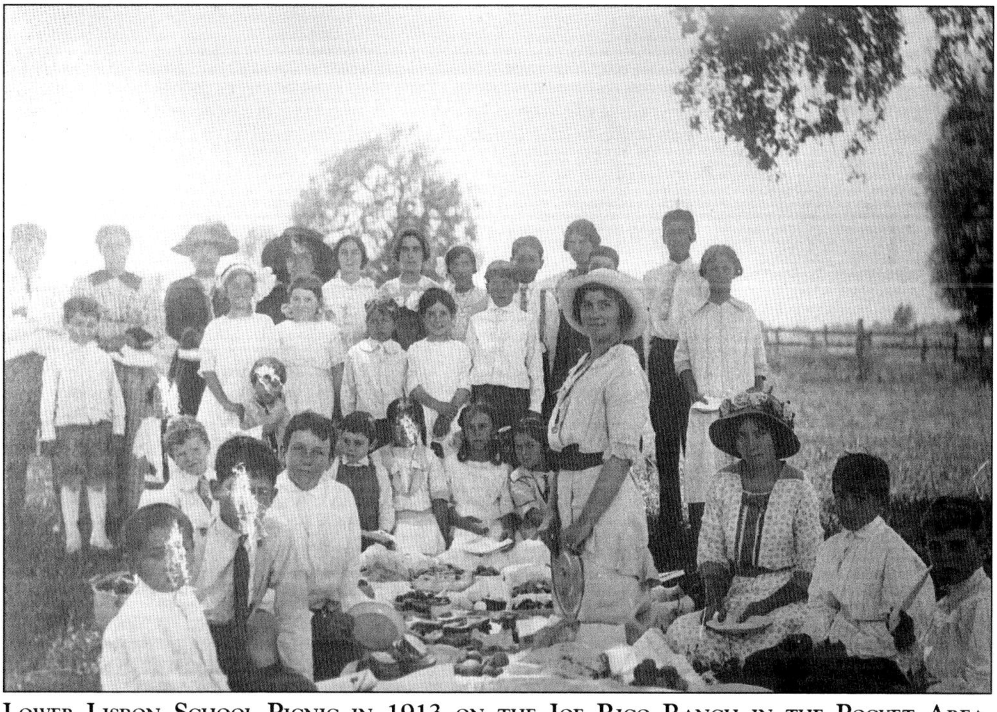

Lower Lisbon School Picnic in 1913 on the Joe Rico Ranch in the Pocket Area. (Courtesy of P.H.C.S.)

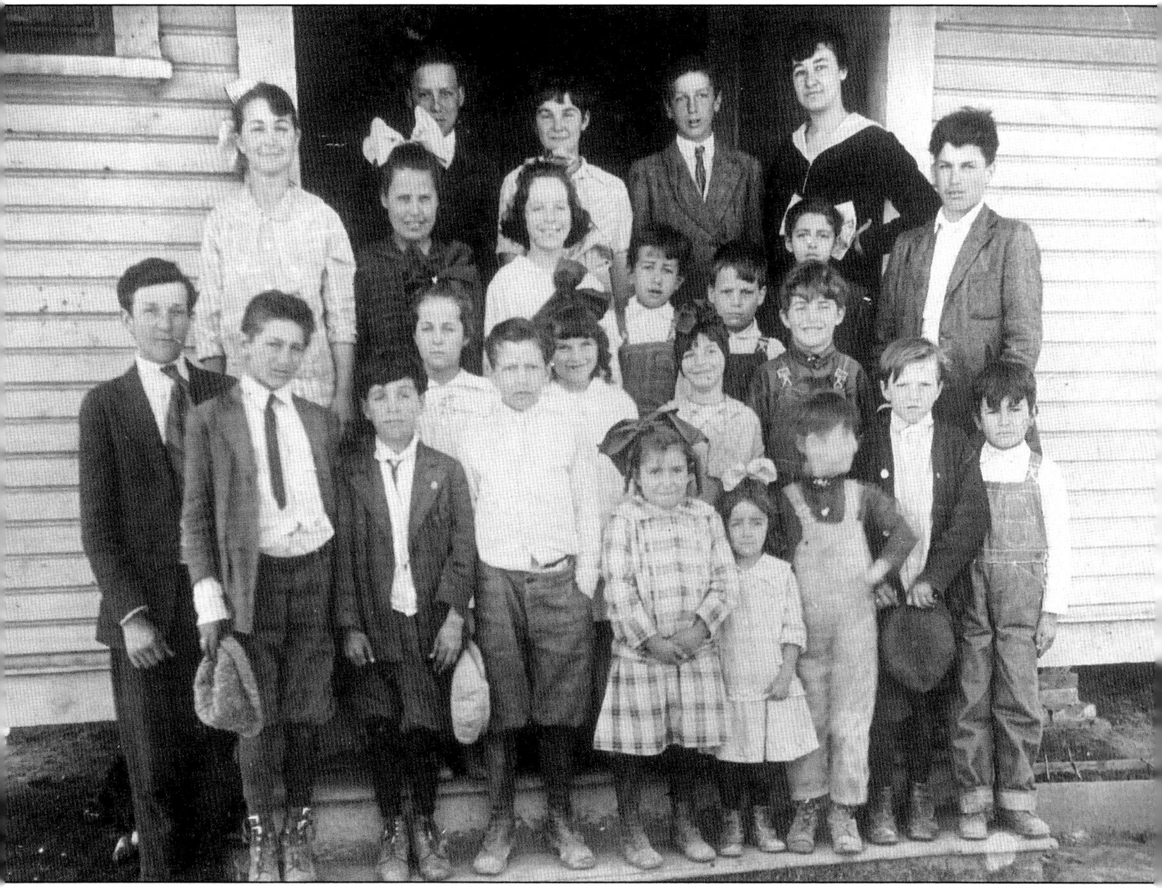

The Lower Lisbon School Class in 1916. Mrs. Lombardi, far left at the top row, is the teacher. Children pictured in the photo include: Eleanor M. Silva, Manuel Ventura, Angelina M. Silva, William Garcia, Alice Ventura, Rose Silva, Frank Dutra, Louis Ventura, Helen Souza, Harry Garcia, Minnie M. Silva, Myrtle Garcia, Hazel Silva, Joaquin "King" M. Silva, Edward Garcia, Melvin Garcia, Anthony L. Silva, Walter Garcia, Mary Dutra, Eva Souza, Manuel M. Silva, Irvin Garcia, and Tony Dutra. (Courtesy of P.H.C.S., donated by Tony Dutra)

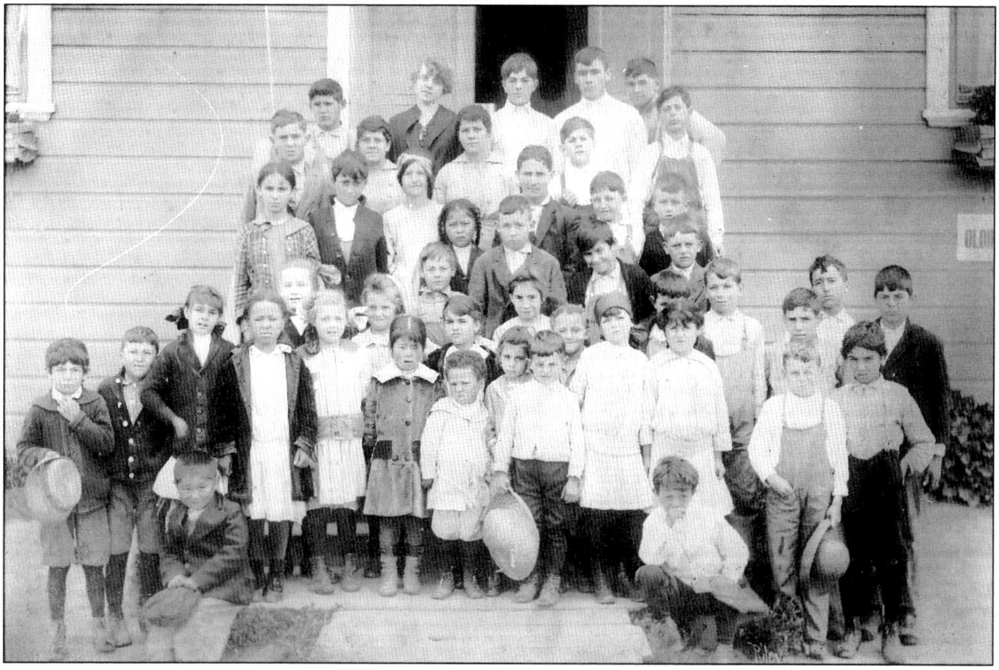

THE UPPER LISBON SCHOOL CLASS c. 1918–1919. (Courtesy of P.H.C.S)

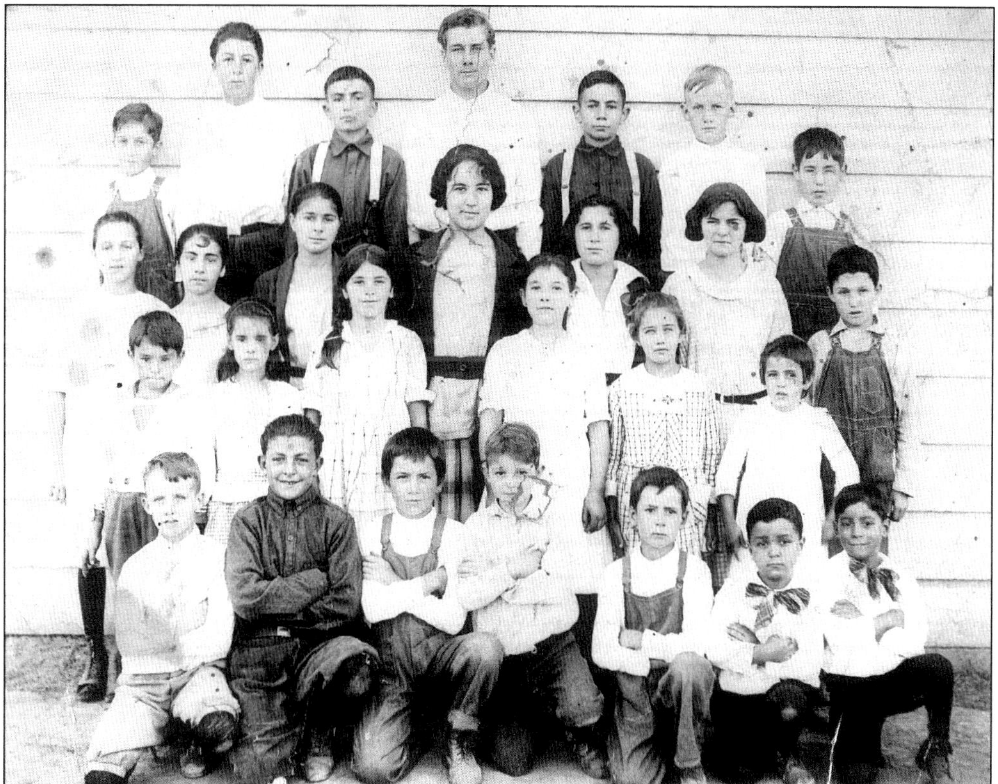

THE UPPER LISBON SCHOOL CLASS IN 1921. (Courtesy of P.H.C.S)

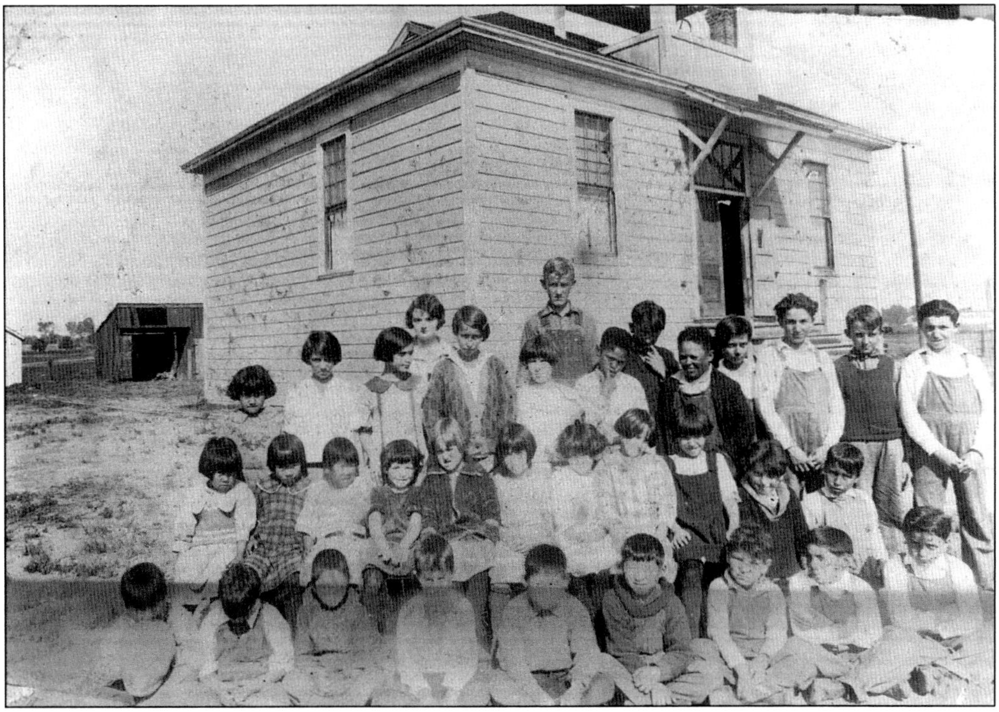

The Upper Lisbon School Class in 1926 With the School Building in the Foreground. (Courtesy of P.H.C.S., donated by Clarence Nevis)

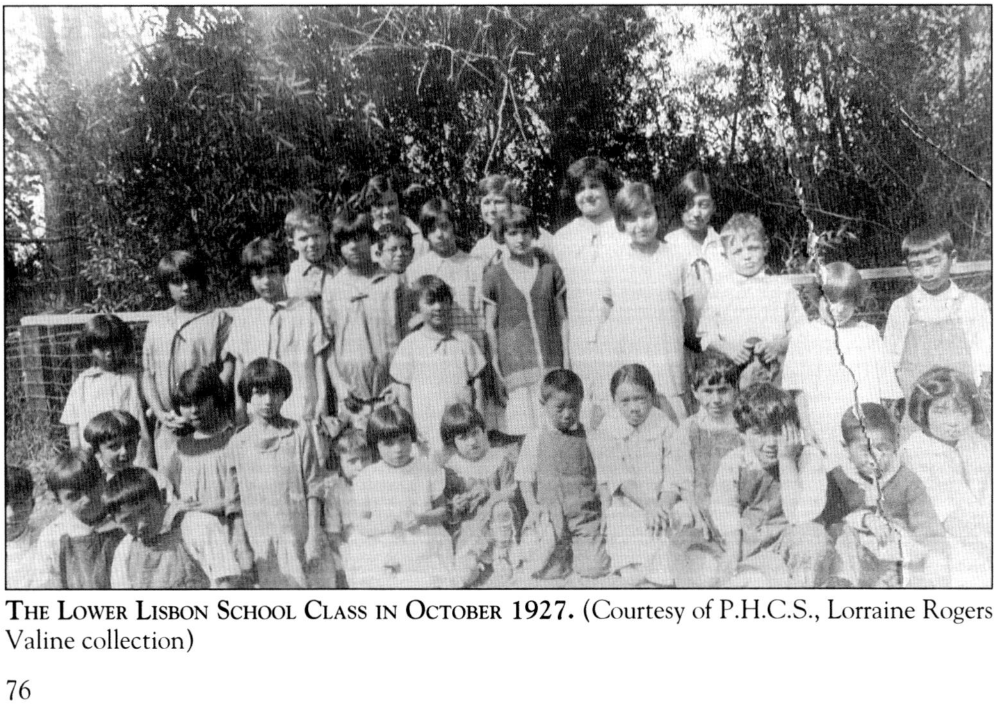

The Lower Lisbon School Class in October 1927. (Courtesy of P.H.C.S., Lorraine Rogers Valine collection)

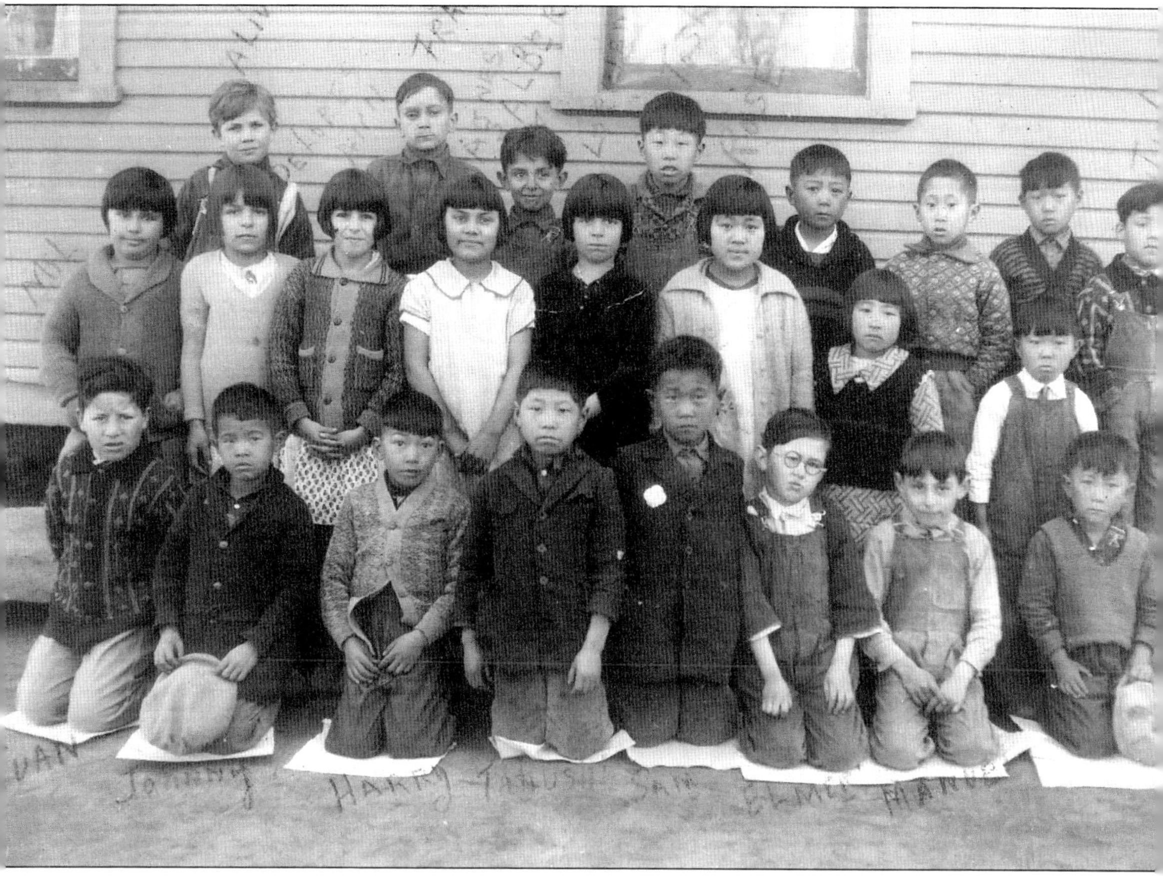

THE LOWER LISBON SCHOOL CLASS IN 1927, WITH MS. MABEL WAKEFIELD AS THE TEACHER (NOT SHOWN IN PICTURE). Pictured, from left to right, are as follows: (first row) Juan Hernandez, John (Johnny) Inouye, Hiroo (Harry) Kashiwada, Takashi Tanaka, Simon (Sam) Inouye, Elmer Silva, Manuel Perry, and Masakuzu Ojima; (second row) Mildred Rogers, Dolores Silva, Anna Perry, Agnes Lee, Lorraine Rogers, Shizuko (Rose) Sakayeda, Kiyoko Ojima, and Shinichi Suyeda; (third row) Alvin Berkencamp, Frankie Lewis, Albert "Goo" Rogers, Toshio Tanaka, Akio Ojima, Makoto Shirai, Thomas Suyeda, and Julio Hernandez. The year after in 1928, the classes were moved to a school building located on the Frank Lewis ranch and rented monthly from the Japanese community, who owned the building. The Japanese language was subsequently taught in this building on weekends. This picture was used on the front cover of the manuscript for the *Strange and Wonderful Harvest Documentary* in 1982. A collaborative project co-sponsored by the Portuguese Historical and Cultural Society and the Japanese American Citizens League, it documented through oral histories how the two cultural groups came together in Sacramento's Riverside/Pocket area to create a positive inter-ethnic community. The documentary was directed by Dr. Gregg Campbell, Professor of History at California State University, Sacramento, and produced by the University Media Services through a grant from the California Council of Humanities. The fact that children from families of Portuguese, Japanese, and other ethnic groups were able to attend school together in the Pocket area was one of the many highlights that this documentary featured regarding their peaceful co-existence. (Courtesy of P.H.C.S., Alvin Berkencamp collection)

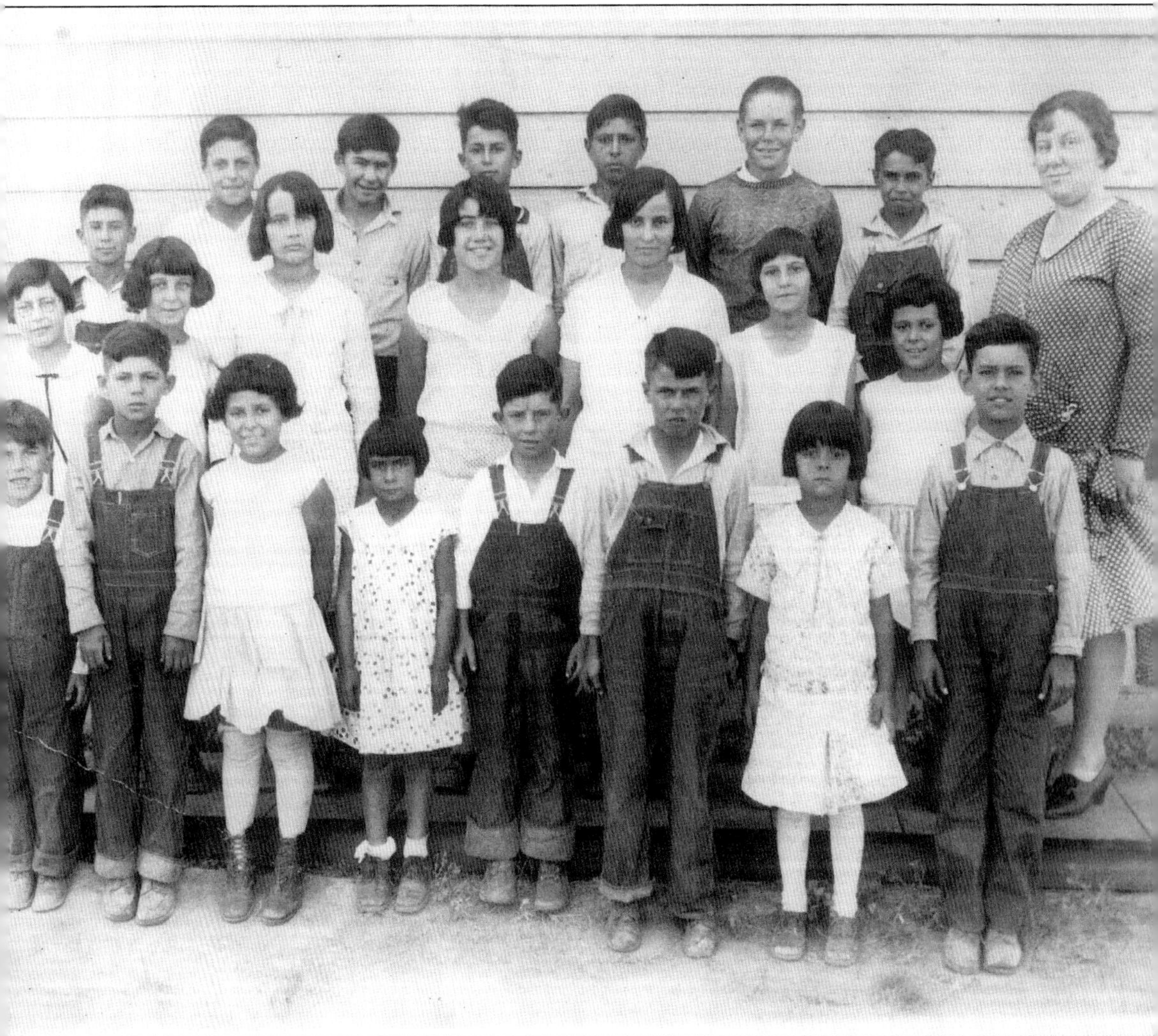

The Upper Lisbon Class in 1928 With School Children from First Through Eighth Grades. At far right is Mrs. Hoschner, the teacher. Pictured here, from left to right, are as follows: (first row) Edward Prady, Ernest Azevedo, Edna Garcia, Marie Gomes, Wilbert Azevedo, Marvin Gomes, Marie Sarmento, and Manuel Sarmento; (second row) Veronica Azevedo, Alvera Nevis, Elise Curry, Lorraine Perry, Irene Curry, Lorene Nevis, and Edith Garcia; (third row) Marvin Silveira, Frank Martin, Lloyd Nevis, Alvin Silveira, Clyde Sarmento, Elmer Holmes, and Elmer Gomes. (Courtesy of P.H.C.S.)

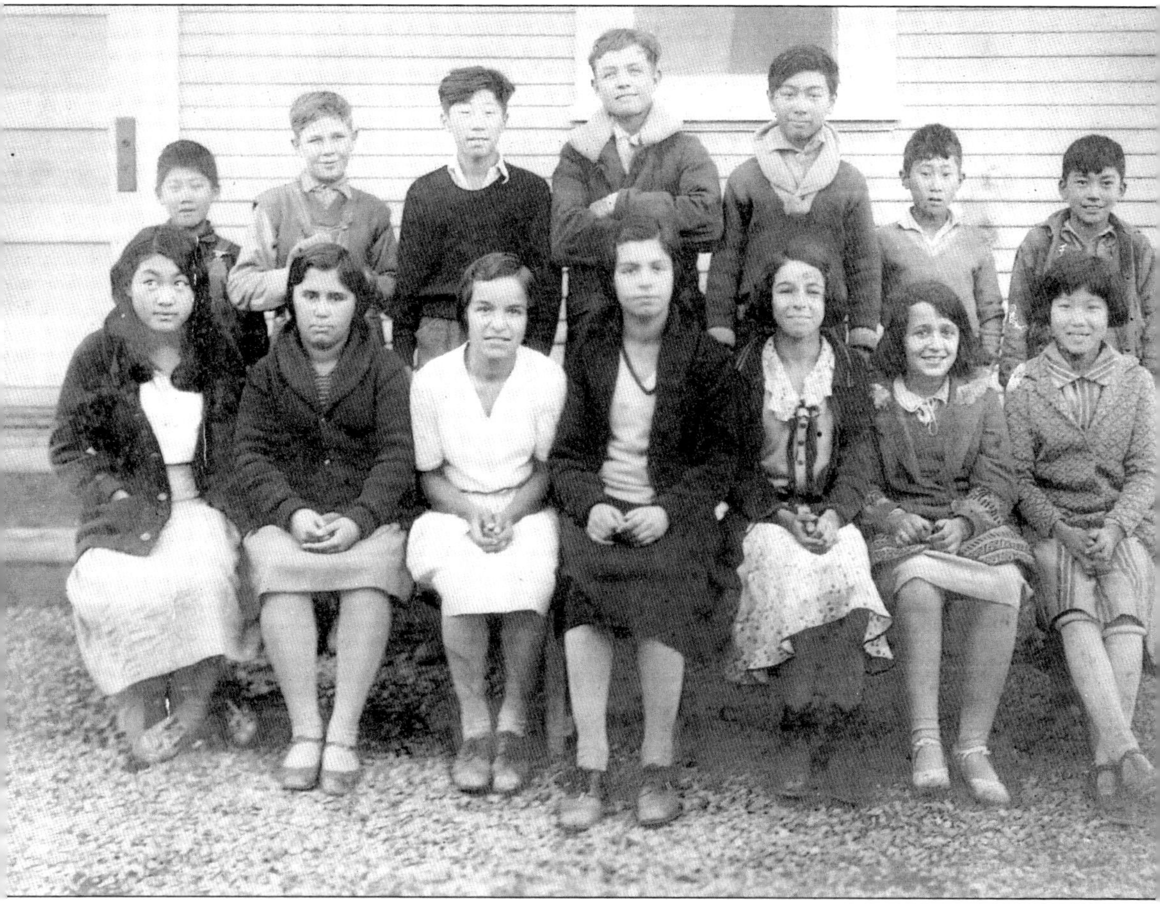

The Lower Lisbon School Class About 1929. The teacher Mrs. Wakefield is not in the picture. (Courtesy of P.H.C.S)

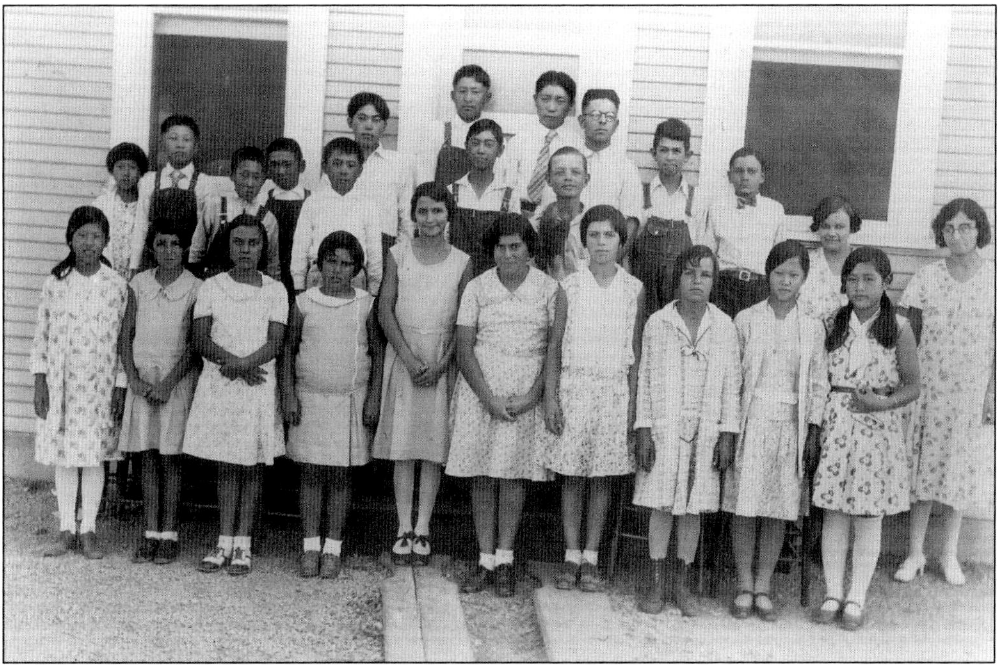

THE LOWER LISBON SCHOOL CLASS c. 1930. Teacher is Emma James Buckley at the far right, who also taught at Sutter Union School. (Courtesy of P.H.C.S.)

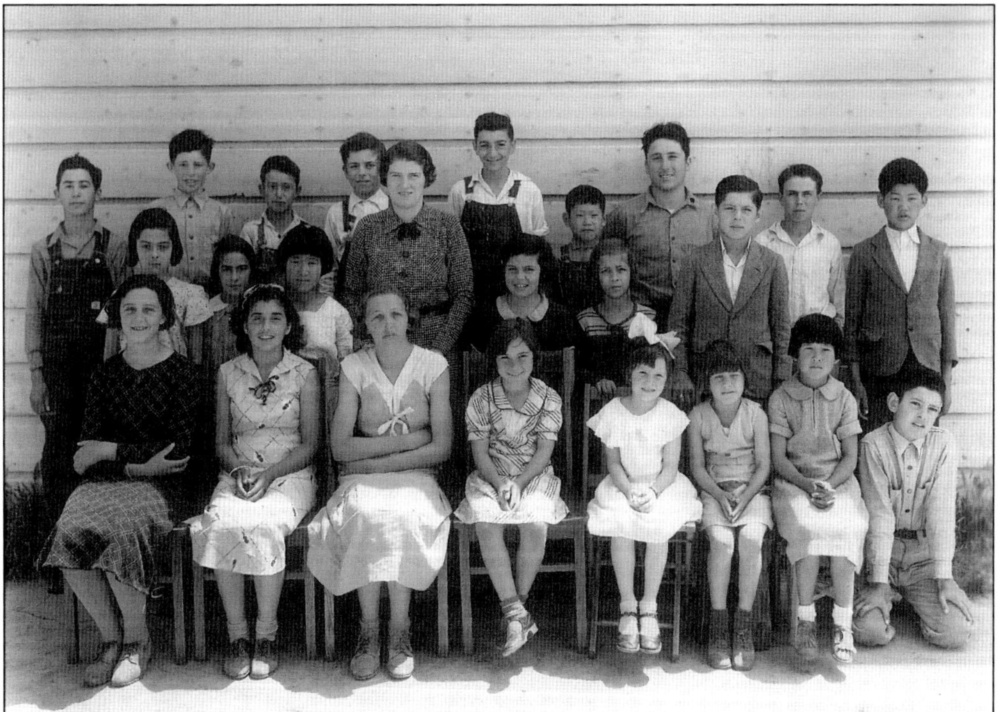

THE UPPER LISBON SCHOOL CLASS IN 1936. The teacher is Mildred Fernandes, in the second row, fourth from left. (Courtesy of P.H.C.S.)

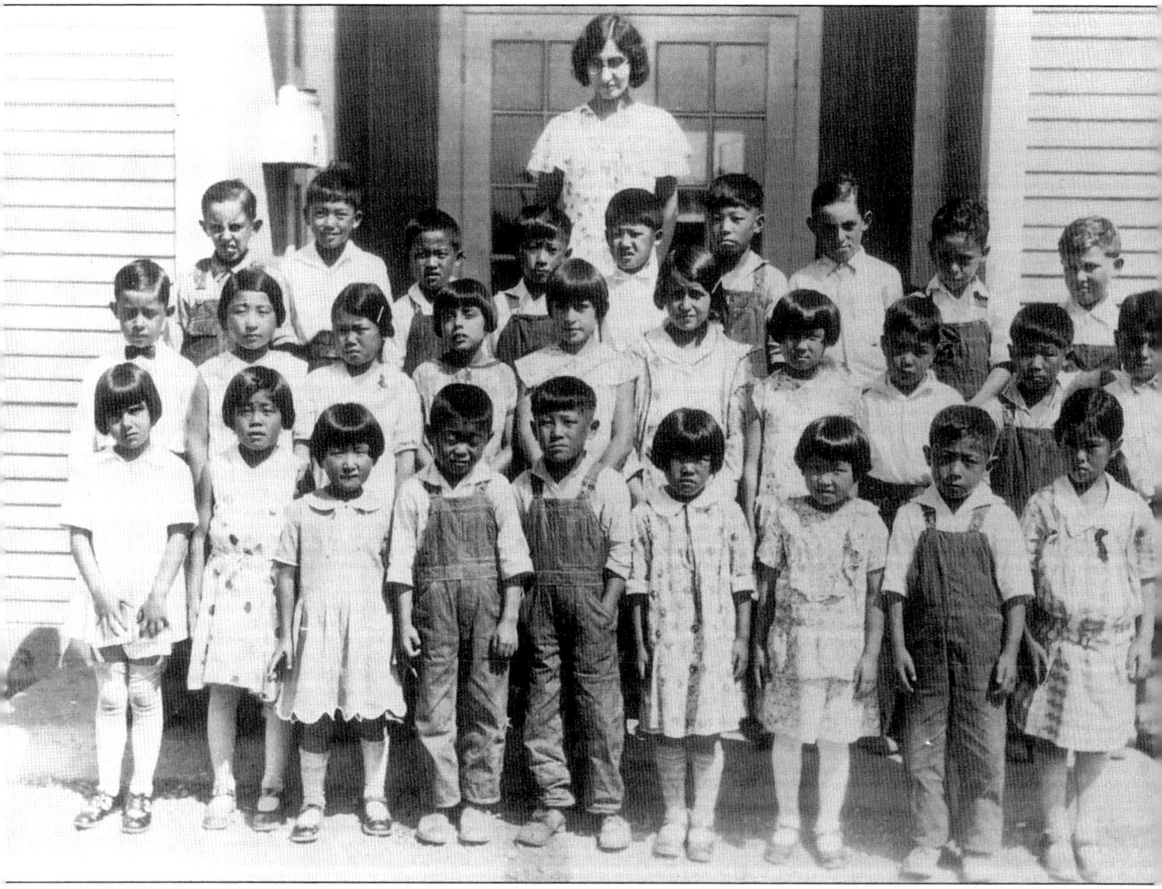

The Upper Lisbon School Class in 1933. Pictured here, from left to right, are as follows: (first row) Athol Souza, Dorothy Sakayeda, Rose Matsunami, Ichiro Nakayama, Satoshi Tanaka, unidentified, unidentified, and Asako Shirai; (second row) Manuel Simas, Masalazo Ojima, Sumi Nakayama, Evelyn "Tootie" Lewis, Aileen Rogers, Margaret Simas, Chisaye Fukumori, Jim Kashiwada, Shigueyuki Tanaka, and Billy Rico; (third row) Albert Rogers, Harry Kashiwada, Toshio Sawamura, Akio Ojima, Joe Matsunami, Takashi Tanaka, Manuel Perry, John Rogers, and Alvin Berkencamp. At back is teacher Emma James Buckley. (Courtesy of P.H.C.S.)

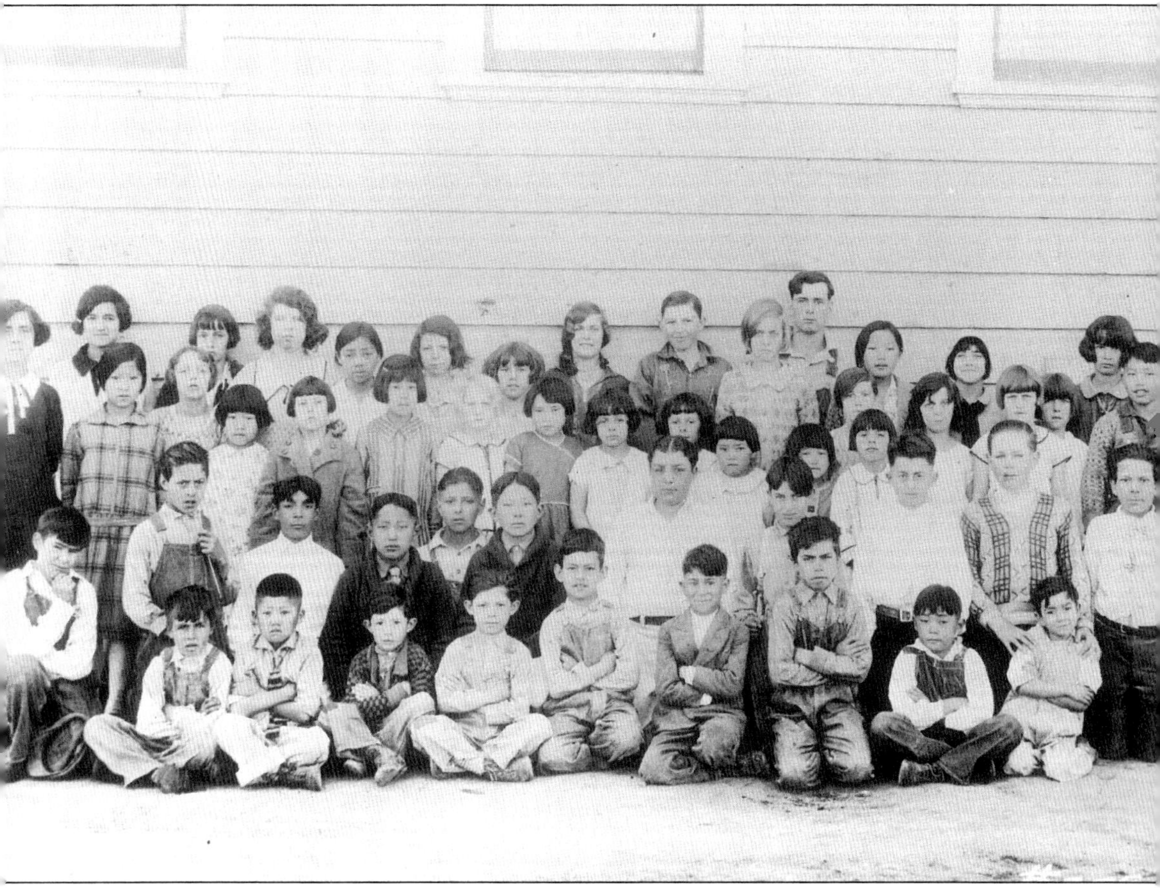

AN UPPER LISBON SCHOOL CLASS. Letitia Seymore at far left is the teacher. (Courtesy of P.H.C.S., Mary Lewis collection)

Five

COMMUNITY LIFE

The Pocket area's community life before suburban development has been described as a cohesive community network, in which families often helped one another. During times of harvest and failure because of weather or the Great Depression, neighboring farmers would give food or other necessities to families in need. Farm equipment would be left on parcel corners for neighbors to use. Verbal leasing agreements of farmland were common, especially between Portuguese and Japanese farmers. When Japanese families in the Pocket area were forced into internment camps during World War II, Portuguese farmers are reported to have generously ranched their property and watched their homes until they returned from the war. And as told in the previous chapter, Portuguese, Japanese, and other children of various ethnic groups attended school together. The large Portuguese community in the Pocket area distinctly celebrated their cultural heritage and their celebrations were a way of life for the community. The Chamarrita, an Azorean folklike dance, often took place at the homes of Portuguese people as well as a Mardi-gras type religious festival found pictured in this chapter. However, the most notable of all Portuguese celebrations in the Pocket area was the Holy Ghost Festival, which is still celebrated in the area today.

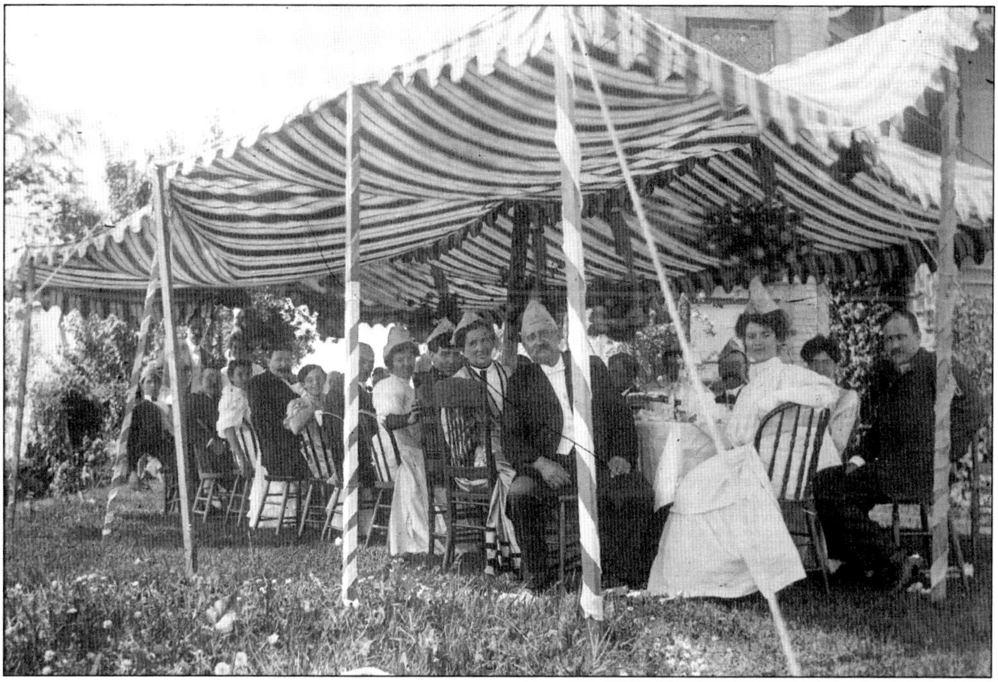

PARTY AT THE GROUNDS AND HOME OF MANUEL AND ROSELINA (ROSALINNA) SEAMAS, OWNERS OF GRANGERS DAIRY. Their daughter Anna is seated at far right in the white dress. (Courtesy of P.H.C.S.)

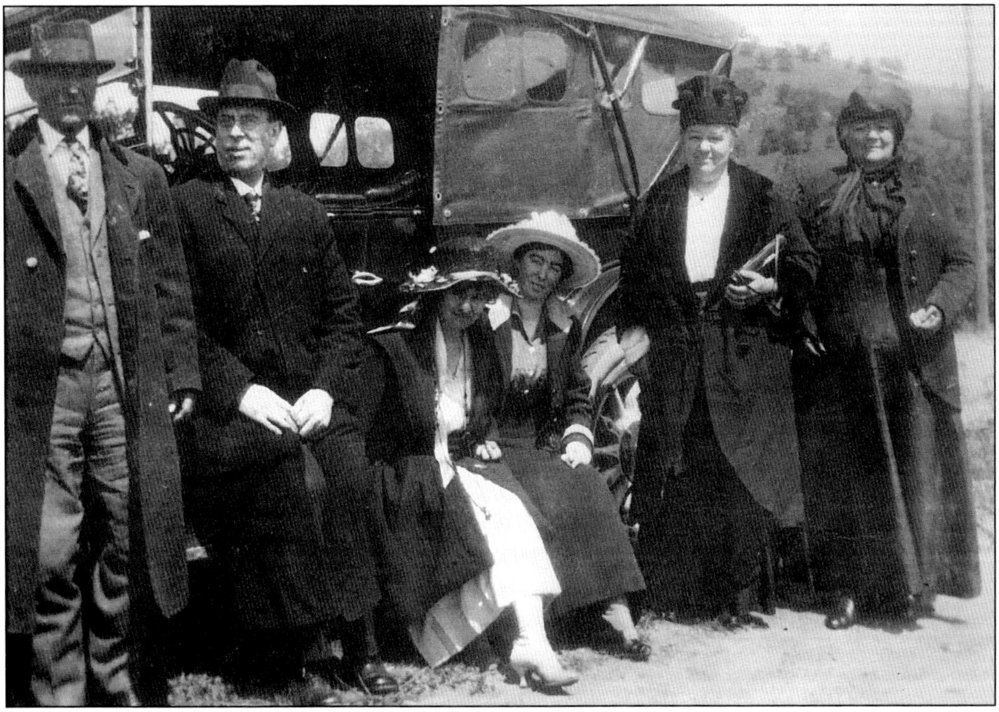

Seamas, Lewis, and Pimentel Family Members During a Family Outing. Pictured from left to right are Manuel Seamas, Manuel Lewis, Anna Lewis, Annie Savoy, Roselina (Rosalinna) Seamas, and Anna Leonora Pimentel. (Courtesy of P.H.C.S., Manuel Seamas collection)

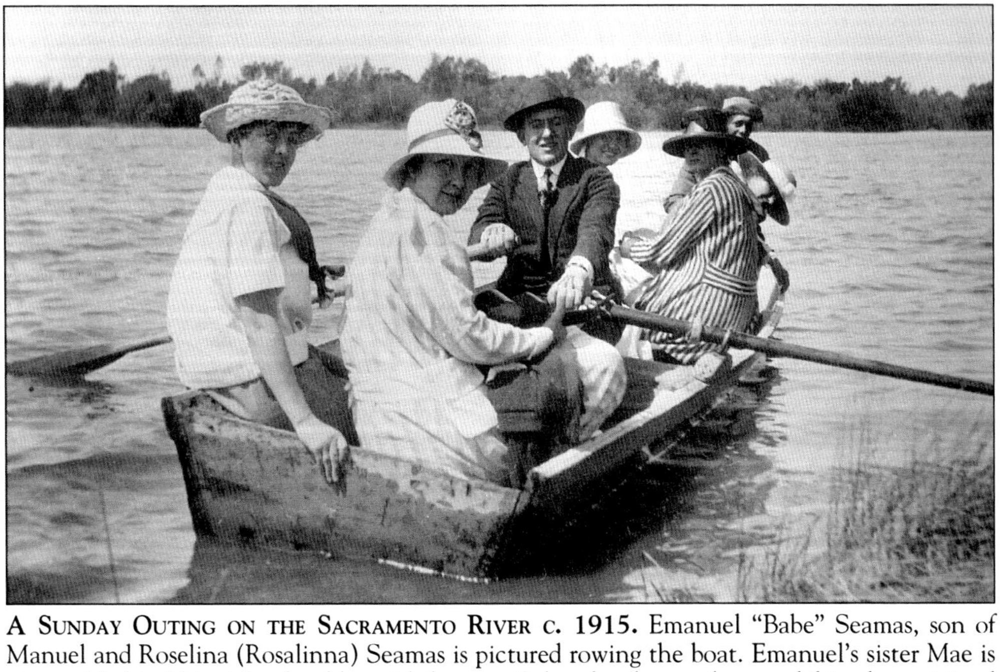

A Sunday Outing on the Sacramento River c. 1915. Emanuel "Babe" Seamas, son of Manuel and Roselina (Rosalinna) Seamas is pictured rowing the boat. Emanuel's sister Mae is pictured behind his right shoulder with hat on. Other family members and friends are joined with them for the outing. (Courtesy of P.H.C.S., Manuel Seamas collection)

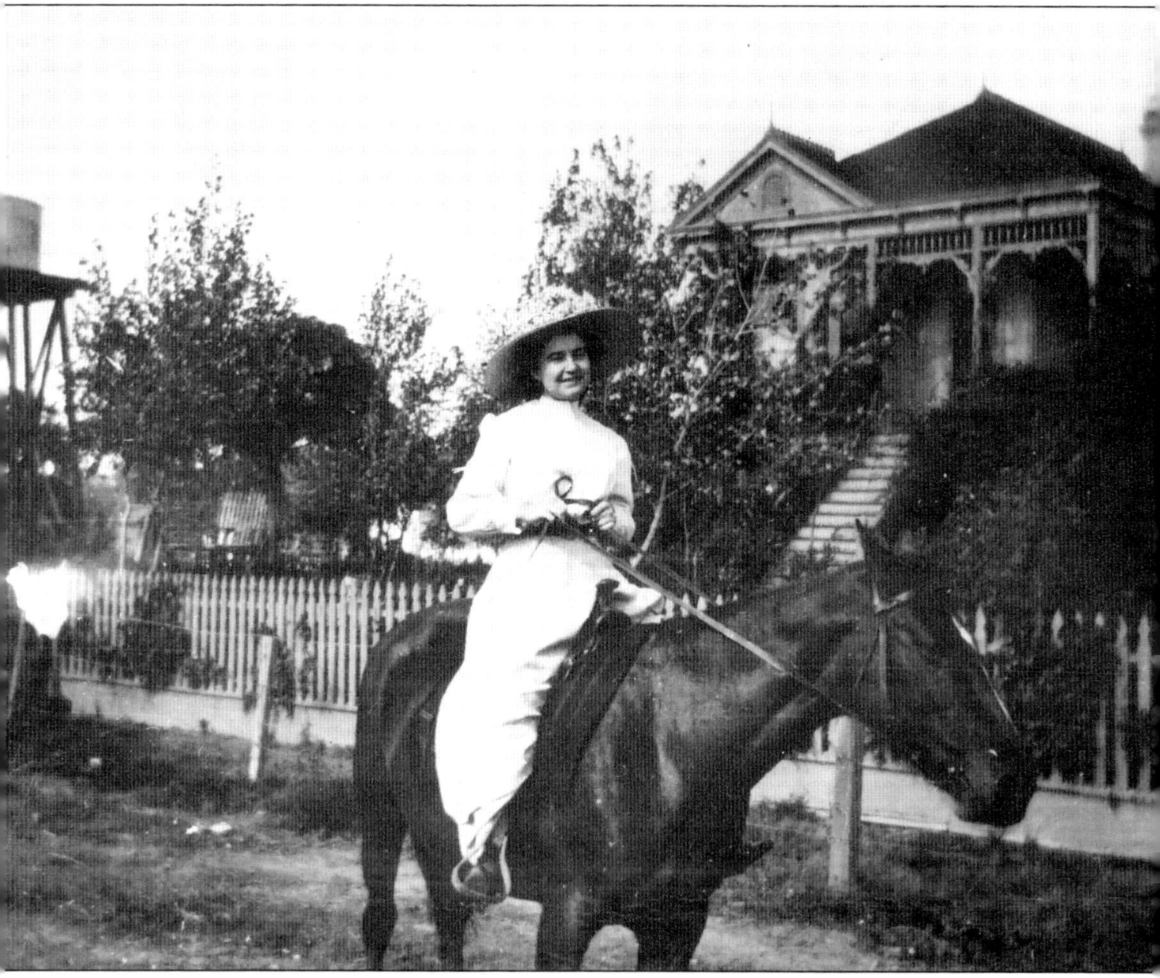

ANNA SEAMAS, DAUGHTER OF MANUEL AND ROSELINA (ROSALINNA) SEAMAS, RIDING A HORSE IN FRONT OF THE SEAMAS FAMILY HOME. (Courtesy of P.H.C.S.)

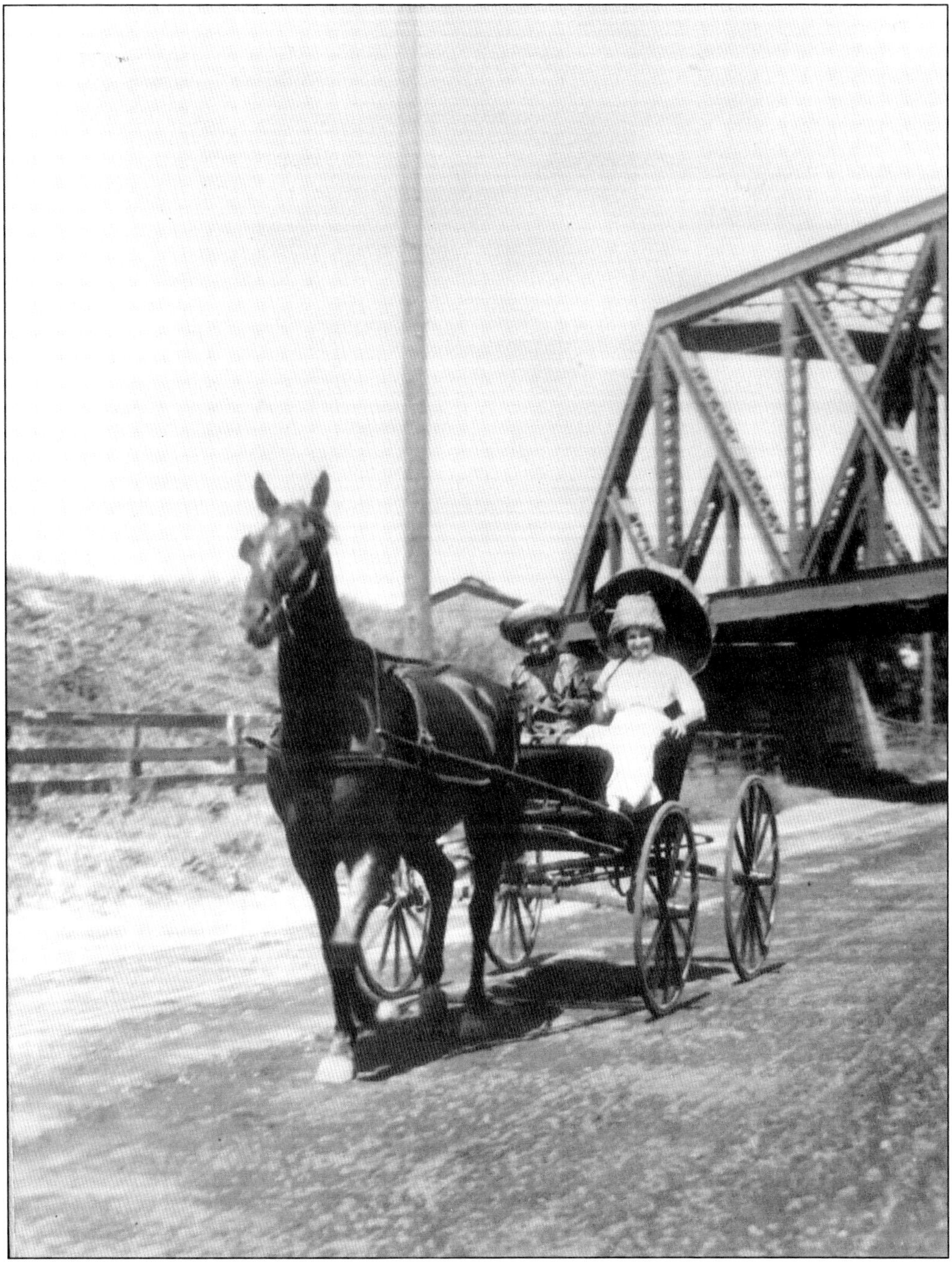

Possibly Amelia Garcia at Left With Her Daughter Mabel Garcia During a Pleasure Ride on Riverside Road. This picture was taken at the railroad trestle just south of present day William Land Park. The Sacramento River levee is to the left of the picture. (Courtesy of P.H.C.S., Manuel Seamas collection)

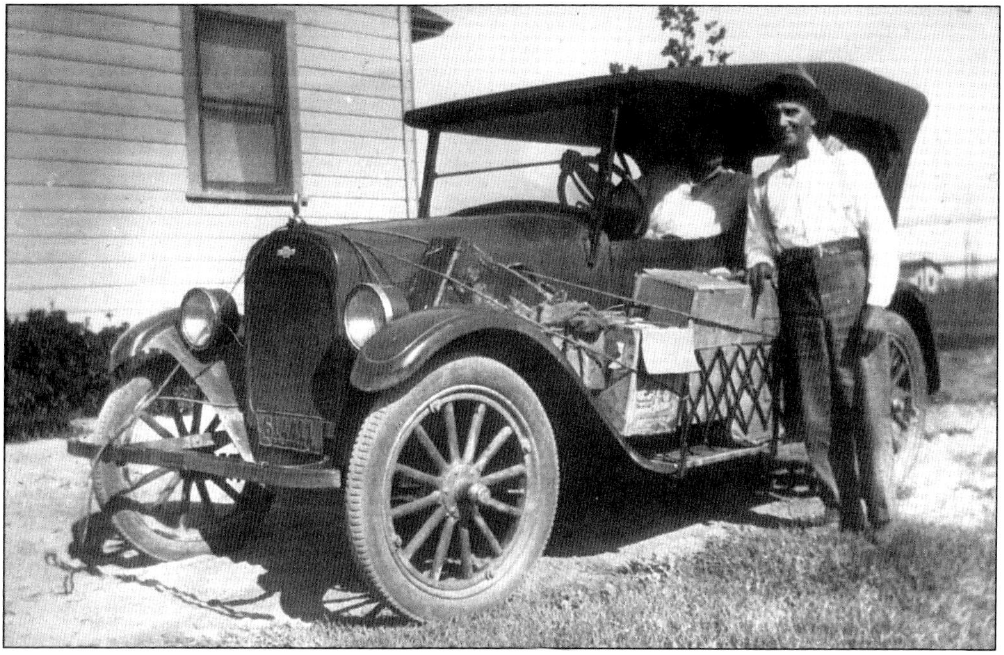

Joseph Perry and Josie (Marshall) Perry Loading Up Their Car for a Trip. Picture taken in front of family home in the Pocket area during the 1920s. (Courtesy of P.H.C.S.)

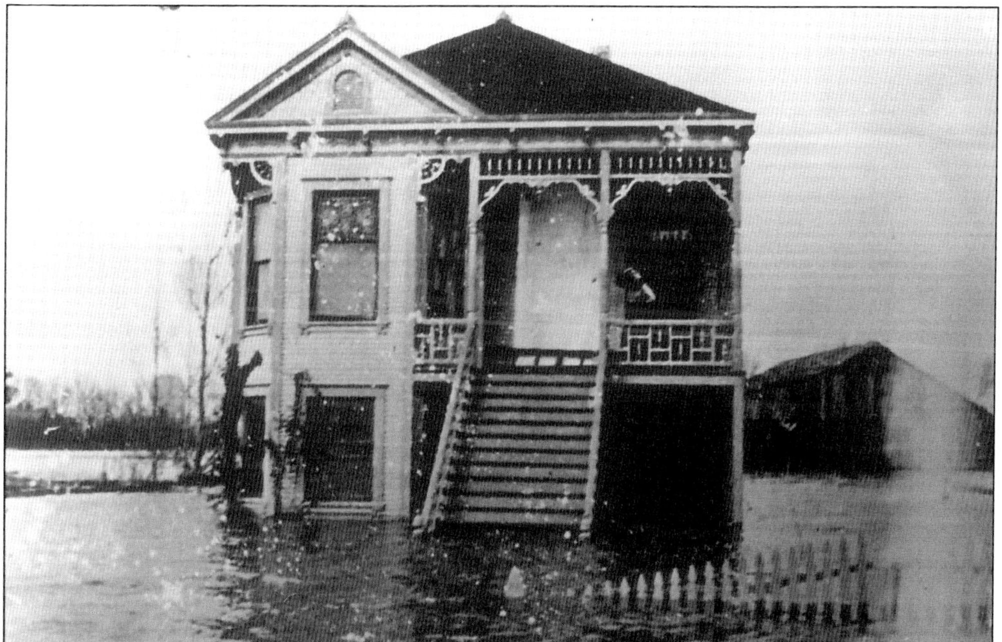

The Manuel Seamas Home in the Pocket Area During the Spring of 1904. The flooding was caused by the Edwards Levee Break. Due to the Pocket area being in a low-lying flood plain next to the Sacramento River, flooding was a common part of everyday life for early day settlers. However, the "Edwards Break" incident was one of the worst floods to occur in the area's history. (Courtesy of P.H.C.S.)

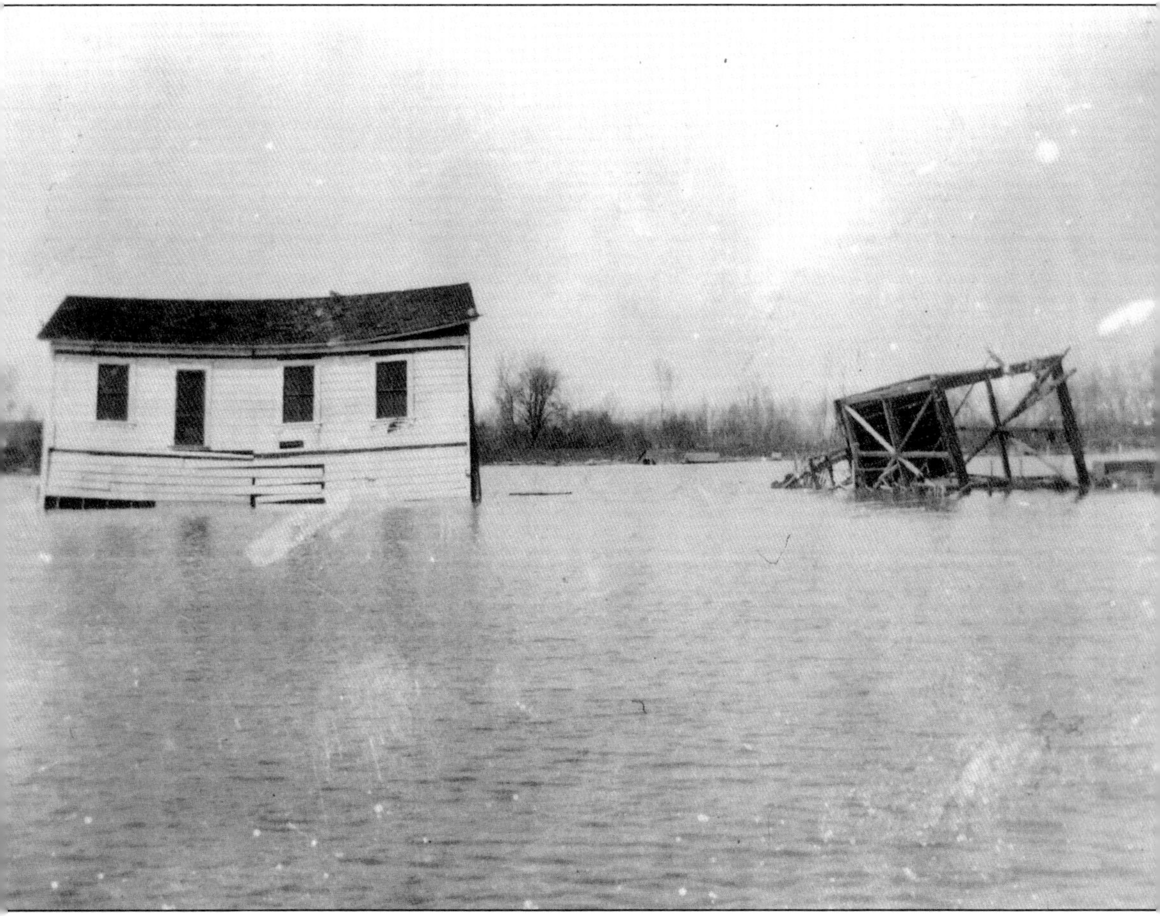

DAMAGE DONE TO THE MANUEL PERRY HOME IN THE RIVERSIDE/POCKET AREA DURING THE "EDWARDS BREAK" FLOOD OF 1904, JUST OPPOSITE OF PRESENT DAY LEWIS PARK. The levee break occurred at Riverside and Sutterville Roads and completely isolated the Pocket area. (Courtesy of P.H.C.S.)

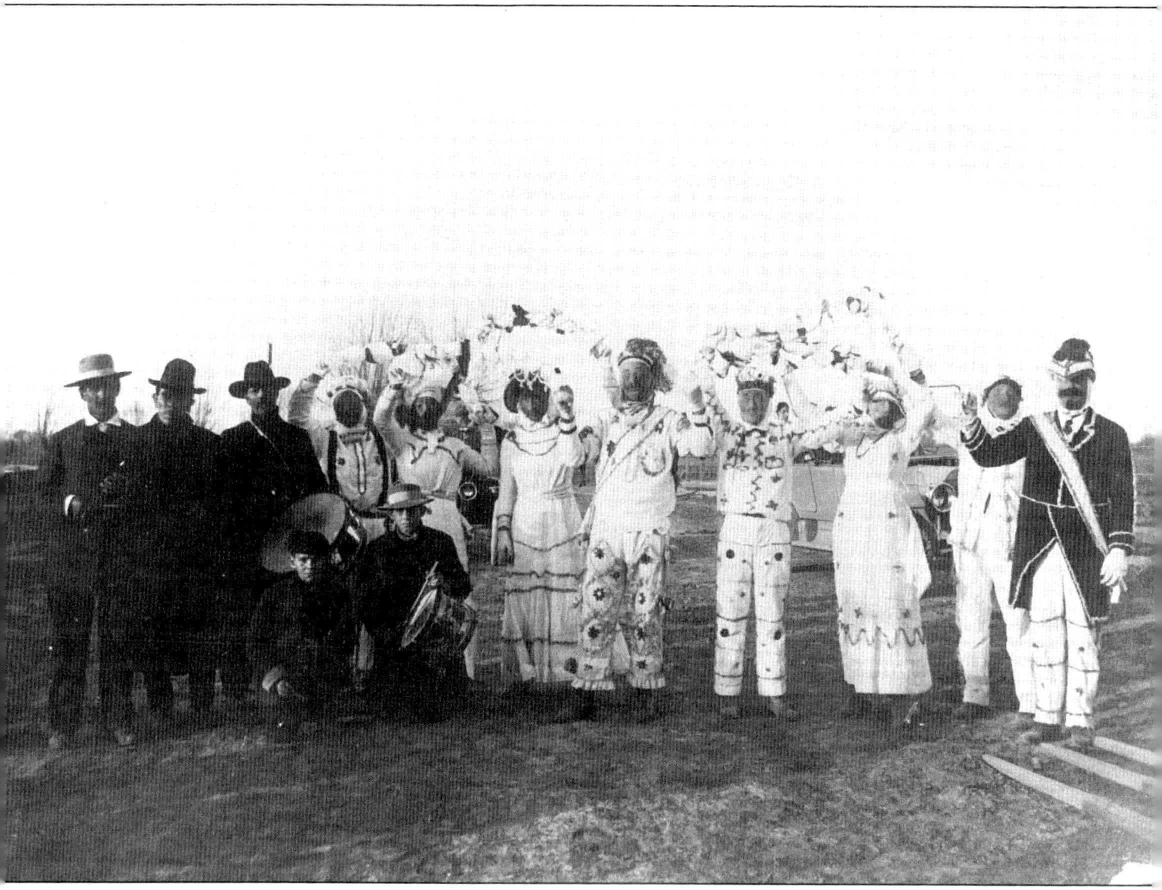

Pictured Are Masqueraders Around 1910 Celebrating a Religious Festival in the Pocket Area. Following a custom started in Portugal, the masqueraders went door to door to only Portuguese homes playing music on string instruments and dancing. Refreshments and food would be served to them at each house. They began by singing a special song pertaining to Flower Day as a greeting to each home. The Masqueraders started at dusk at the home of the Pimentel's near the Trap and continued around the Pocket. (Courtesy of P.H.C.S.)

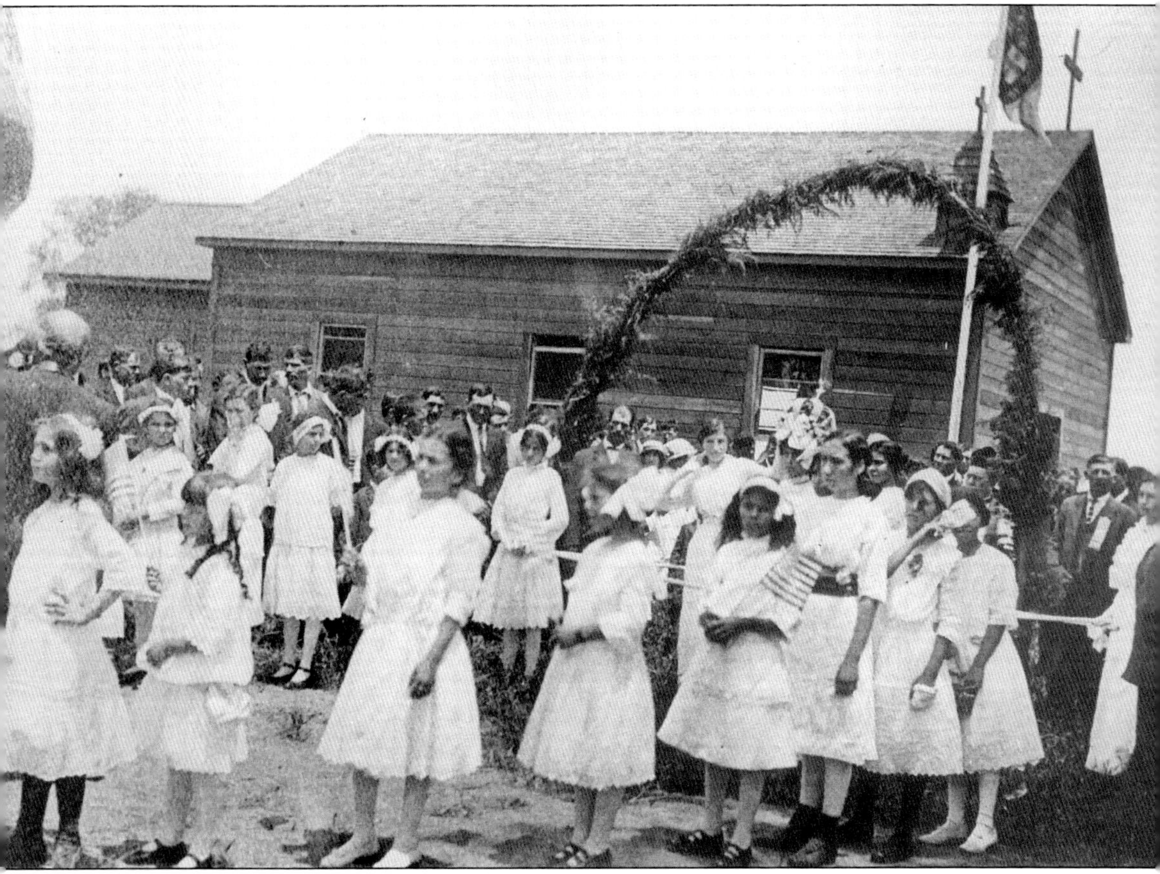

Church of St. Mary, c. 1914, During the A.A.D.E.S. (Azorean Association of the Divine Holy Spirit) Holy Ghost Festa. The A.A.D.E.S. was the Portuguese organization in charge of the festa celebration before it merged with the O.D.E.S. (Order of the Divine Holy Spirit) Portuguese organization from downtown Sacramento in 1967. Located on Old Pocket Road, the Church of St. Mary building was moved in two sections by wagon and horses from Sacramento's Grant District to the Pocket in 1909. (Courtesy of P.H.C.S.)

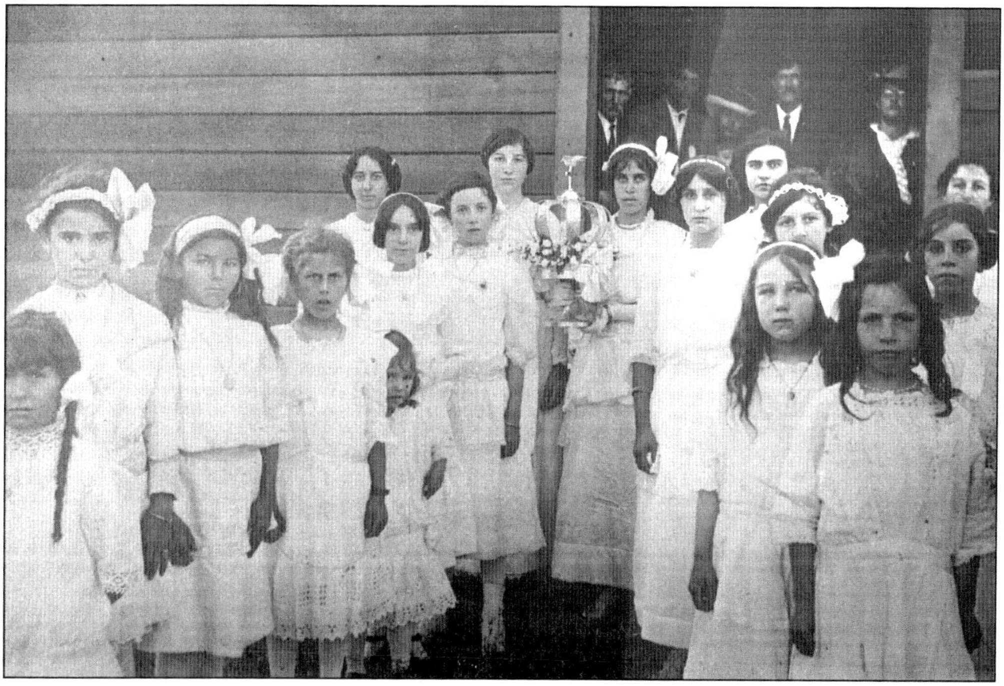

RIVERSIDE HOLY GHOST FESTA IN 1914. Mary Silva (Rogers), holding the crown, is the queen of the festivities. Partial identifications, from left to right, are as follows: (back row) Mary Silveira, Carrie Nevis, queen Mary Silva (Rogers), Minnie Gomes, and Mary Nevis. In front of queen to the right is Rosalyn Waxon. Front at left is Mary Perry. Mary Vargas is the lady standing in the doorway at left. (Courtesy of P.H.C.S.)

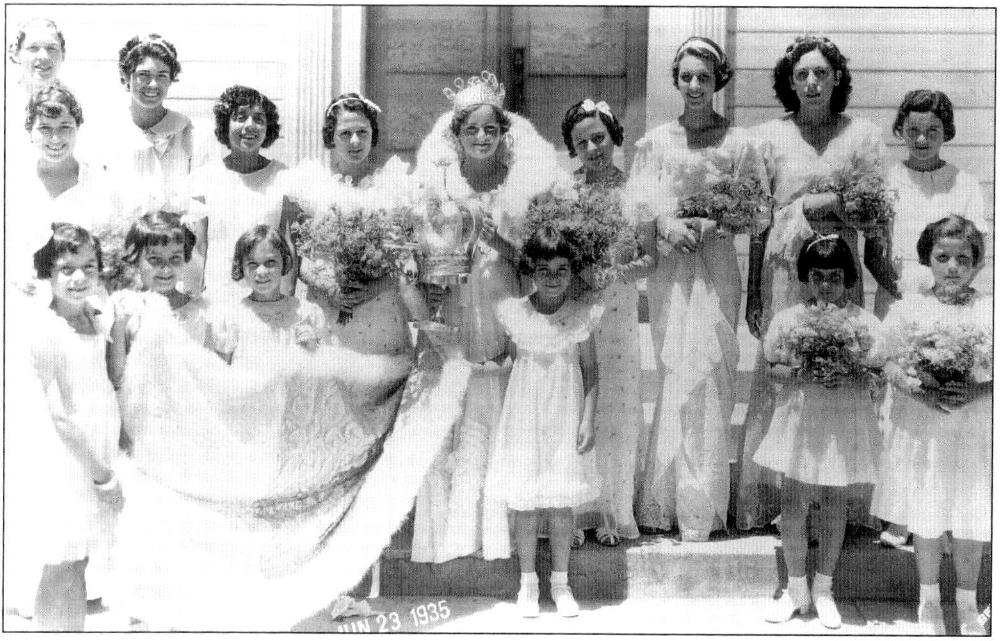

QUEEN, SIDEMAIDS, AND ATTENDANTS IN FRONT OF THE CHURCH OF ST. MARY DURING THE RIVERSIDE HOLY GHOST FESTA. (Courtesy of P.H.C.S.)

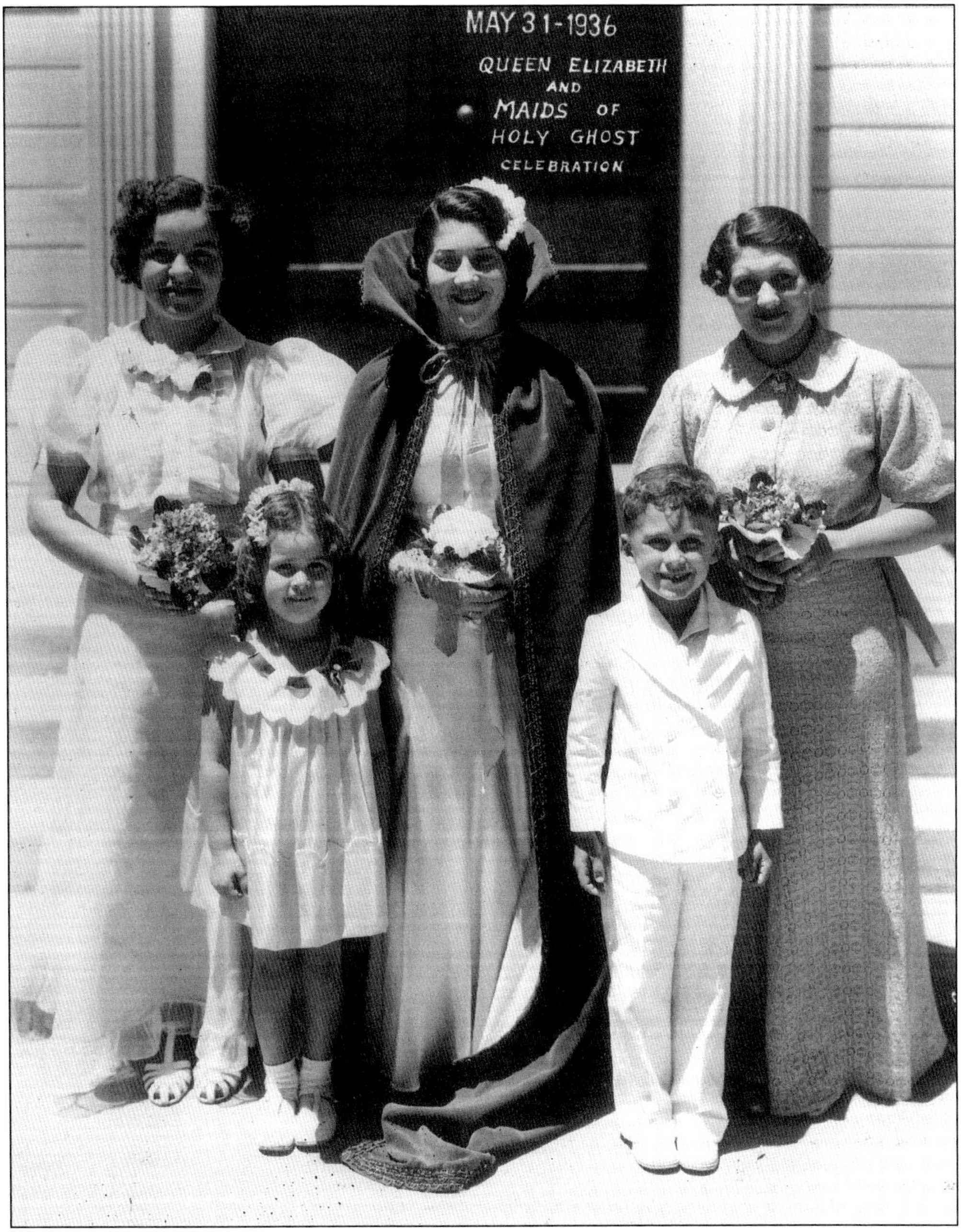

A.A.D.E.S. Riverside Festa Queen Lorraine Perry in 1936. Her sidemaids at left are Dolores Silva and at right her sister Evelyn Perry. The children at front are Elsie Silva and Faustino "Snookie" Silva Jr. A uniquely religious tradition from the Azores Islands, where a majority of the Portuguese immigrants from the Pocket area came from, it is celebrated six to seven weeks after Easter during Pentecost and Trinity Sundays. The Holy Ghost Festival commemorates Queen Saint Isabel of 13th century Portugal, who sold her jewels to help feed the poor in Portugal and united its people through her dedication and belief in the Holy Spirit. A young girl from the Portuguese community was crowned each year as queen of the festa celebration. (Courtesy of P.H.C.S.)

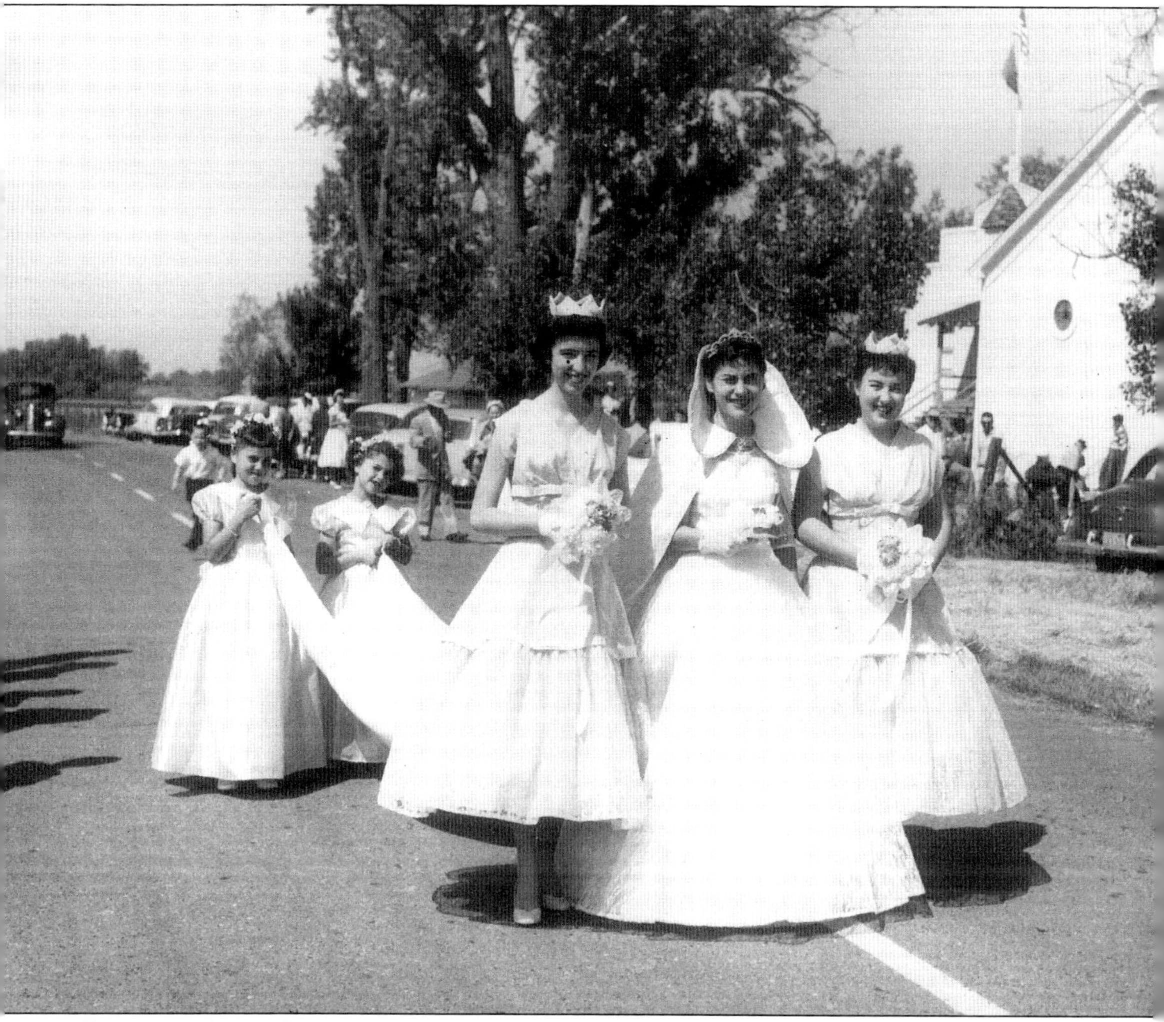

RIVERSIDE FESTA QUEEN AND SIDEMAIDS ON OLD POCKET ROAD PASSING THE PORTUGUESE HALL AND THE CHURCH OF ST. MARY. Pictured from left to right are Rosemary Valine, Queen Antoinette D'Alessandro, daughter of Lorraine Perry (queen in previous picture), and Marian Lewis. Susan D'Alessandro is at right behind her sister and sidemaids. (Courtesy of P.H.C.S.)

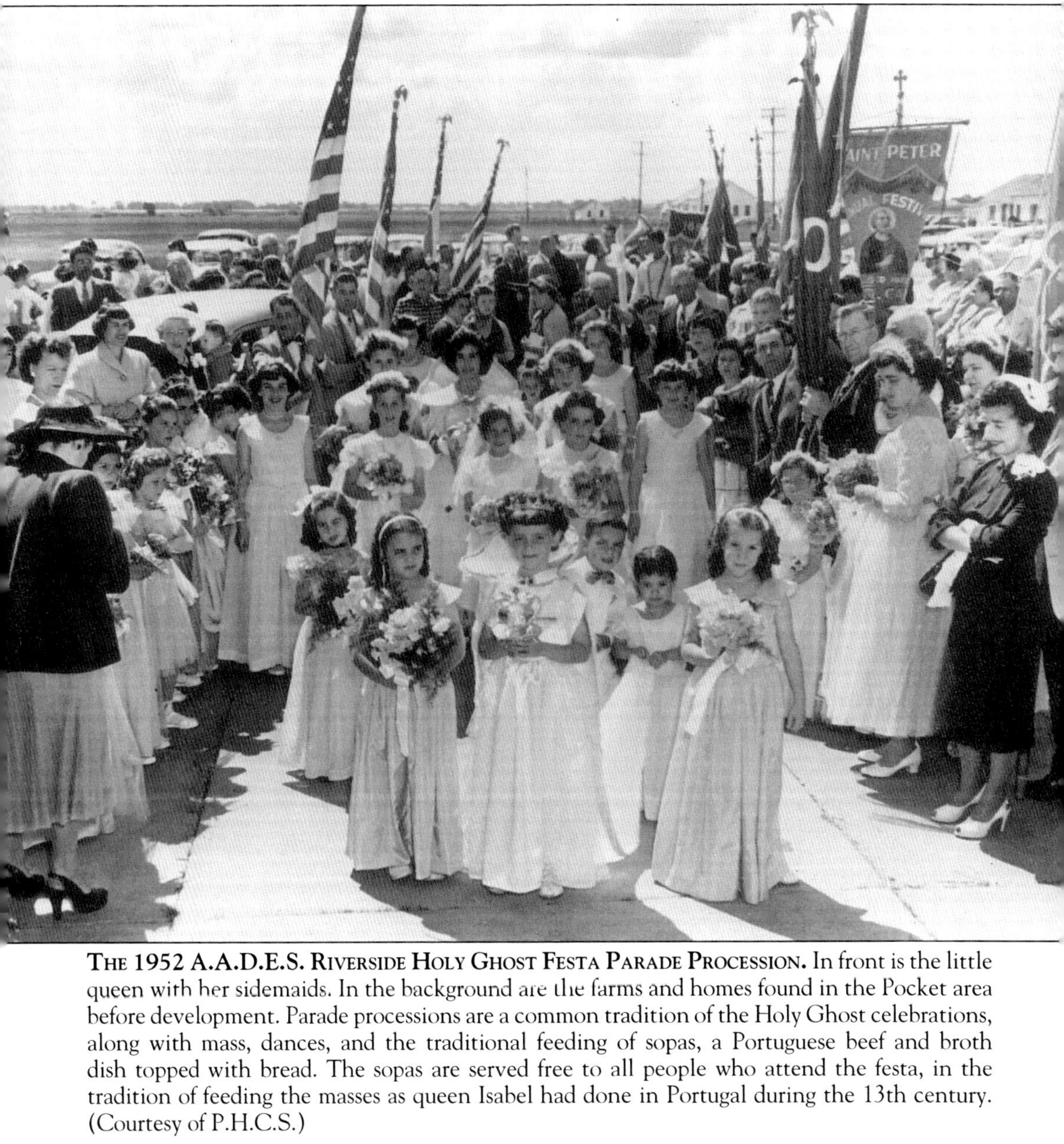

The 1952 A.A.D.E.S. Riverside Holy Ghost Festa Parade Procession. In front is the little queen with her sidemaids. In the background are the farms and homes found in the Pocket area before development. Parade processions are a common tradition of the Holy Ghost celebrations, along with mass, dances, and the traditional feeding of sopas, a Portuguese beef and broth dish topped with bread. The sopas are served free to all people who attend the festa, in the tradition of feeding the masses as queen Isabel had done in Portugal during the 13th century. (Courtesy of P.H.C.S.)

Riverside A.A.D.E.S. Festa Celebration in 1952. Bob Garcia (Gracia) presents the crown to the little queen at the Joe Tash ranch. The little queen in turn will take the crown to the Church of St. Mary's to be blessed for the celebration. Frank Lewis Jr. is in background. (Courtesy of P.H.C.S.)

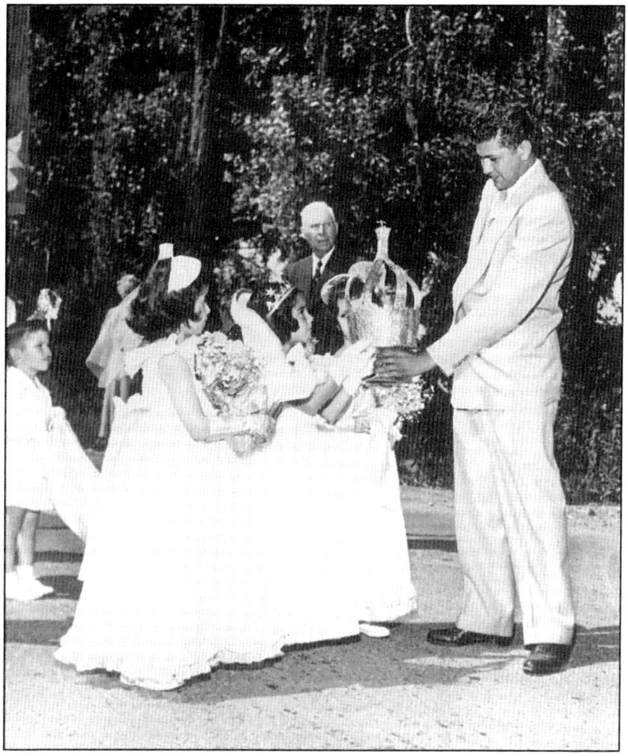

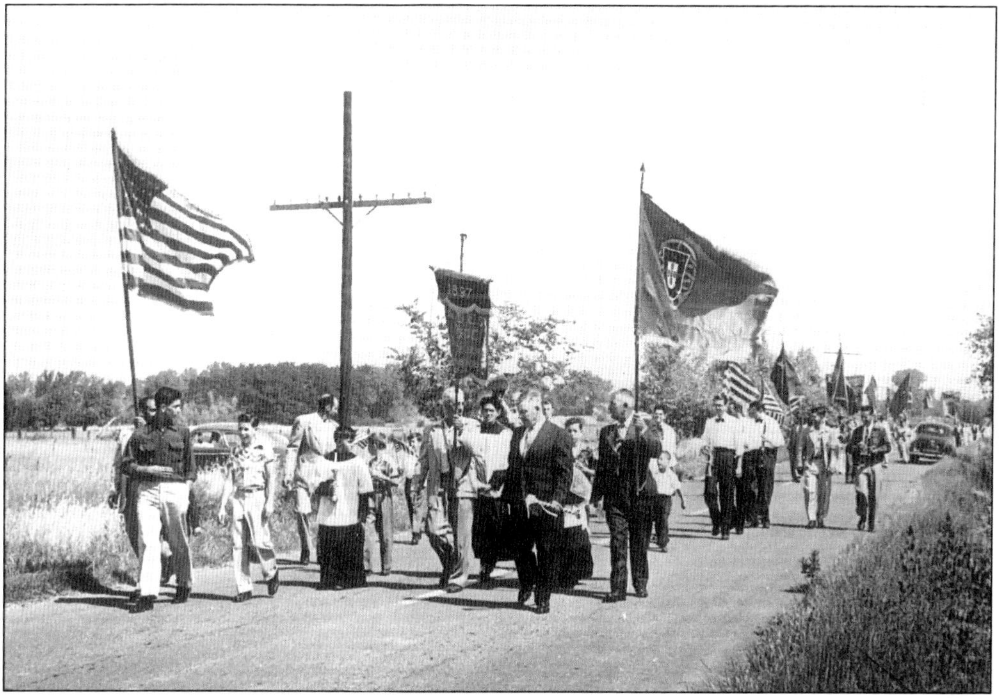

Riverside A.A.D.E.S. Festa Parade Procession in 1952 Marching to the Joe Tash Ranch to Receive the Crown. Pictured is Joe Silva (son of A.L. Silva) carrying the A.A.D.E.S. banner and Frank Tash carrying the marshal's staff. (Courtesy of P.H.C.S.)

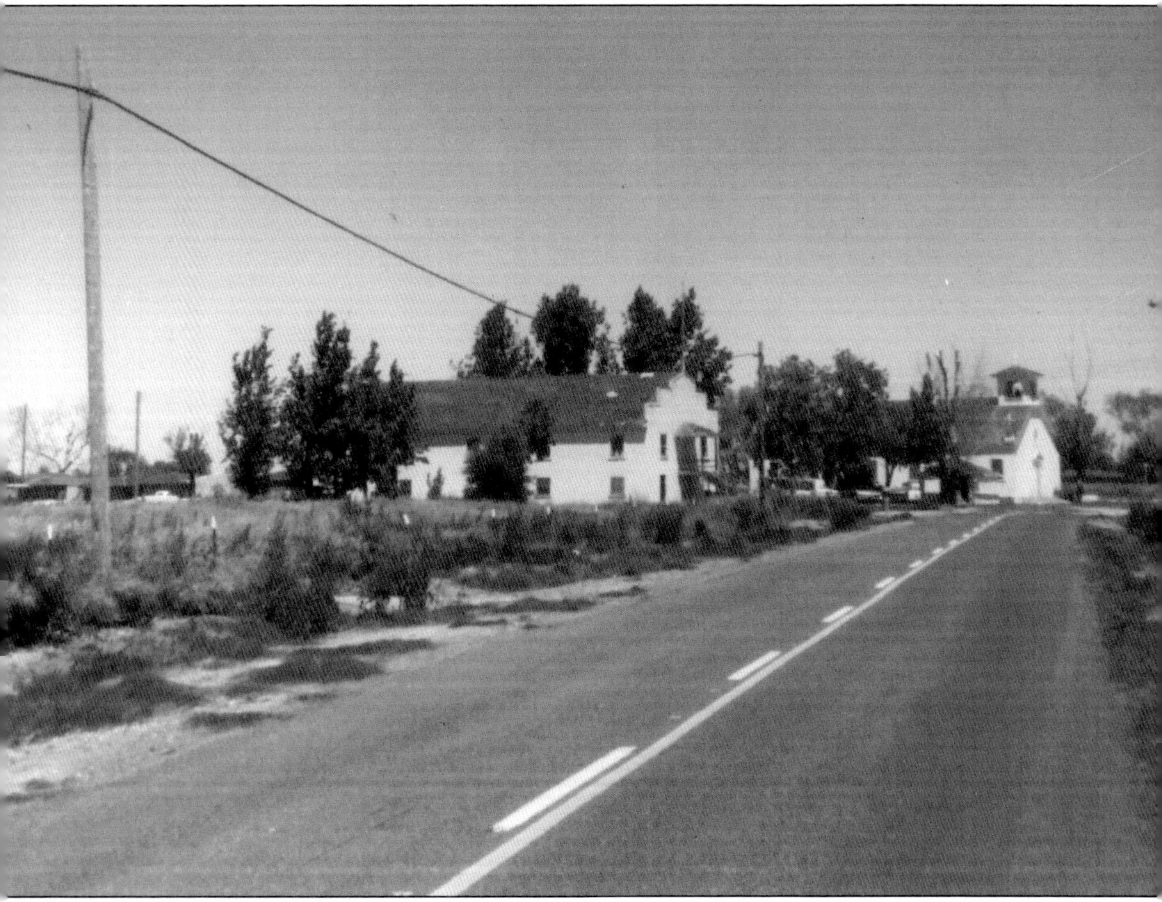

PICTURE OF OLD POCKET ROAD TO THE NORTH WITH SIDE VIEWS OF THE ORIGINAL A.A.D.E.S. PORTUGUESE HALL (AT LEFT) AND THE CHURCH OF ST. MARY'S (AT RIGHT). The Portuguese hall and church were the "community centers" of the large Portuguese population settlement in the Pocket area. The land, owned by Frank Lewis Sr., was deeded to the local Portuguese organizations for sole purpose of being used for the Holy Ghost festival celebration. (Courtesy of P.H.C.S.)

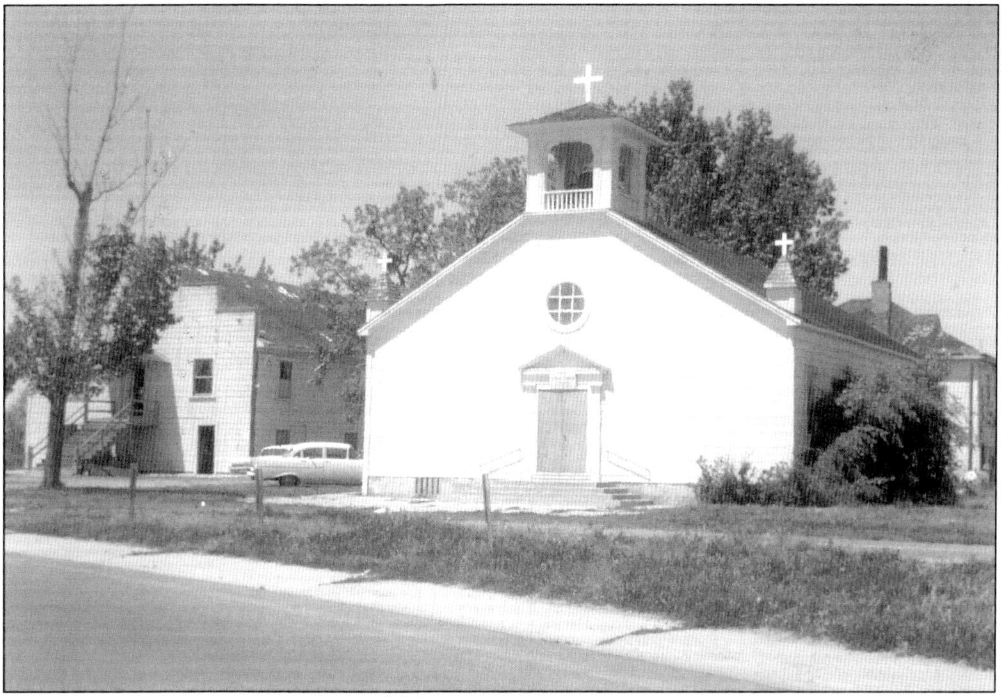

THE A.A.D.E.S. HALL AT LEFT, BUILT IN 1912, WAS DEMOLISHED STARTING ON MAY 8, 1967. This photo was taken just before demolition. The Church of St. Mary at right has the Upper Lisbon School building located at the back of the church. The old school building was used as a clubhouse after the school closed down and was subsequently demolished when the hall was torn down. (Courtesy of P.H.C.S., Grace Rose collection)

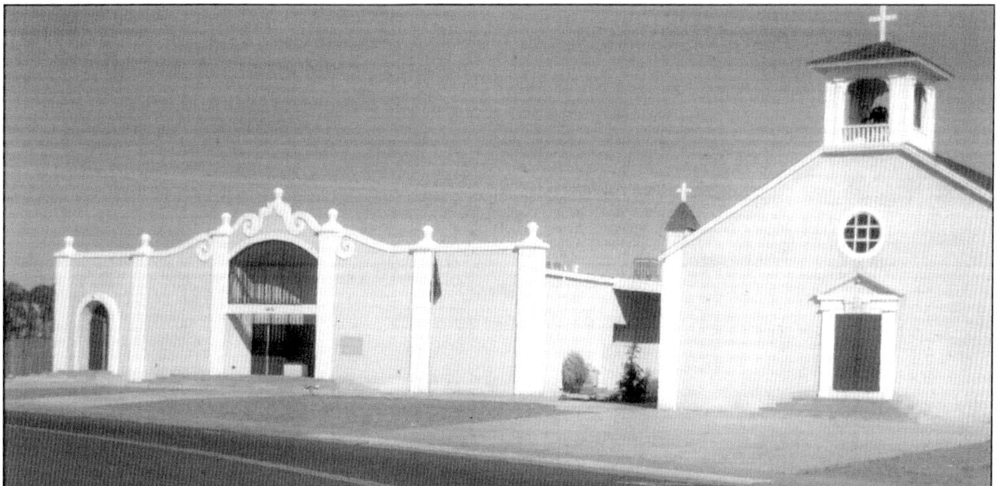

THE NEWLY COMPLETED SACRAMENTO PORTUGUESE HOLY SPIRIT SOCIETY (S.P.H.S.S) PORTUGUESE HALL IN 1967. The grand opening banquet and dance dedication took place on October 21, 1967. This hall replaced the A.A.D.E.S. Riverside Hall, when the O.D.E.S. and A.A.D.E.S. Portuguese organizations merged into one, S.P.H.S.S. Frank Dias was the last O.D.E.S. president and became the first president of S.P.H.S.S.(Courtesy of P.H.C.S.)

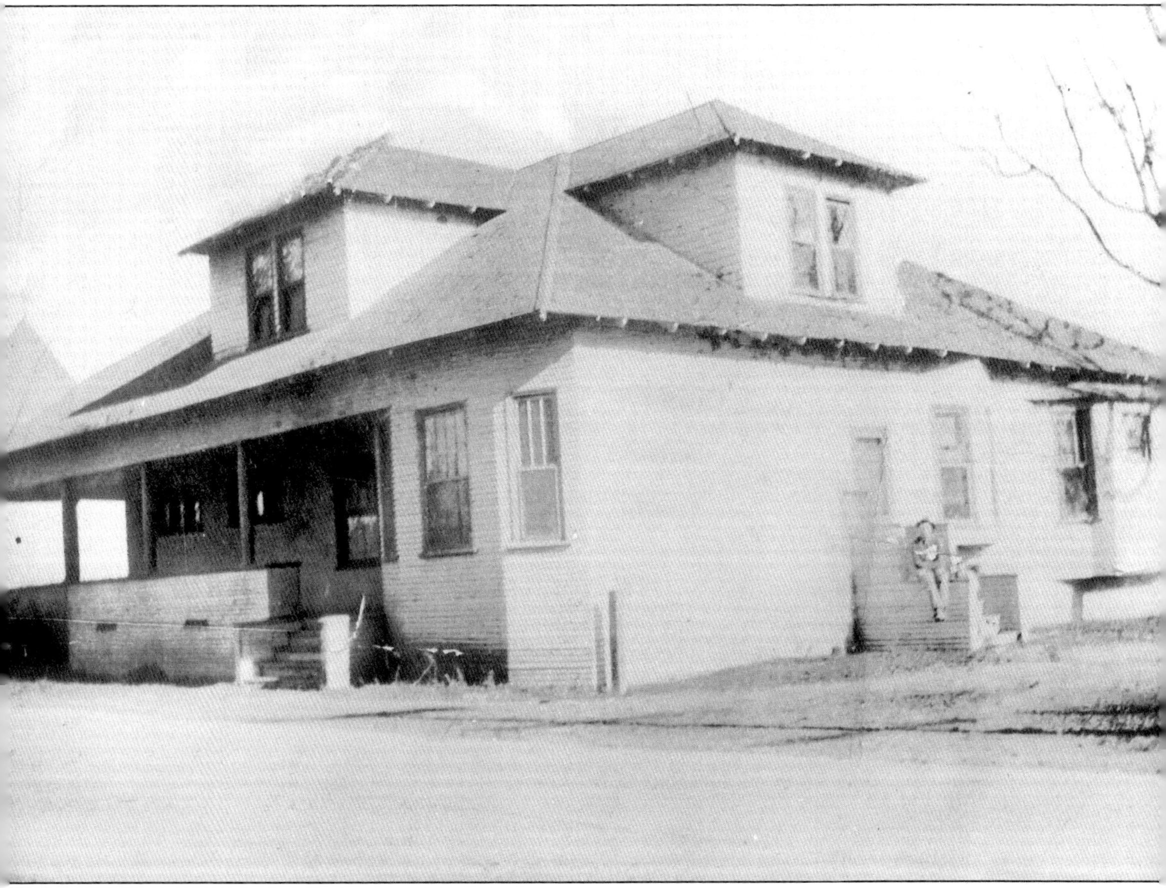

OAK HALL IN THE RIVERSIDE/POCKET AREA AROUND 1920. Manuel Mauricio Sr. at far right siting on the side porch is holding Manuel Jr. The Mauricios at one time owned the Oak hall building and the land that it was on. It was a plush dance hall rumored to also be a brothel. (Courtesy of P.H.C.S.)

Six

Recent Years

Today, the Greenhaven/Pocket area is considered one of the most desirable areas in the City of Sacramento. It had a 1990 census population of 40,397 and 85 percent of its housing units are single-family homes, the majority of which are custom-built. The community also has multi-unit housing available in the form of townhouses, apartments, and condensed housing units. The area is home to a number of professionals who find the community adequate for raising families based on the high number of sports leagues, good schools, and recreational facilities. The area has five shopping centers providing goods and services. Many of the businesses in these shopping centers are independently owned and have been serving the community for a number of years. The development of the Pocket area has considerably changed the way the area used to look, based on previous chapters found in this book, but many relic landscape features exist in the area today as a reminder of its historic past.

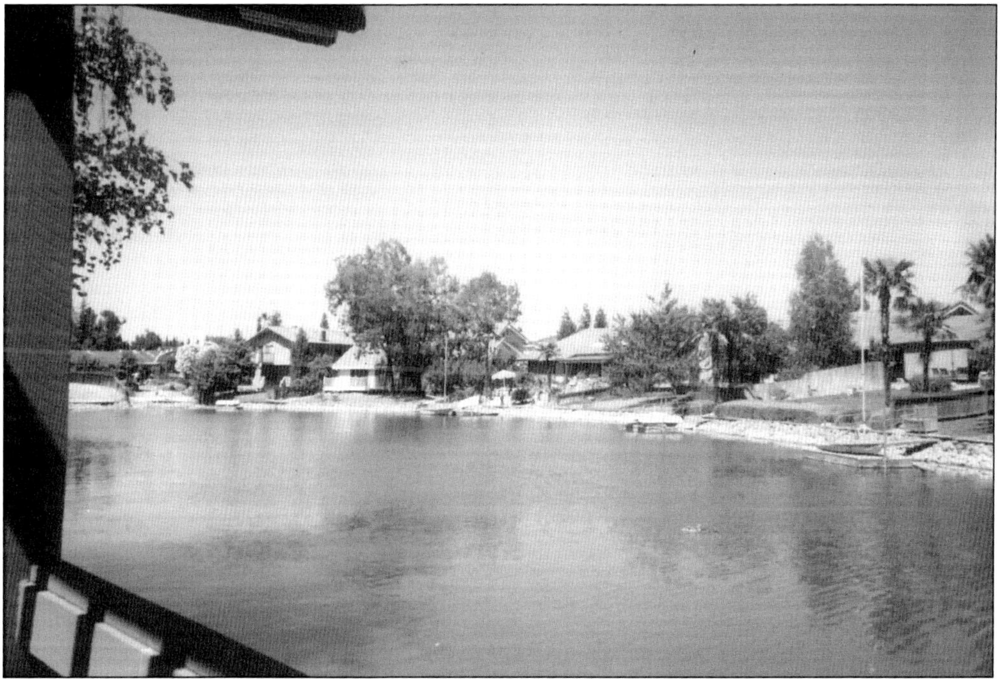

Greenhaven Lake and Surrounding Lakefront Homes in 2001. Greenhaven Lake was once a clay pit, providing an abundant source of clay for the nearby brickyard. During the development of the Greenhaven community, Lincoln and Parker Development Company envisioned that the clay pit would be a public recreational area for Greenhaven residents. Later, it was decided that homes would surround the lakefront. Greenhaven Lake is home to a variety of waterfowl such as mallards and Egyptian geese.

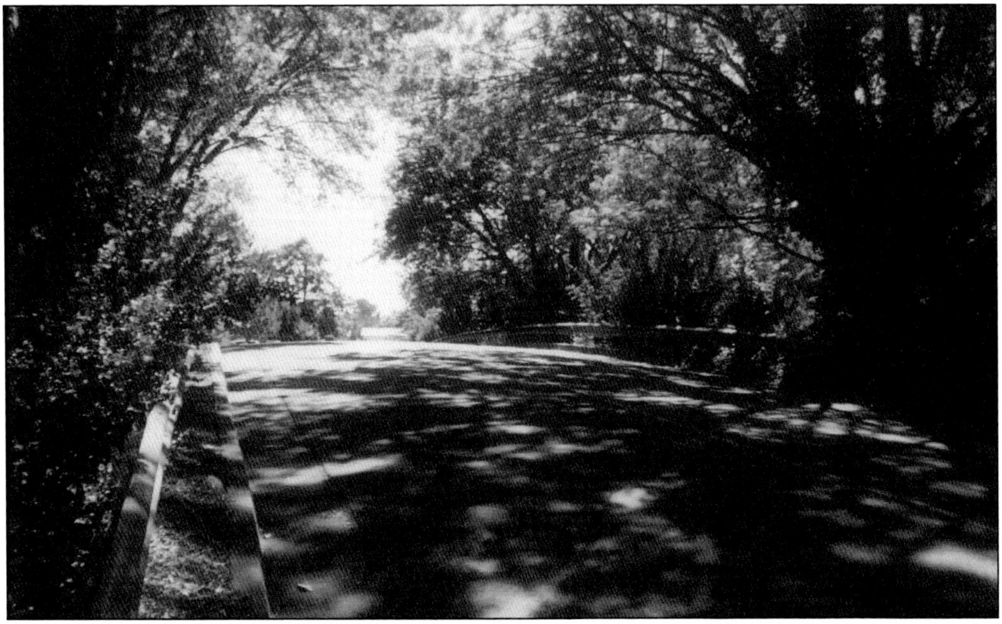

Pictured is Parklin Street in the Original Greenhaven 70 development Above the Seymour Park Pedestrian Underpass. The street was named after the Greenhaven 70 developers Kermit Lincoln and Harold Parker of Lincoln and Parker Development Company.

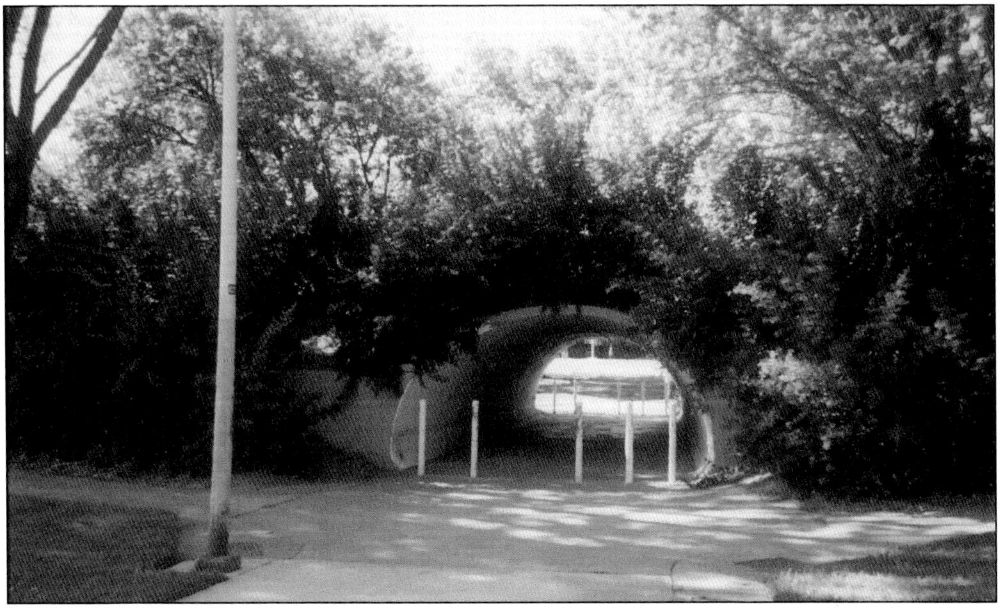

Pedestrian Underpass. One of the major innovative features for the Greenhaven 70 plan by Lincoln and Parker Development Company in 1961 was the pedestrian underpass located along the Seymour Park Greenbelt. The pedestrian underpass and accompanying overpasses were designated to separate automobile traffic from pedestrian traffic in conjunction with the usual adequate recreational facilities such as playgrounds and softball/baseball fields within the open space network. The above pedestrian underpass, located under Parklin Avenue, was the only one built in Greenhaven.

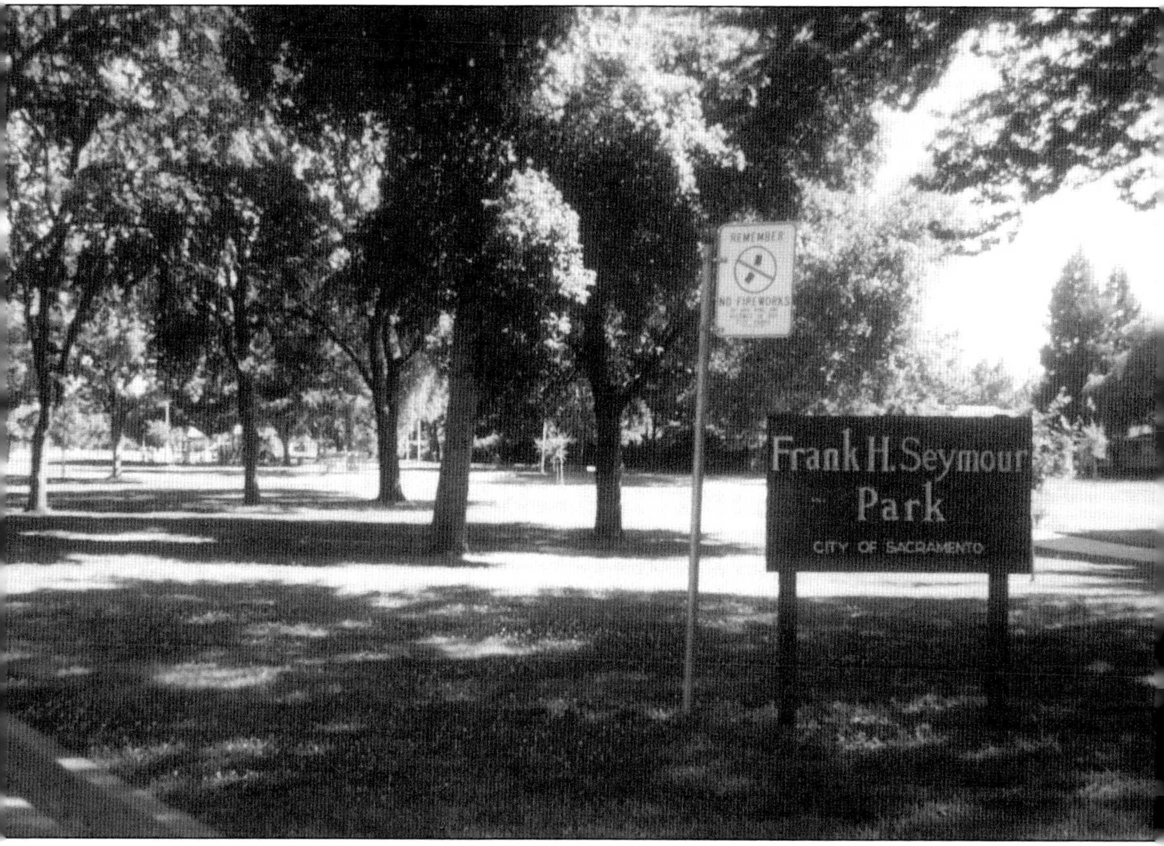

A View of the Seymour Park Greenbelt in the Original Greenhaven 70 Development. The park network extends as a corridor into the South Pocket area, crossing the Greenhaven neighborhood. The greenbelt was created as part of the original development in the 1960s so that housewives could walk safely to shopping and children could walk safely to school without crossing any automobile traffic.

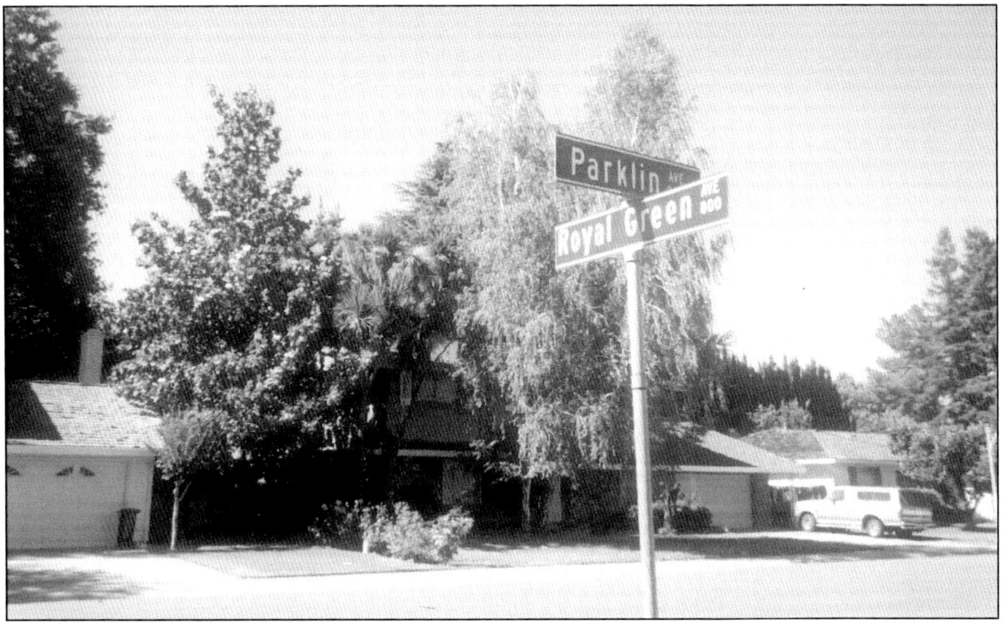

The Intersection of Parklin Avenue and Royal Green Avenue in the Original Greenhaven 70 Development. Suburban ranch style homes were the common architectural feature of Greenhaven homes, despite the majority of them being custom-built. Architectural controls were strongly in place early on in the development to maintain the highest standards of community orientation and character throughout Greenhaven. This included the restriction that clotheslines, TV antennas, and RV recreational vehicles were to be hidden from view.

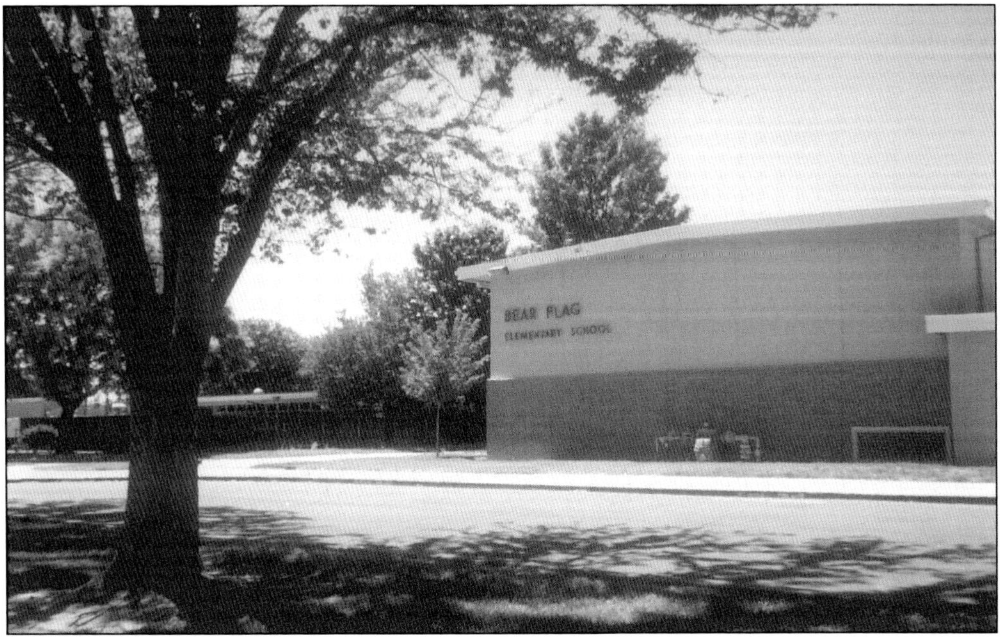

Bearflag Elementary School, Located Along the Seymour Park Greenbelt. It was the first public school to open in 1965 for elementary school children residing in the Greenhaven 70 development.

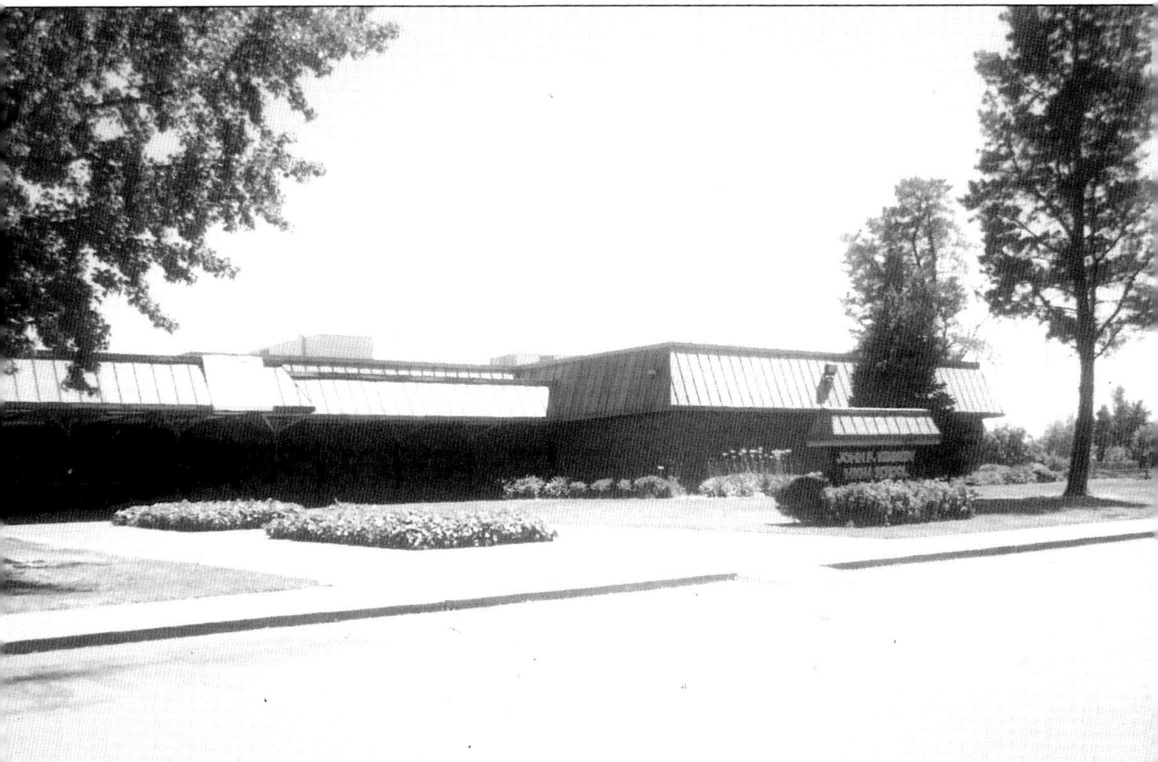

JOHN F. KENNEDY HIGH SCHOOL. The only high school located in the Greenhaven/Pocket area opened in the fall of 1967 to 1,400 students. The Dutra family once farmed tomatoes on the land where the school stands today. Today, the high school has many outstanding academic programs and its athletic teams have been Metro League Champions in virtually every field over the past 17 years. (Information provided by Anthony Dutra, Diane Dutra, and Barb Chandler)

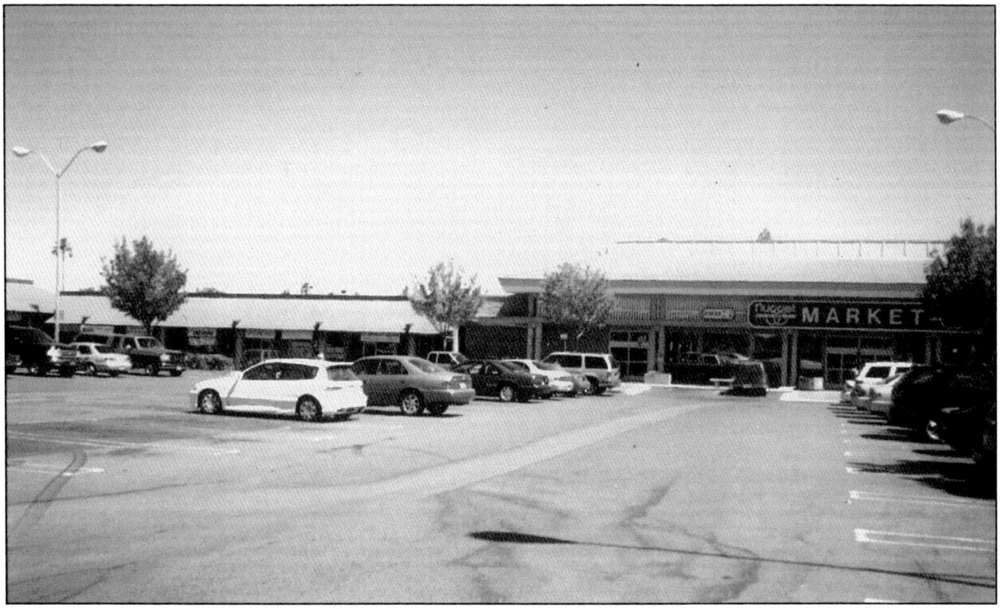

The Nugget Market Shopping Center, Located Next to Greenhaven Lake in the North Pocket Area in 2001. This shopping center is part of the Greenhaven/Riverside Plaza Center on Florin Road. Nugget Market is this neighborhood shopping center's anchor and features a lot of independently owned restaurants and businesses. The only gas station in the Greenhaven/Pocket area, Shell Gas Station, is also located in this center.

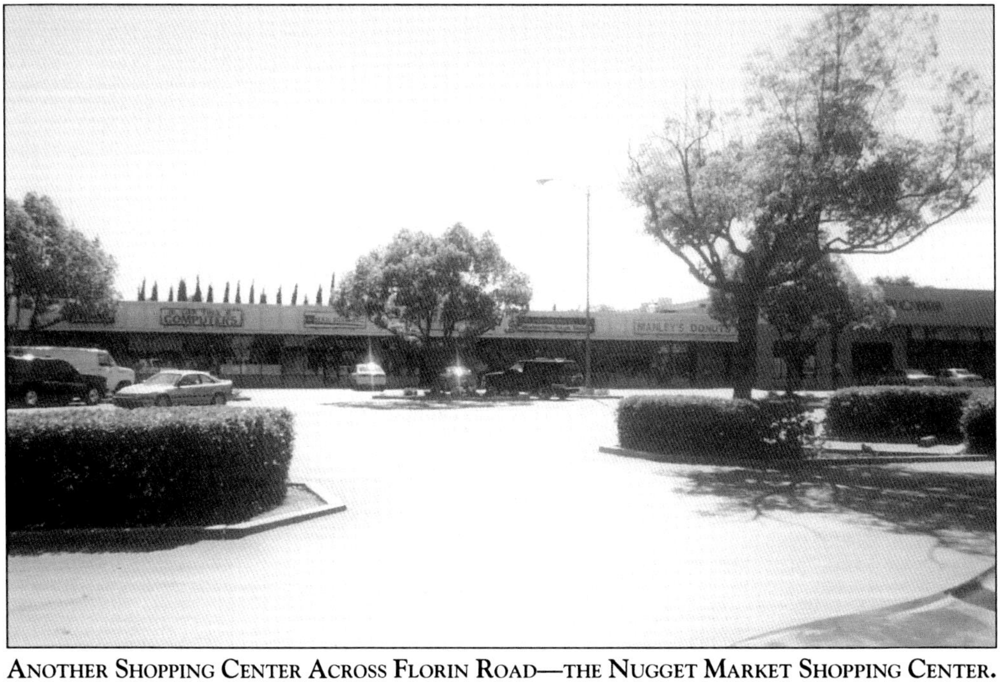

Another Shopping Center Across Florin Road—the Nugget Market Shopping Center. This center is one of the oldest in the Pocket area, built in the late 1960s. Pictured is the Rainbow's End Restaurant and Manleys Donuts, two independently owned businesses that have served locals in the Greenhaven/Pocket area for a number of years.

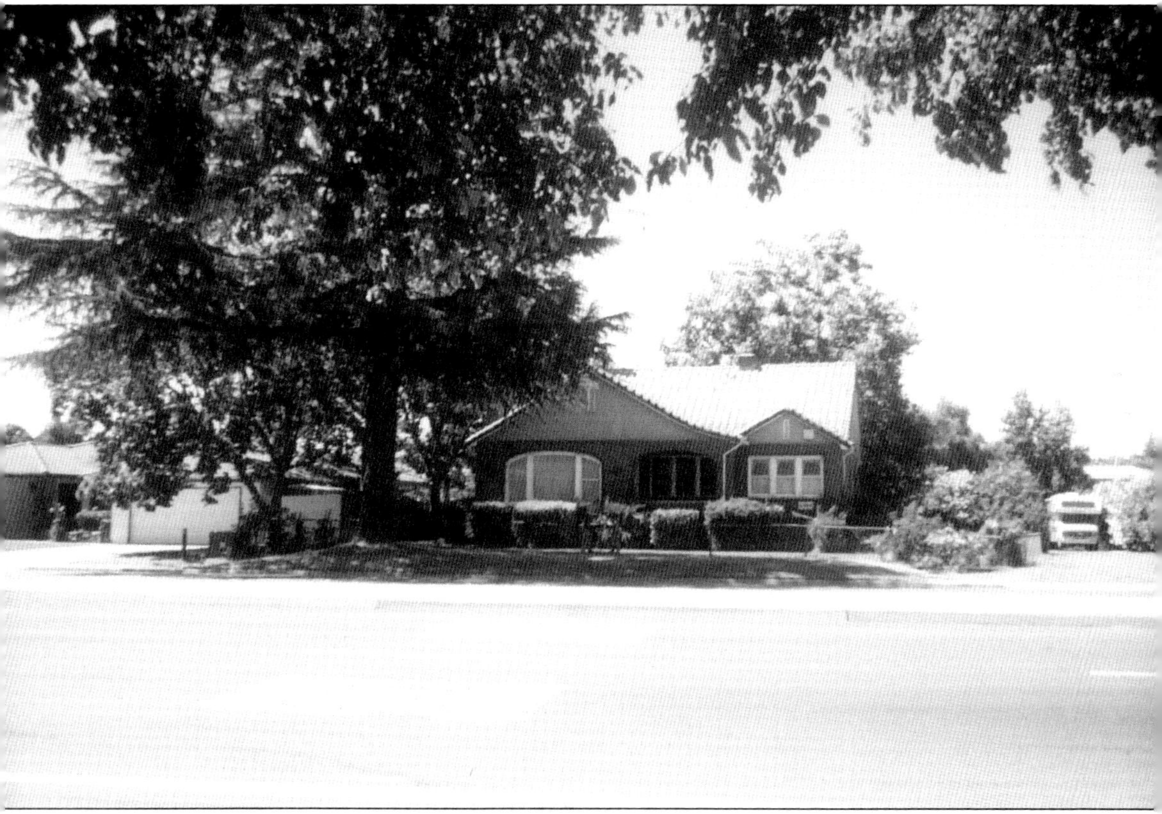

The Manuel Garcia Home, Located in the North Pocket Area Across from the Nugget Shopping Center. Manuel Garcia was the brother of Manuel Bento Simas who took the surname of Garcia after his godfather to avoid confusion. The home was built by the Terra brothers and Manuel's widow lived there with one of her twin daughters for many years.

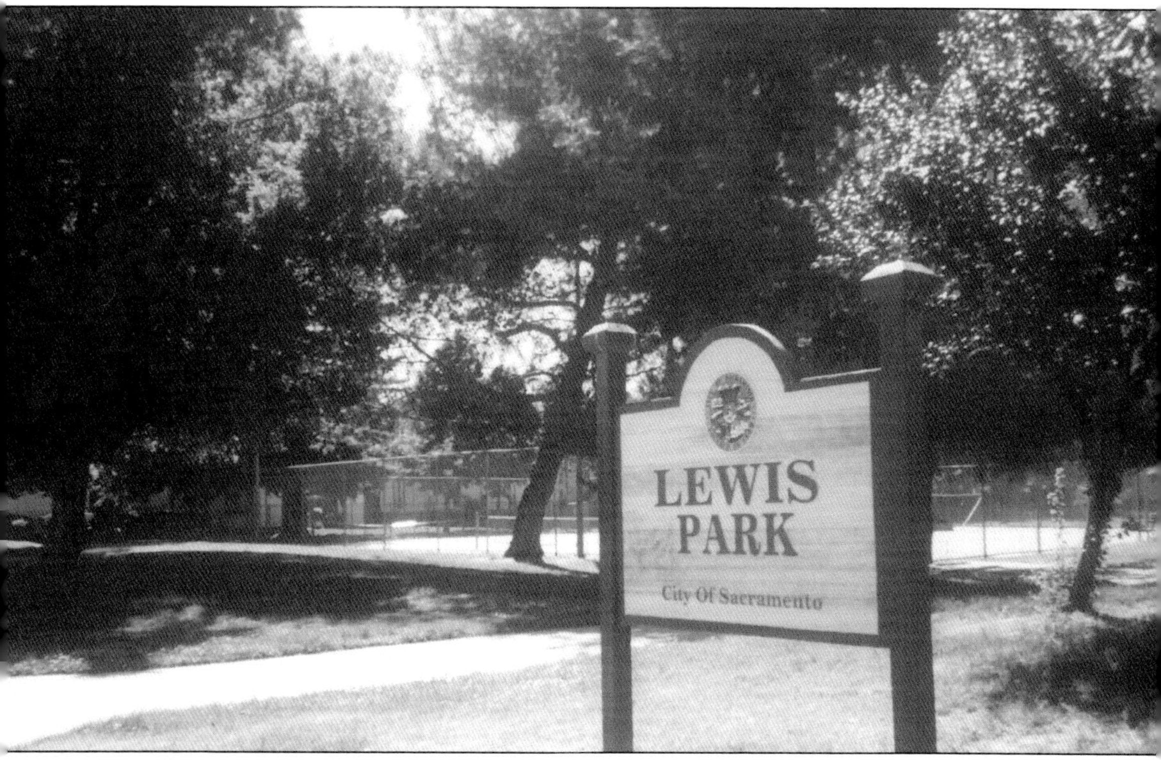

LEWIS PARK IN THE NORTH POCKET AREA WITH ITS TENNIS COURTS IN THE BACKGROUND. The Lewis Park playground was once the site of many baseball games for children in the area. It was located on a lot in front of the Joe Perry property, in which he allowed area children to play baseball.

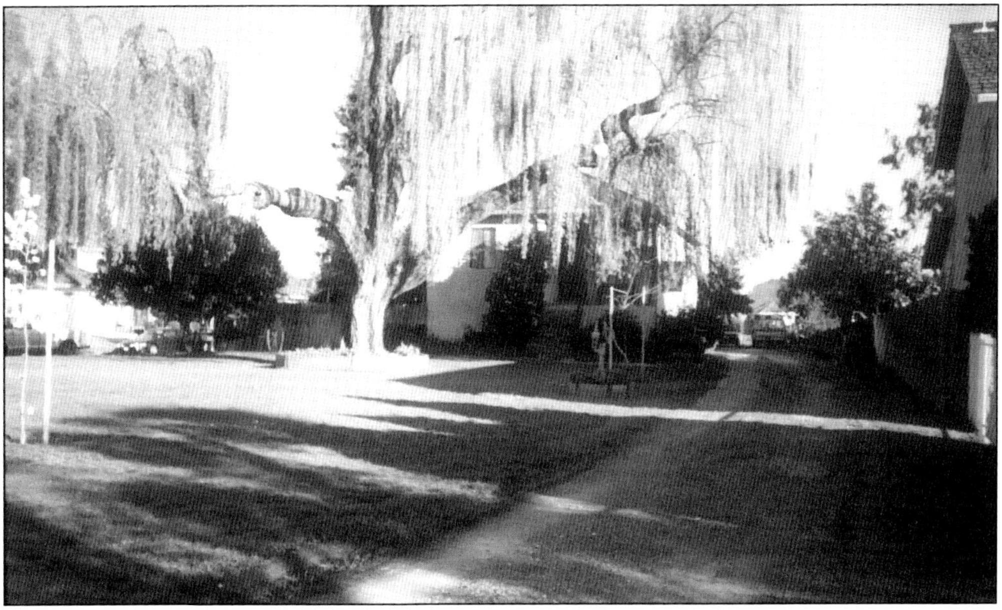

The Lawrence Perry Family Home in the North Pocket Area on Park Riveira Way in 1997. The historic home is also pictured in Chapter 3. At one time the neighborhood where this house was located was known as "Dog Town" because dogs were in abundance in the area and were used to drive waterwheels to pump well water for irrigation. Mr. Lawrence Perry kept older farm equipment in his front yard, reminiscent features of the community's bygone farming days.

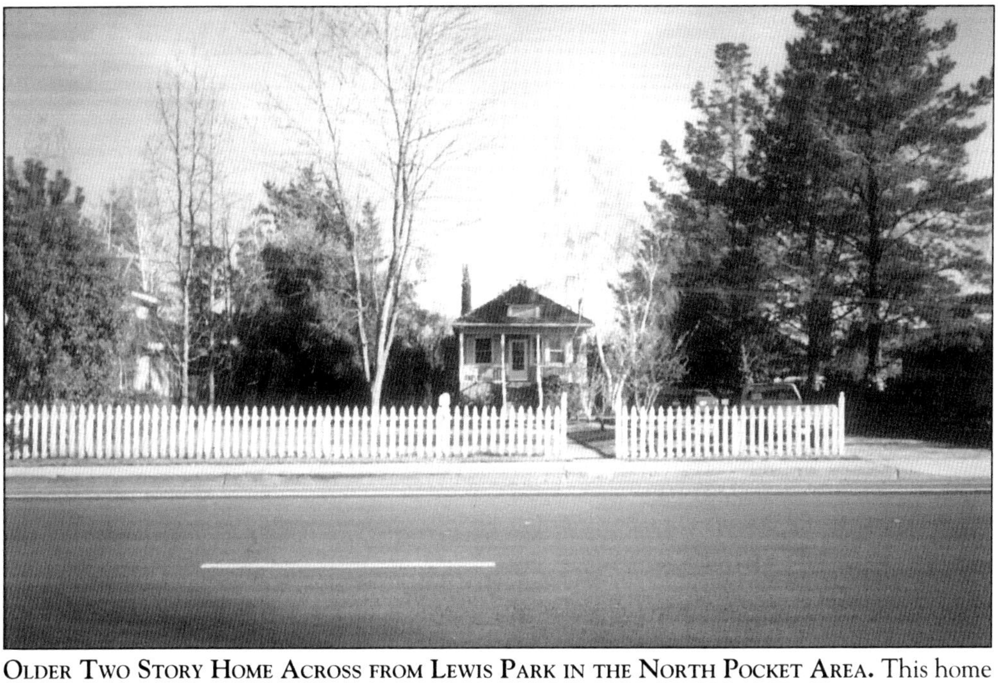

Older Two Story Home Across from Lewis Park in the North Pocket Area. This home was possibly the Azevedo family home at one time. It is one of the few remaining homes found in the Pocket area before suburban development, located in a cluster of older homes of this type in the neighborhood. (Information provided by Lucille Carter)

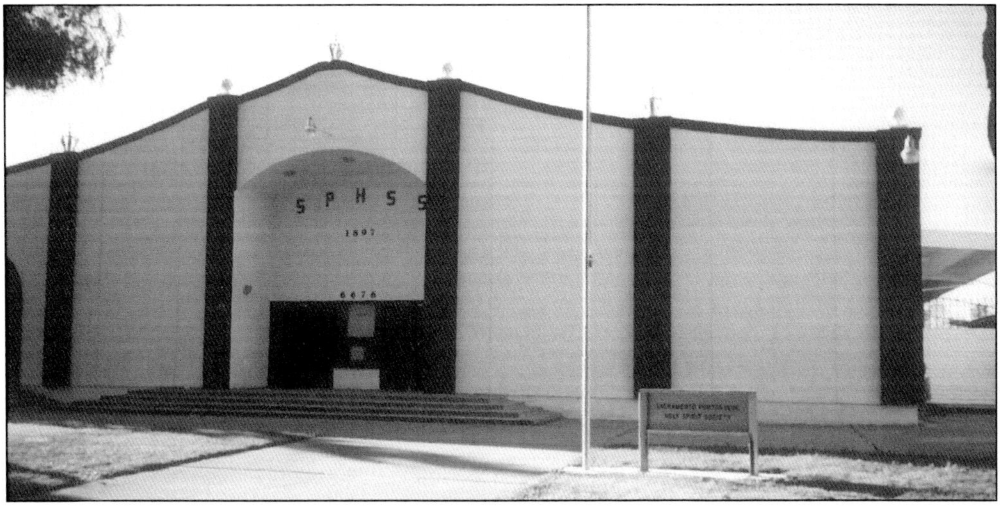

The Sacramento Portuguese Holy Spirit Society Hall on Old Pocket Road in 1997. The hall was painted white at that time and bears silver Holy Ghost crowns at the top of the building. S.P.H.S.S. regularly hold its meetings and functions here as well as rents out the hall to other local community groups and organizations for functions. The hall is also used annually for Sacramento's Holy Ghost Festival celebration.

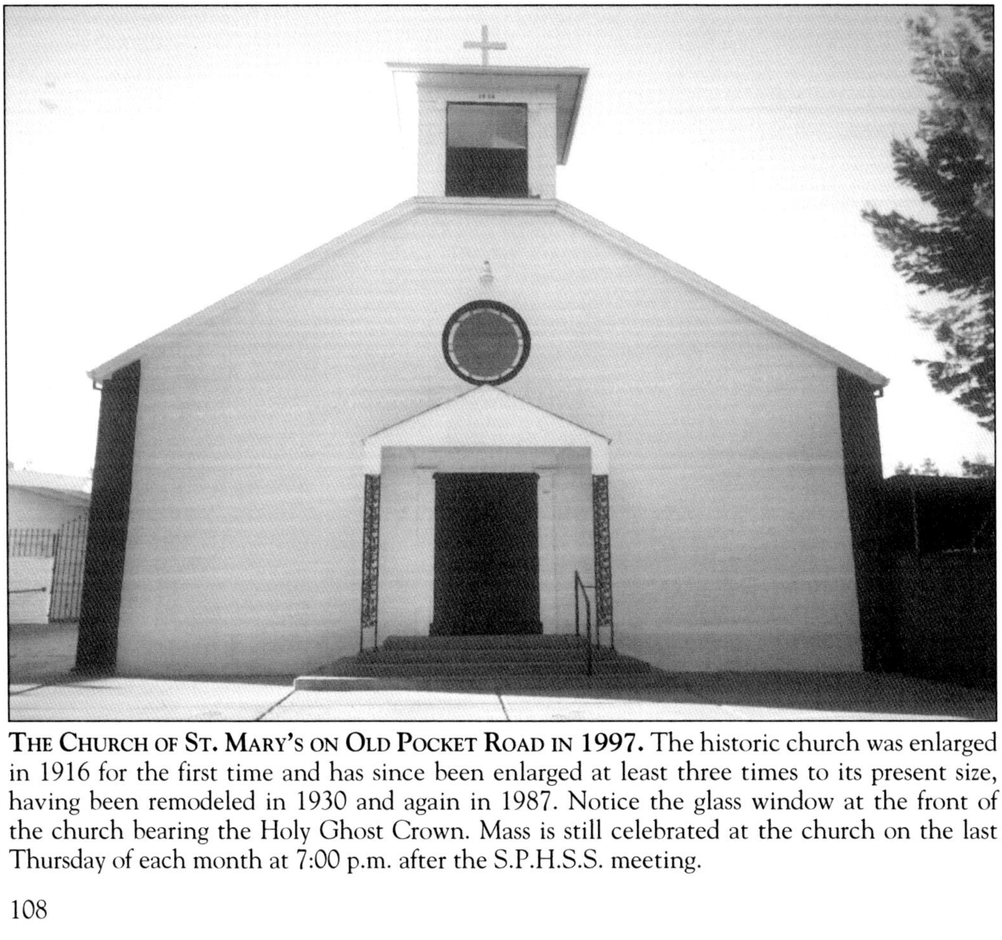

The Church of St. Mary's on Old Pocket Road in 1997. The historic church was enlarged in 1916 for the first time and has since been enlarged at least three times to its present size, having been remodeled in 1930 and again in 1987. Notice the glass window at the front of the church bearing the Holy Ghost Crown. Mass is still celebrated at the church on the last Thursday of each month at 7:00 p.m. after the S.P.H.S.S. meeting.

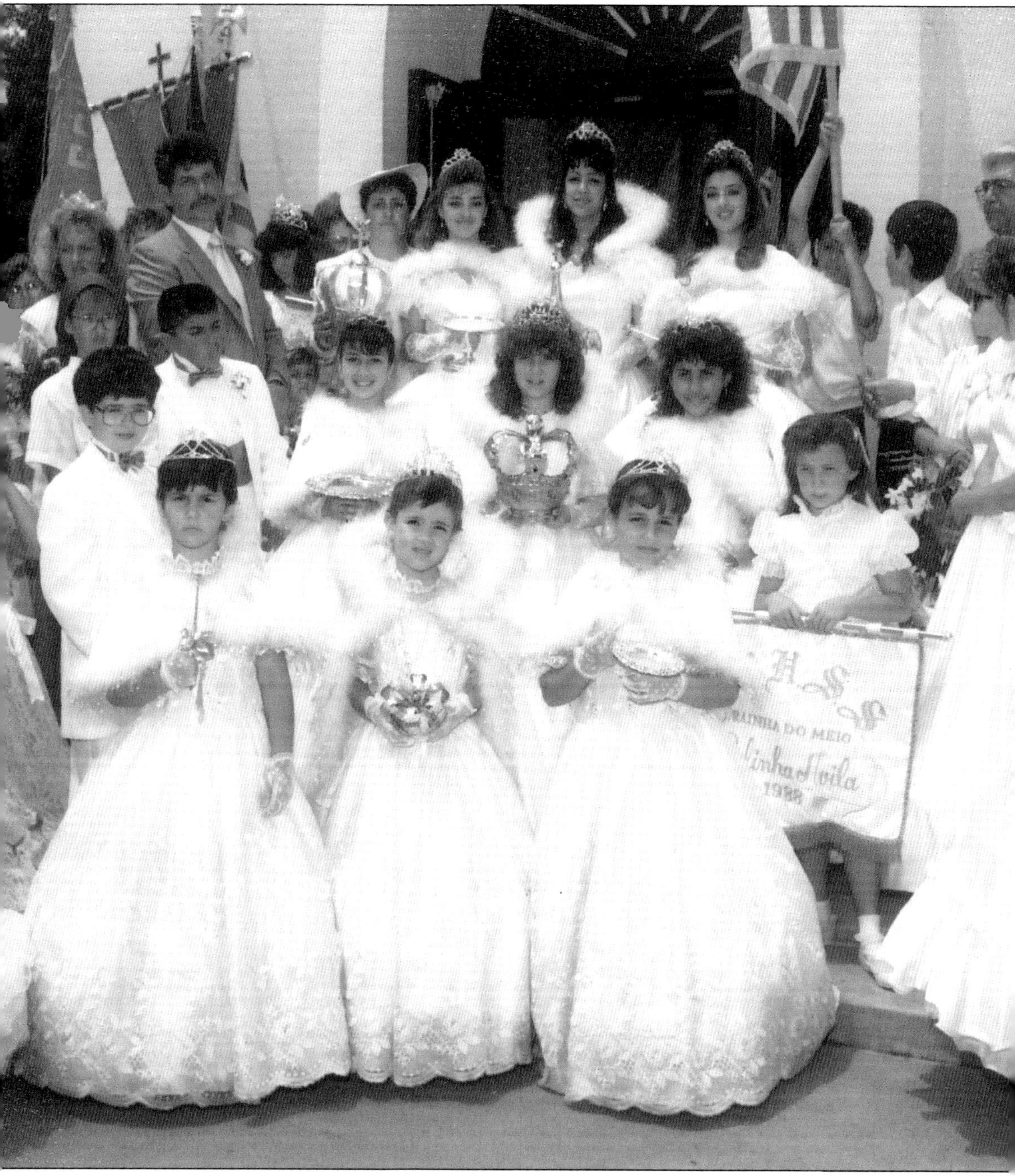

Sacramento Portuguese Holy Spirit Society (S.P.H.S.S.) Holy Ghost Festival in 1988. Pictured, from left to right, are: (front row) Nancy Queresma, Marlene Freitas (Little Queen), and Rosemary Ferreira; (middle row) Fernando Silva (wearing glasses) and Elizabeth Faria (holding banner); (second middle row) Allison Barsotti, Oscar Machado, Sandy Mendes, Belinha Avila (middle queen), and Suzette Machado; (back row) Miguel Azevedo, Belmira Azevedo (president of S.P.H.S.S. holding crown), Yvonne Mendes, Eugenia Olivera (big queen), and Margaret Mendes. Father Jose Ribeiro is at far right. (Courtesy of P.H.C.S.)

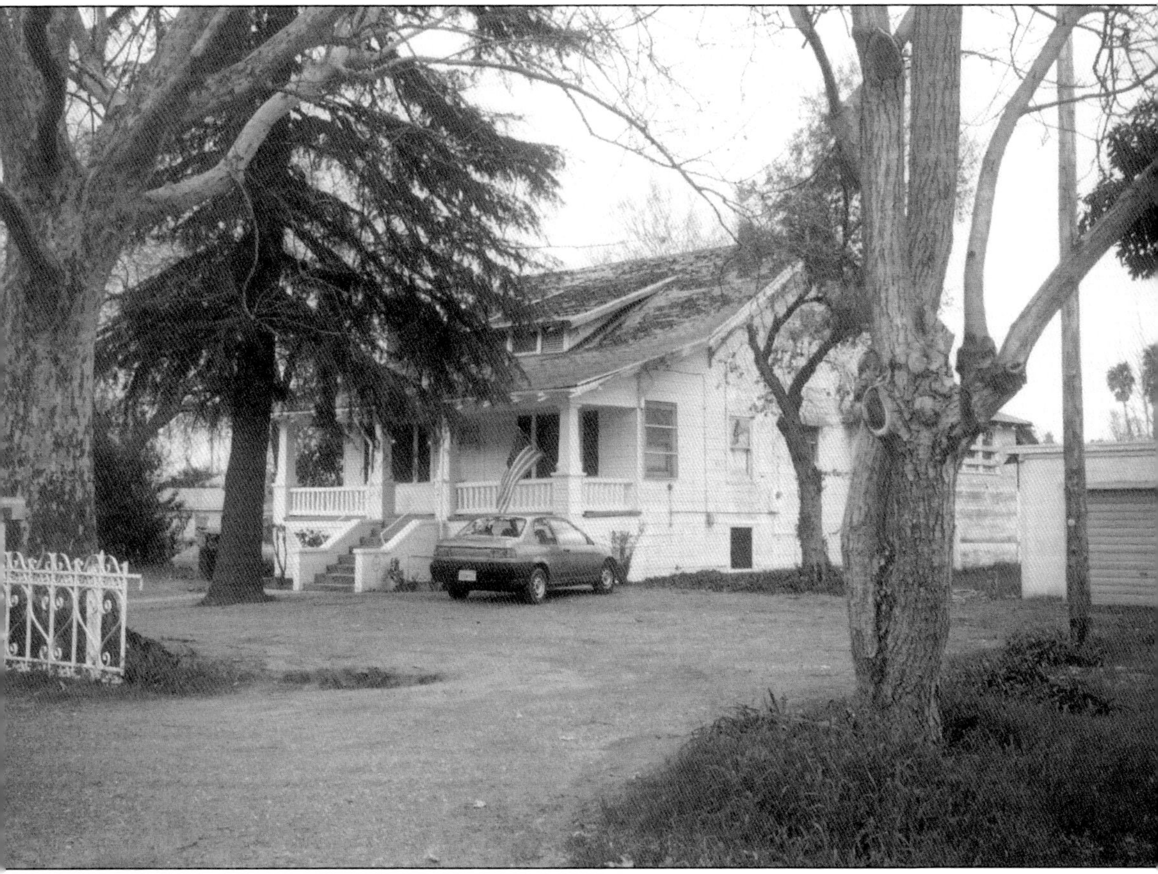

THE FORMER ANTONE AND MAGGIE PIMENTEL HOME ON RIVERSIDE BOULEVARD IN MARCH 1998, NEXT TO THE TRAP. Today, Pocket Security Patrol, a local security company that patrols Greenhaven/Pocket neighborhoods, is housed here. The filigree white gate at the front of the house was added when Pocket Security Patrol moved there. A pump house to the right of the home was removed and replaced with the garage seen in the photo. The base of the pump house was once used as living quarters. (Courtesy of P.H.C.S., photo taken by Dolores Silva Greenslate)

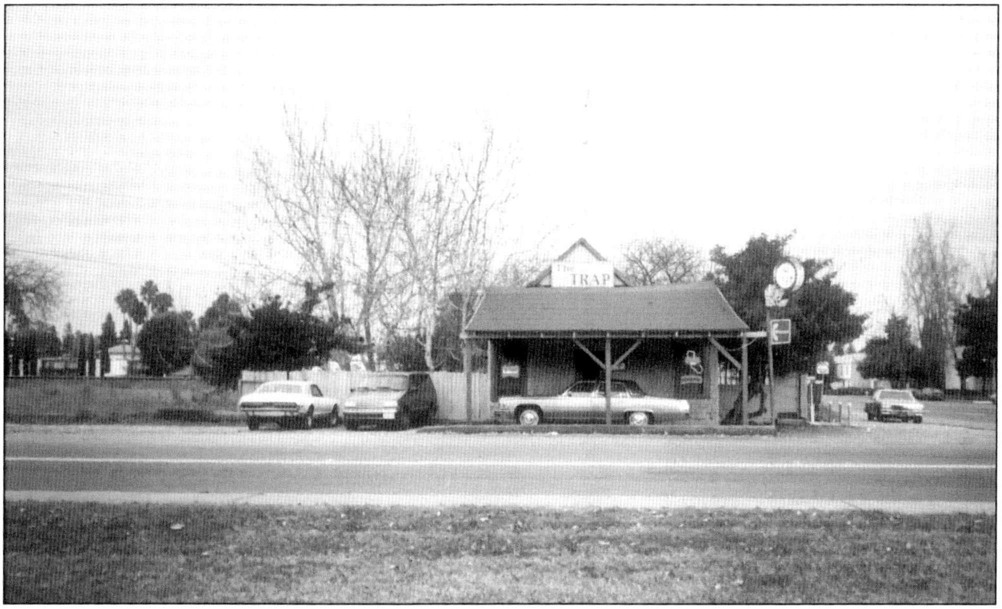

The Trap. Above in a 1997 picture, it is the oldest still-active establishment in the South Sacramento region identified at one-time with the Portuguese. Although somewhat seedy looking, it is considered a landmark by old-time residents of the Greenhaven/Pocket area. Today, it is a local bar and hang-out for residents and visitors of the area. A newer and bigger sign is now fronting the property with the sign in this picture now located on the right side of the establishment.

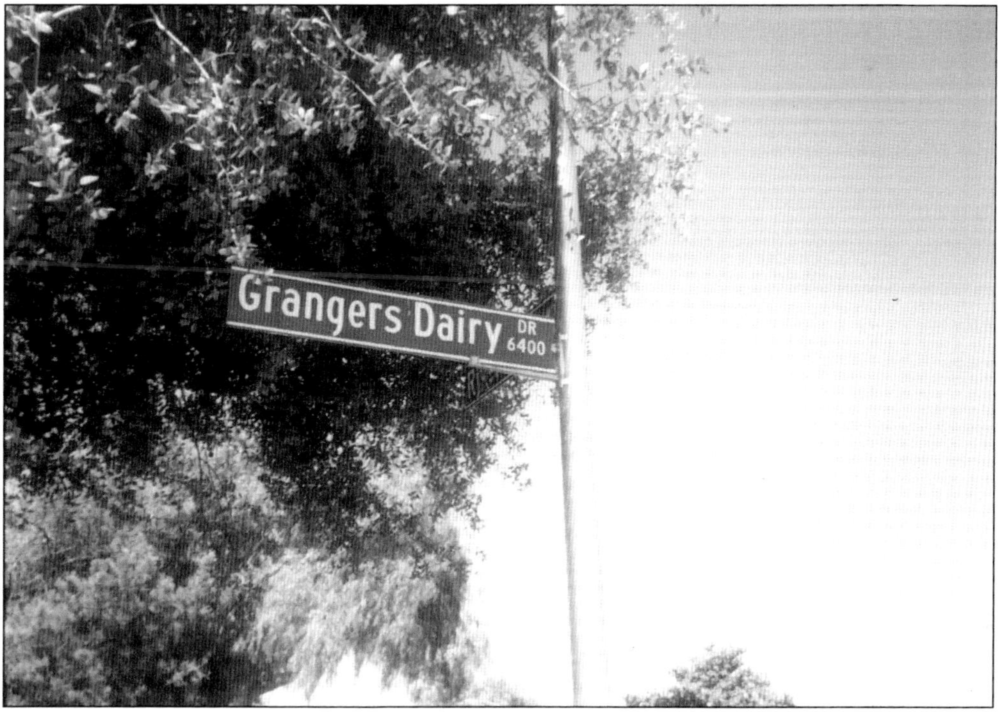

Grangers Dairy Street Sign in the North Pocket Area. The street name is the only remnant of Grangers Dairy, once located where its named after today.

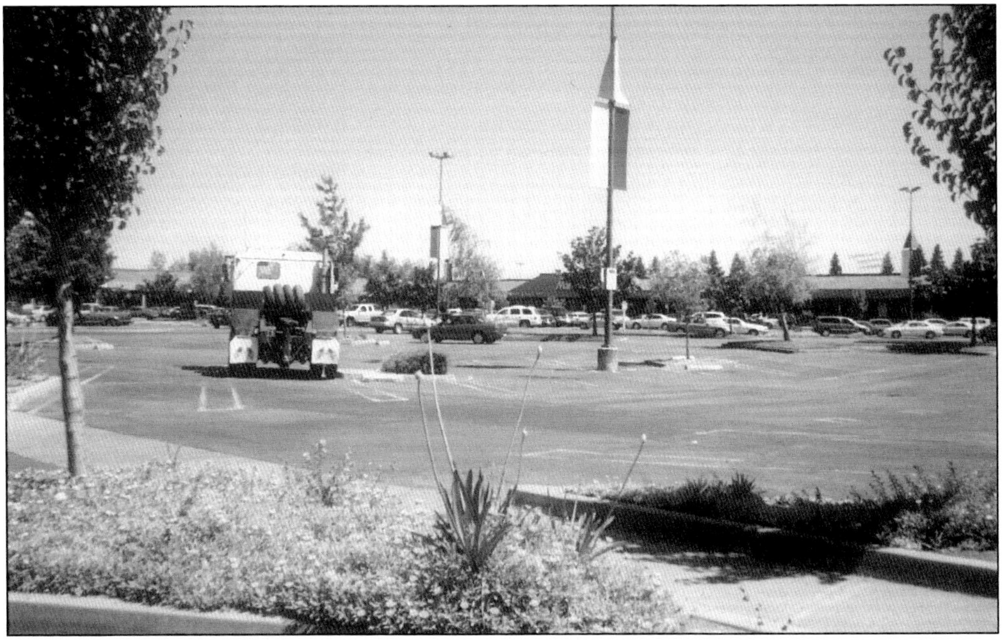

The Lakecrest Village Shopping Center, Located at the Intersection of Florin Road and Greenhaven Drive in 2001. This shopping center was intended to be the large-scale Greenhaven Commons center in the original Greenhaven 70 plan, but area residents in the 1970s lobbied the City of Sacramento to considerably reduce the size of the proposed development, especially with nearby Florin Mall as a prime competitor. Lakecrest Village is the largest shopping center in the Greenhaven/Pocket area however, and it is the only center in the area where residents can buy clothes and shoes.

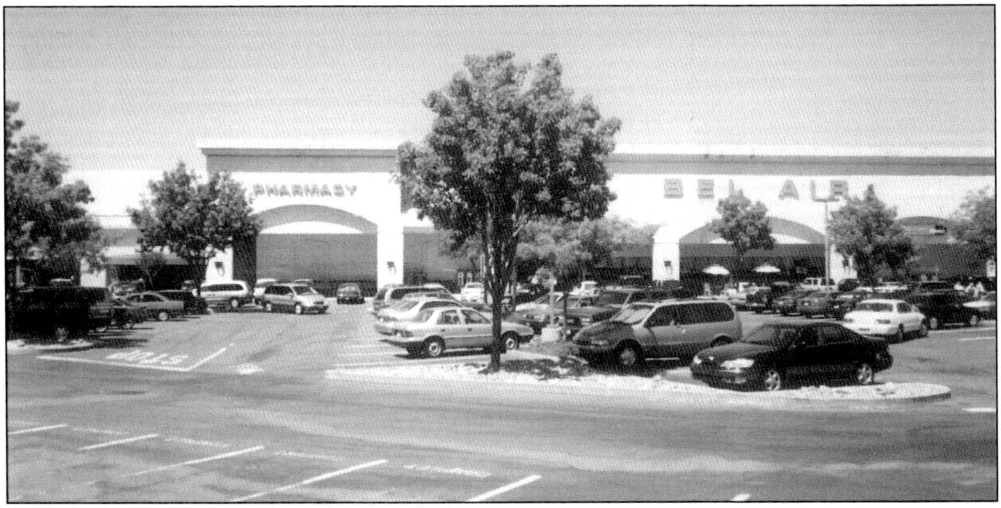

The Promenade Shopping Center in the South Pocket Area, Located at the Intersection of Rush River Drive and Windbridge Drive. Bel-Air Market is this shopping center's anchor. Built in the late 1980s–early 1990s, its architectural style has the look of a tropical, vaguely Arabic oasis with copper light fixtures and an orange/pinkish colored exterior. The Pocket Police Service Center is also located in this shopping center, established by City Councilman Robbie Waters, where volunteers take resident calls about crime in the area.

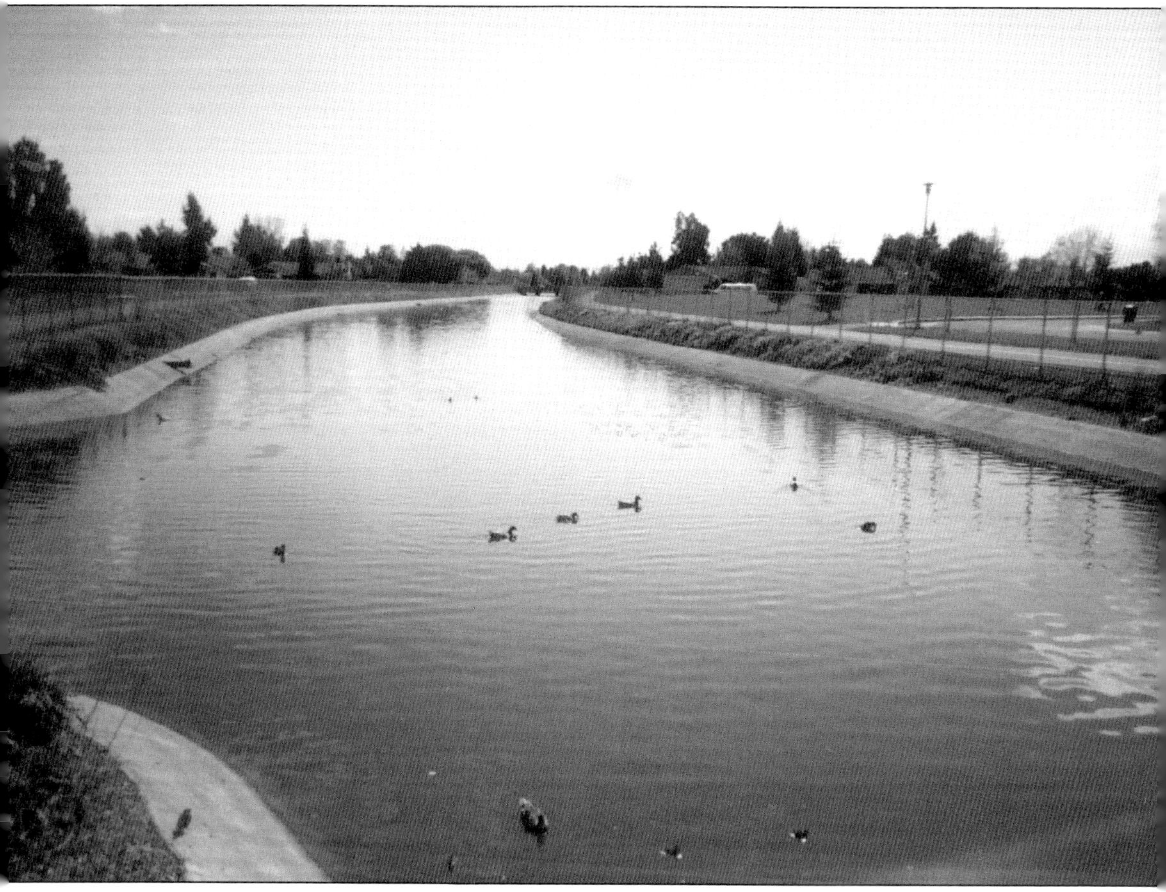

The Pocket Drainage Canal at Portuguese Community Park in the South Pocket Area. The Pocket canal is an extension of the Seymour Park Greenbelt, so that an open space network continues throughout the Pocket area. The canal trails are commonly used by residents for jogging, bicycling, and rollerblading. The canal is also home to ducks and fish. Residents are often seen fishing at the canal. The drainage canal was built in the Pocket area to alleviate any potential flooding problems due to its low-lying elevation.

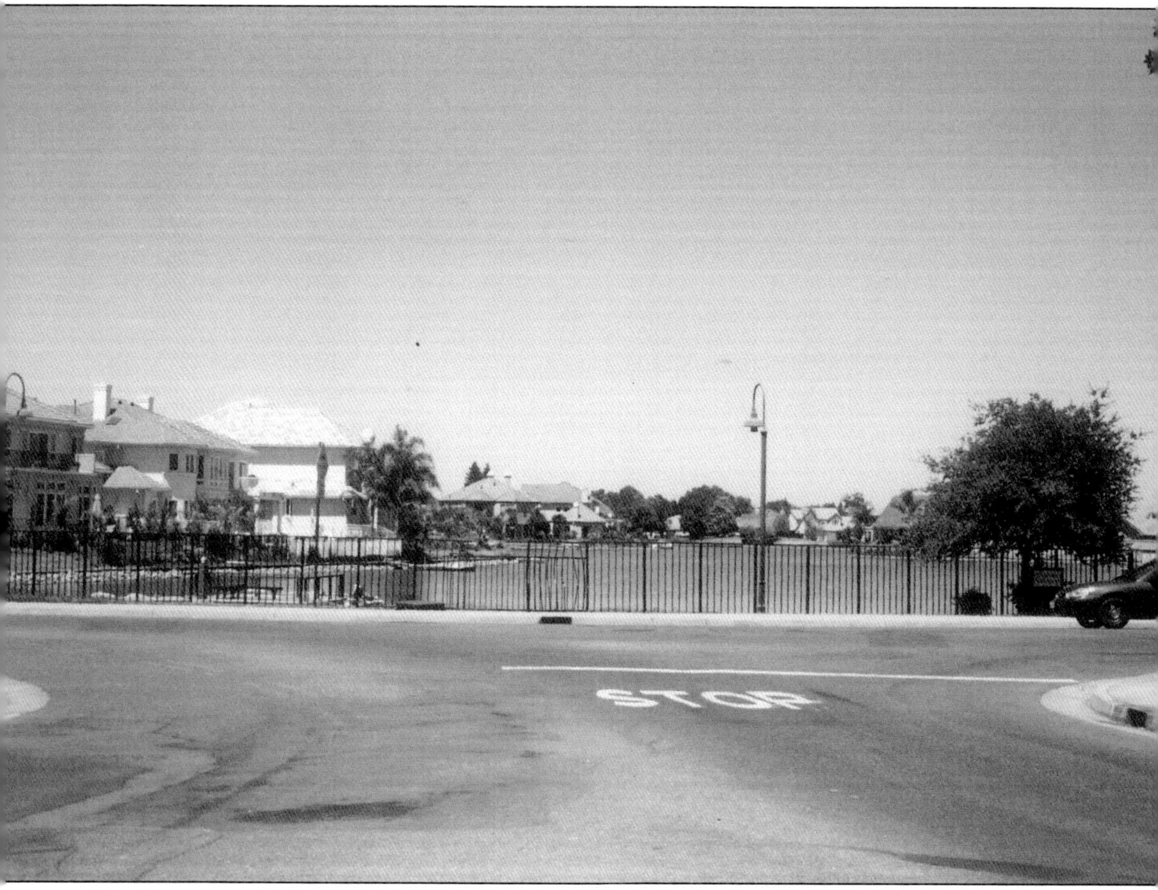

The Riverlake Development in the South Pocket Area, Built by the Parker Development Company. Riverlake is the second man-made lake in the Pocket area, designed to provide drainage for its low-lying elevation. It is also an amenity for lakefront residents. Bill Parker, the son of developer Harold Parker from the original Greenhaven 70 development, continued to provide high quality subdivisions in the Pocket area with a number of amenities as his father did years earlier.

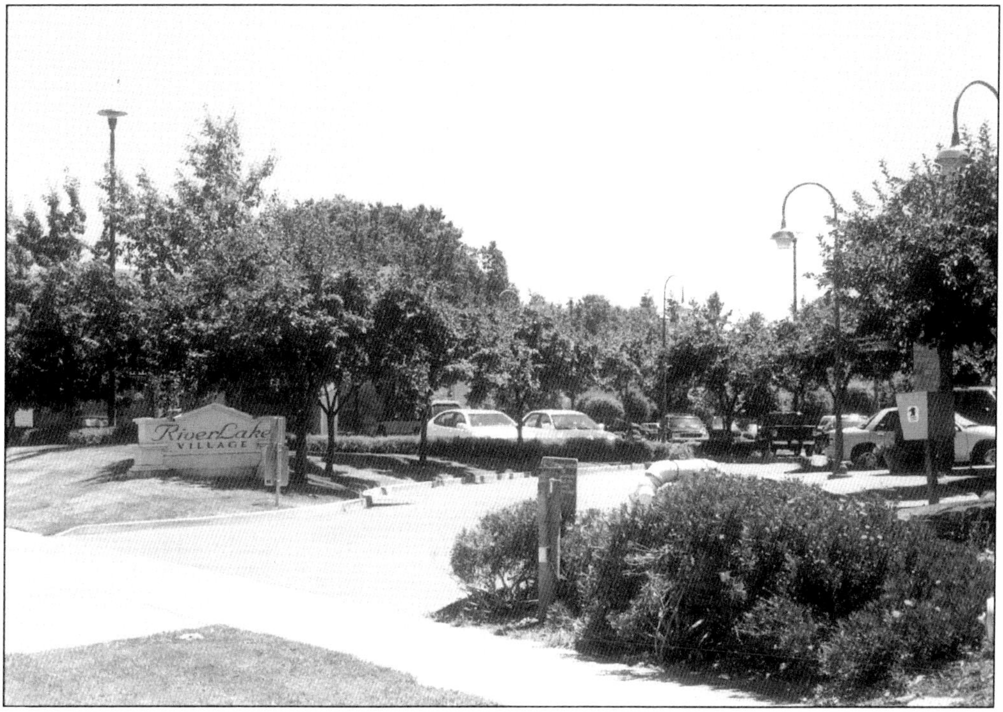

THE RIVERLAKE VILLAGE SHOPPING CENTER, LOCATED AT THE INTERSECTION OF GREENHAVEN DRIVE AND POCKET ROAD IN THE SOUTH POCKET AREA. This is a smaller scale neighborhood shopping center compared to others found in the area. It has a modern village center look and a trendy service orientation.

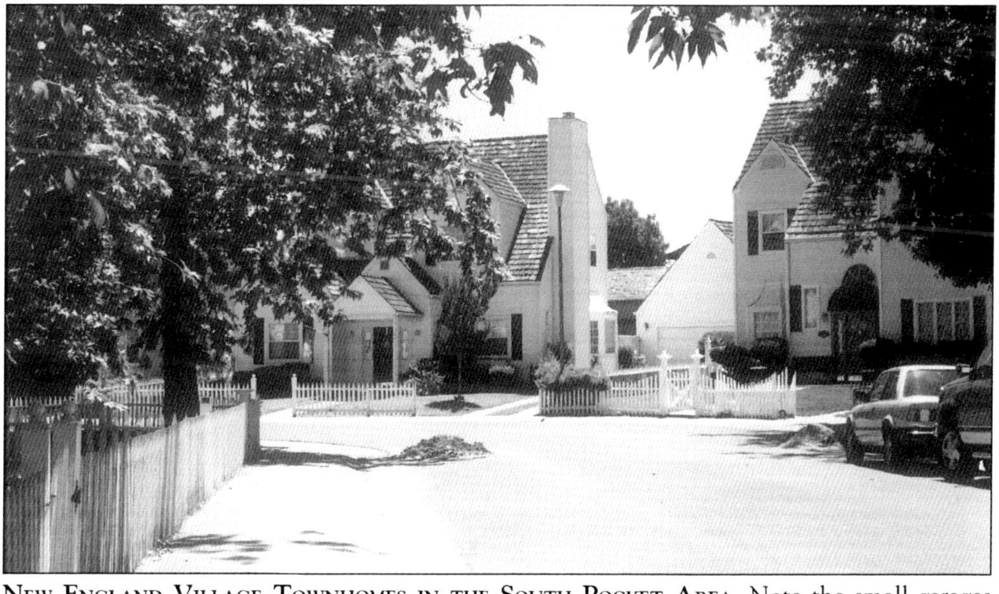

NEW ENGLAND VILLAGE TOWNHOMES IN THE SOUTH POCKET AREA. Note the small garages at the side of these homes. The Greenhaven/Pocket area has a variety of housing stocks and styles, from large-lot, gated community mansions, for which the Pocket area is noted for, to the suburban custom-built ranch home styles of Greenhaven.

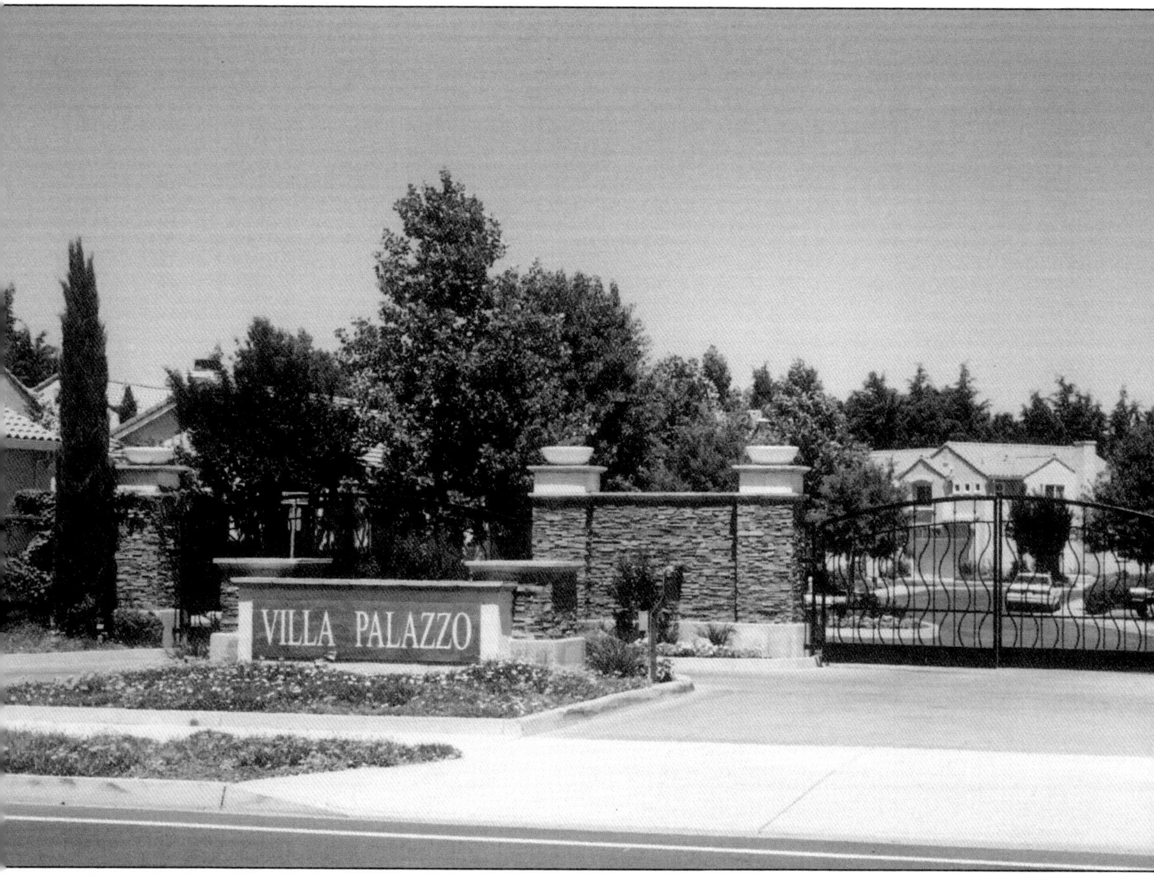

The Villa Palazzo Multi-Unit Housing Development in the South Pocket Area, Located Across From the Dutra House. This townhouse development, built in the mid to late 1990s, is of Italian theme and represents the many housing styles found in the Pocket area.

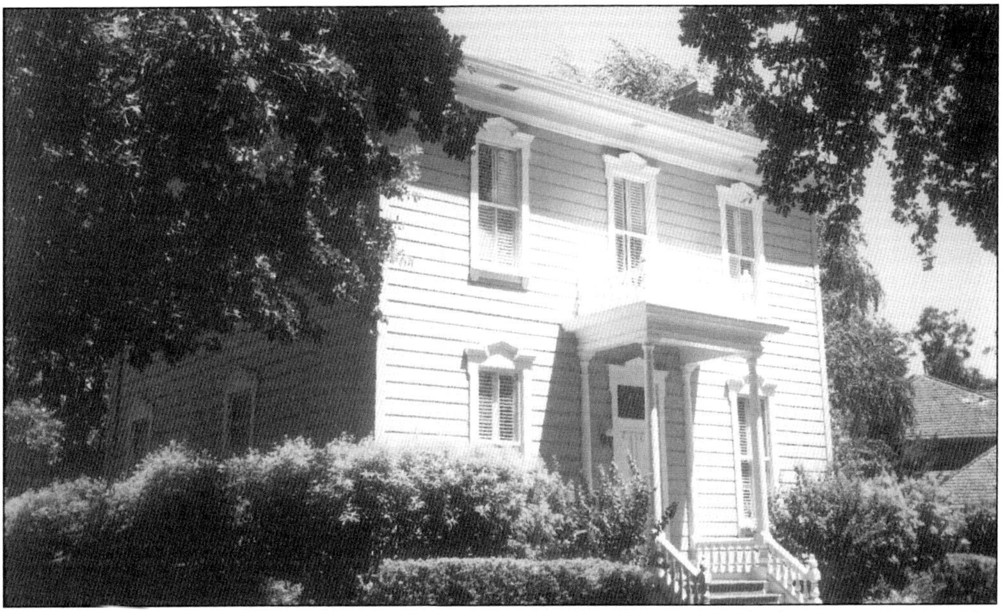

THE RESTORED DUTRA HOUSE IN THE SOUTH POCKET AREA IN 2001. The house was restored by L and P and Pacific/Teichert, land developers for the Riverlake community in the Pocket area. The house cost $1,200 to build but was restored at a cost of $350,000, completed in December of 1986 after nine months of work. The Italianate ranch house was restored to closely resemble the way it looked at the turn-of-the century. The house is currently the sales office of Parker Development Company and it stands as a reminder of the Pocket's early Portuguese settlement and agricultural heritage.

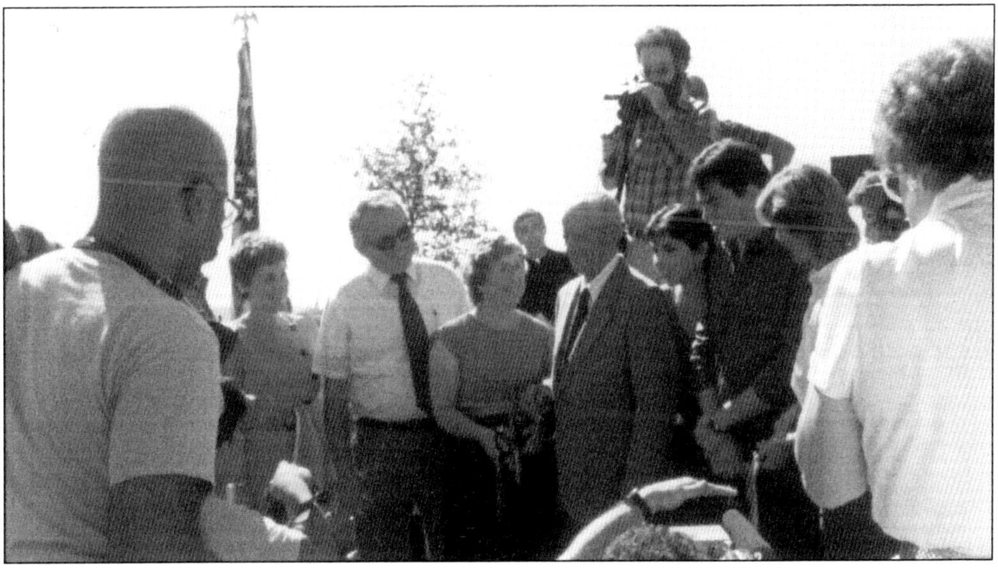

DEDICATION CEREMONY OF THE EILEEN DUTRA PARK IN 1984. The park, located in the North Pocket area is named in honor of Eileen Dutra, a Pocket area native from the Coleman family. At center is Tony Dutra, Eileen's husband. At right is son Anthony Dutra (wearing sunglasses) and daughter Diane Dutra. The park was planned and designed through the efforts of nearby neighborhood residents. (Photo taken by Marie Dutra Gambrel)

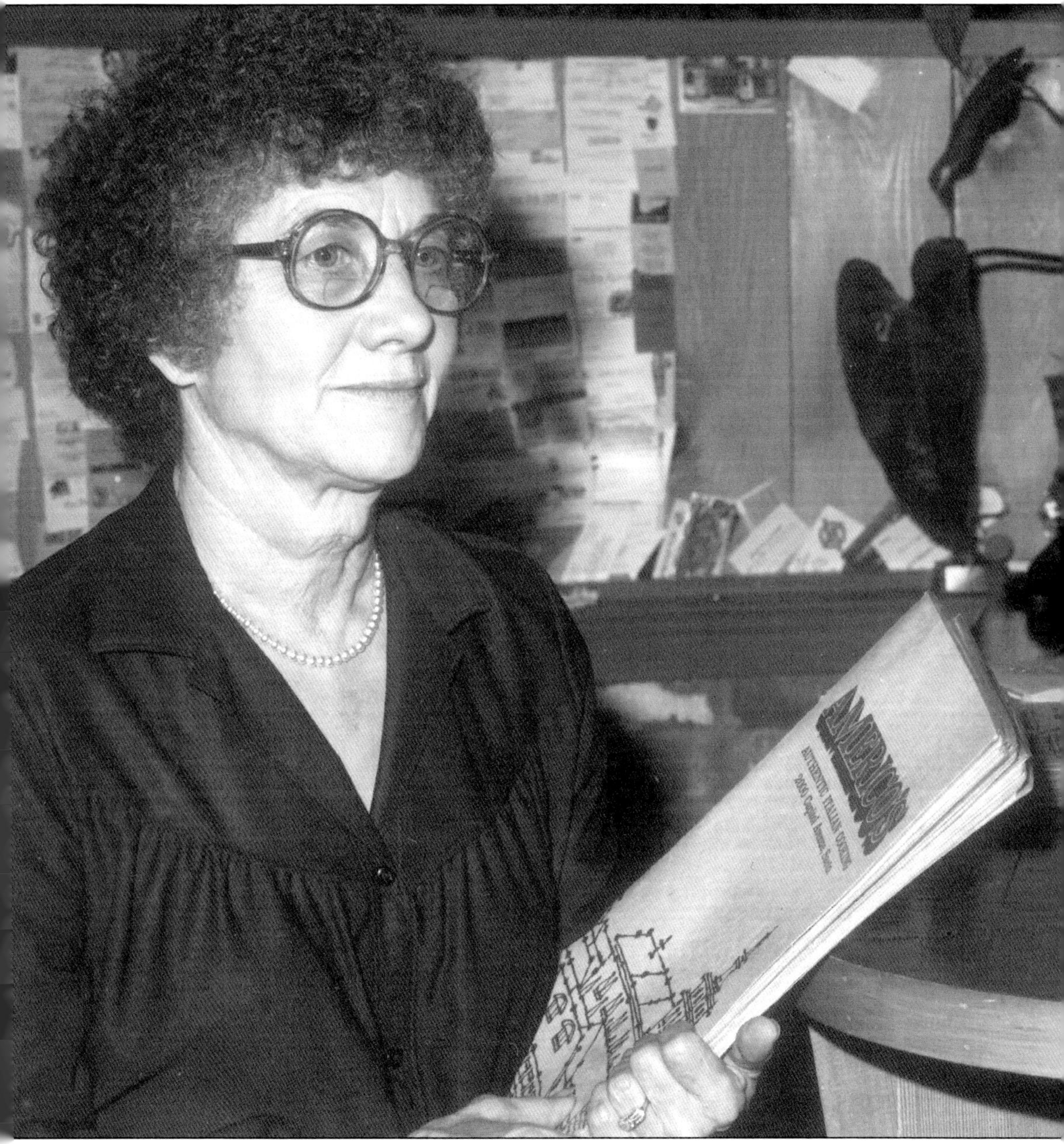

Lorraine Perry D'Alessandro at Americo's Restaurant in 1984. Mrs. D'Alessandro was a native Pocket area resident who helped established the Portuguese Historical and Cultural Society with her son, Joseph D'Alessandro. The Portuguese Historical and Cultural Society was founded in 1979 (then called the Sacramento-Area Historical Committee) to promote and preserve the historic heritage of the Portuguese settlement in the Pocket area. It was later expanded to include the preservation of Portuguese history and settlement in the greater Sacramento area. Mrs. D'Alessandro was an active community leader in both the Portuguese community and Sacramento area at large, as well as a local business owner in downtown Sacramento. The gazebo found in the Portuguese Community Park plaza area is dedicated in her memory. (Courtesy of P.H.C.S.)

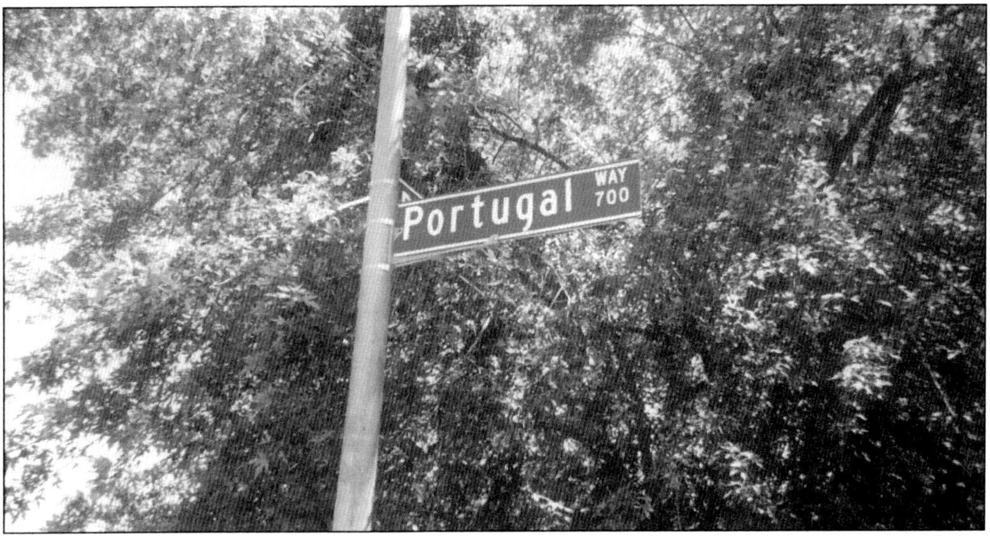

The Portugal Way Street Sign in the South Pocket Area, Across the Street From the Portuguese Community Park. One of the goals of the Portuguese Historical and Cultural Society (P.H.C.S.) was to have street names in the Pocket area bear Portuguese place and family names, in honor of this ethnic group's historic settlement in the area. The development of an ethnic-themed park and the naming of a new elementary school in the area after the historic Lisbon schools were also the goals of the organization. Portugal Way was the first street sign in the Pocket area to be named based on P.H.C.S.'s efforts.

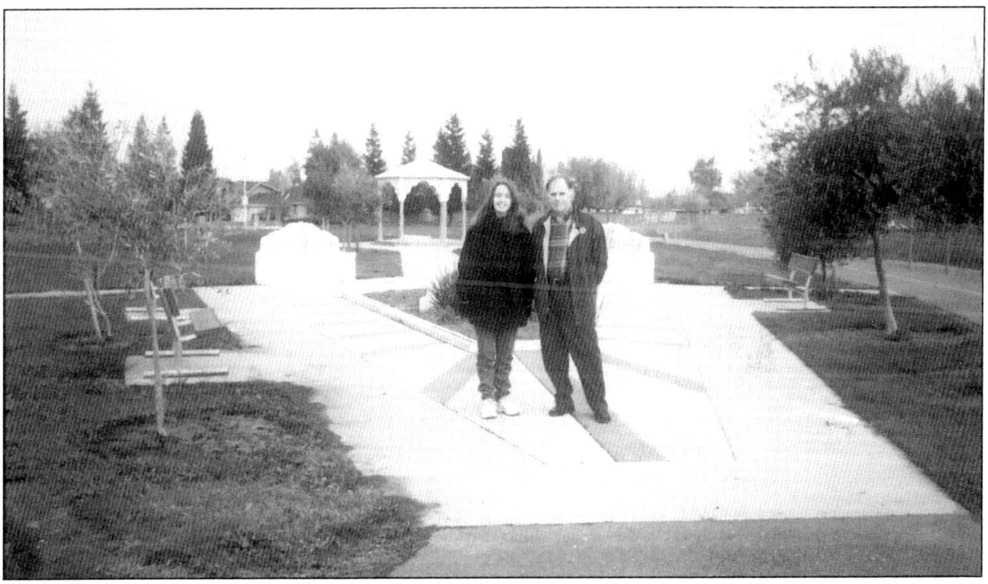

Pictured is the Plaza Area of the Portuguese Community Park in 1997, with Carol Ann Gregory at Left and Herb Perry at Right. Mr. Perry was the President of the Portuguese Historical and Cultural Society during the park's dedication in November 1988. The plaza features cobblestone flooring designed after parks found in the Azores Islands. The gazebo is of Manueline architecture, a distinctive rope-like feature at the gazebo's columns. The plaza also has two concrete whitewash benches displaying azulejo tiles created and donated by the Portuguese government. (Photo taken by Mary Ann Gregory)

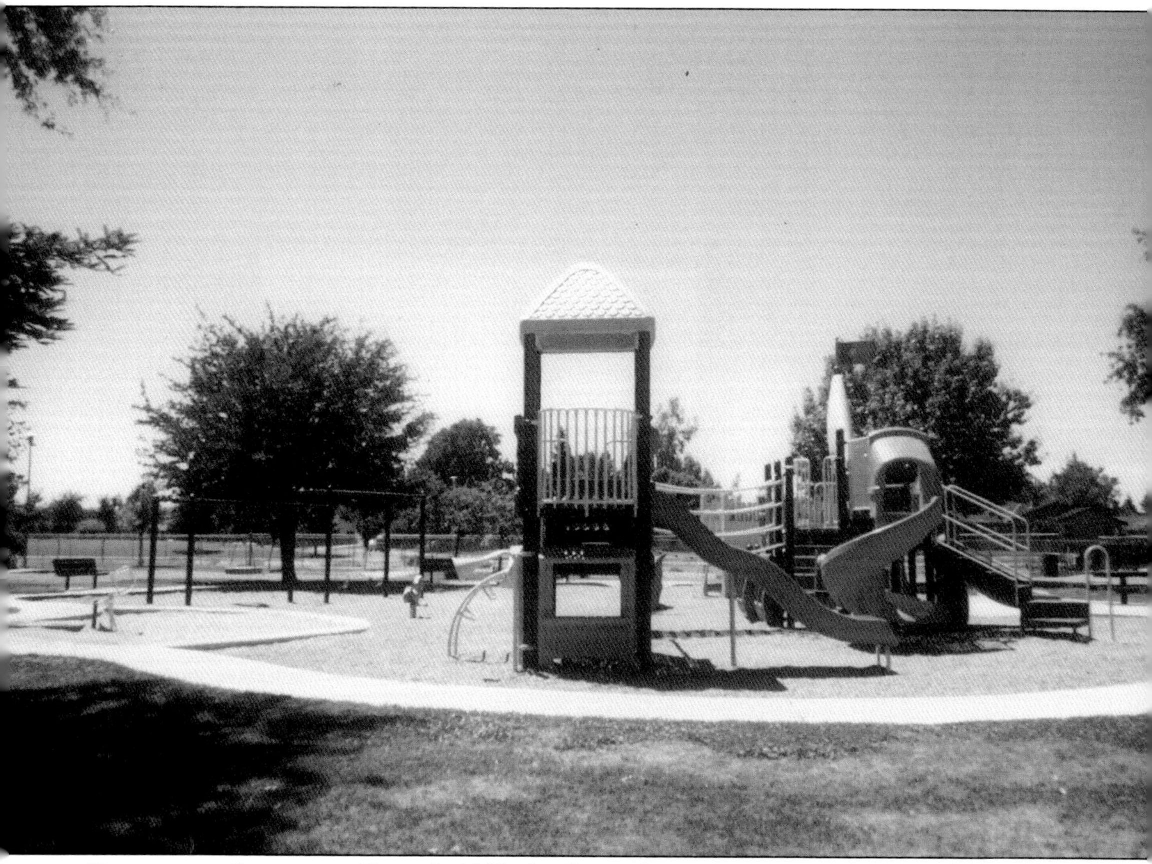

PORTUGUESE COMMUNITY PARK. In 1999, the City of Sacramento received a grant of $50,000 to renovate the then 11-year-old Portuguese Community Park. The majority of the grant money went to the remodeling of the park's playground to meet safety standards. A major addition to the playground was a navigational play ship, commemorating the importance of exploration to the history of Portugal. A Portuguese flag is located at the top of the play ship. The wooden castle, a replica of the Tower of Belem in Lisbon, was also restored and repainted. The concrete mythical sea serpent, commonly found in Portuguese folktales, maps, architecture, and azulejo mosaic tiles, was also kept in the playground. The children of the local neighborhood expressed a liking to the sea serpent during community meetings for the playground's renovation.

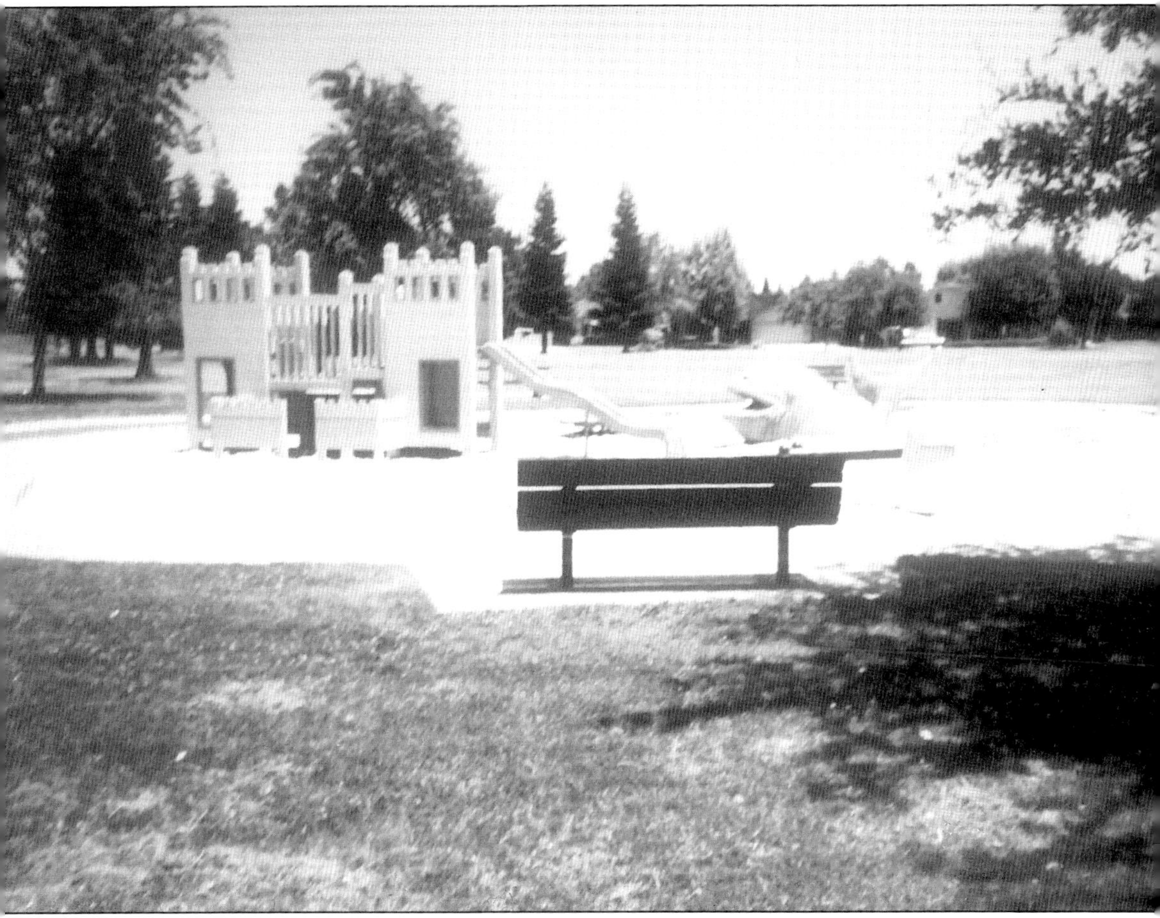

THE PORTUGUESE COMMUNITY PARK PLAYGROUND IN 1997 BEFORE IT WAS REMODELED.

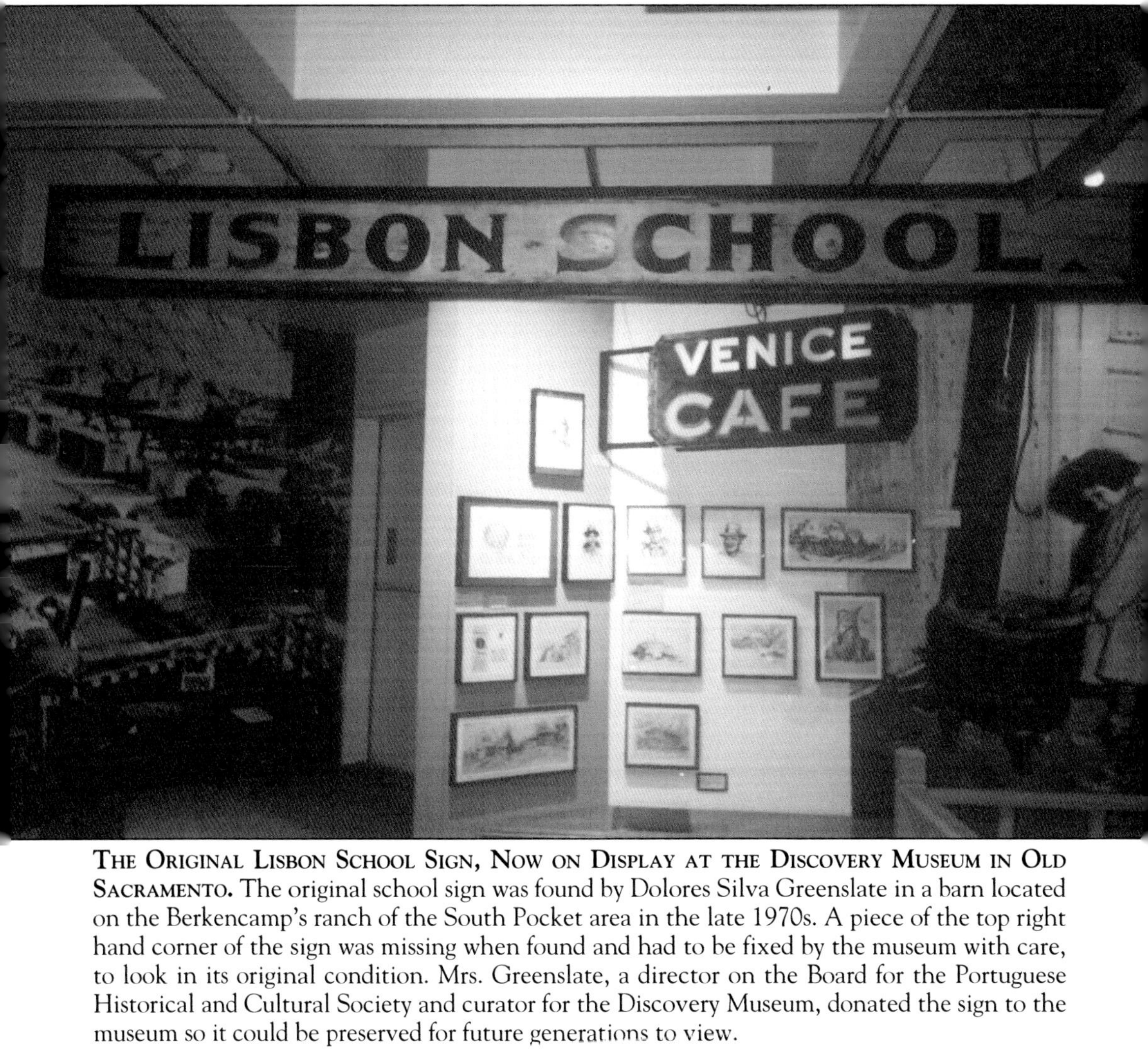

The Original Lisbon School Sign, Now on Display at the Discovery Museum in Old Sacramento. The original school sign was found by Dolores Silva Greenslate in a barn located on the Berkencamp's ranch of the South Pocket area in the late 1970s. A piece of the top right hand corner of the sign was missing when found and had to be fixed by the museum with care, to look in its original condition. Mrs. Greenslate, a director on the Board for the Portuguese Historical and Cultural Society and curator for the Discovery Museum, donated the sign to the museum so it could be preserved for future generations to view.

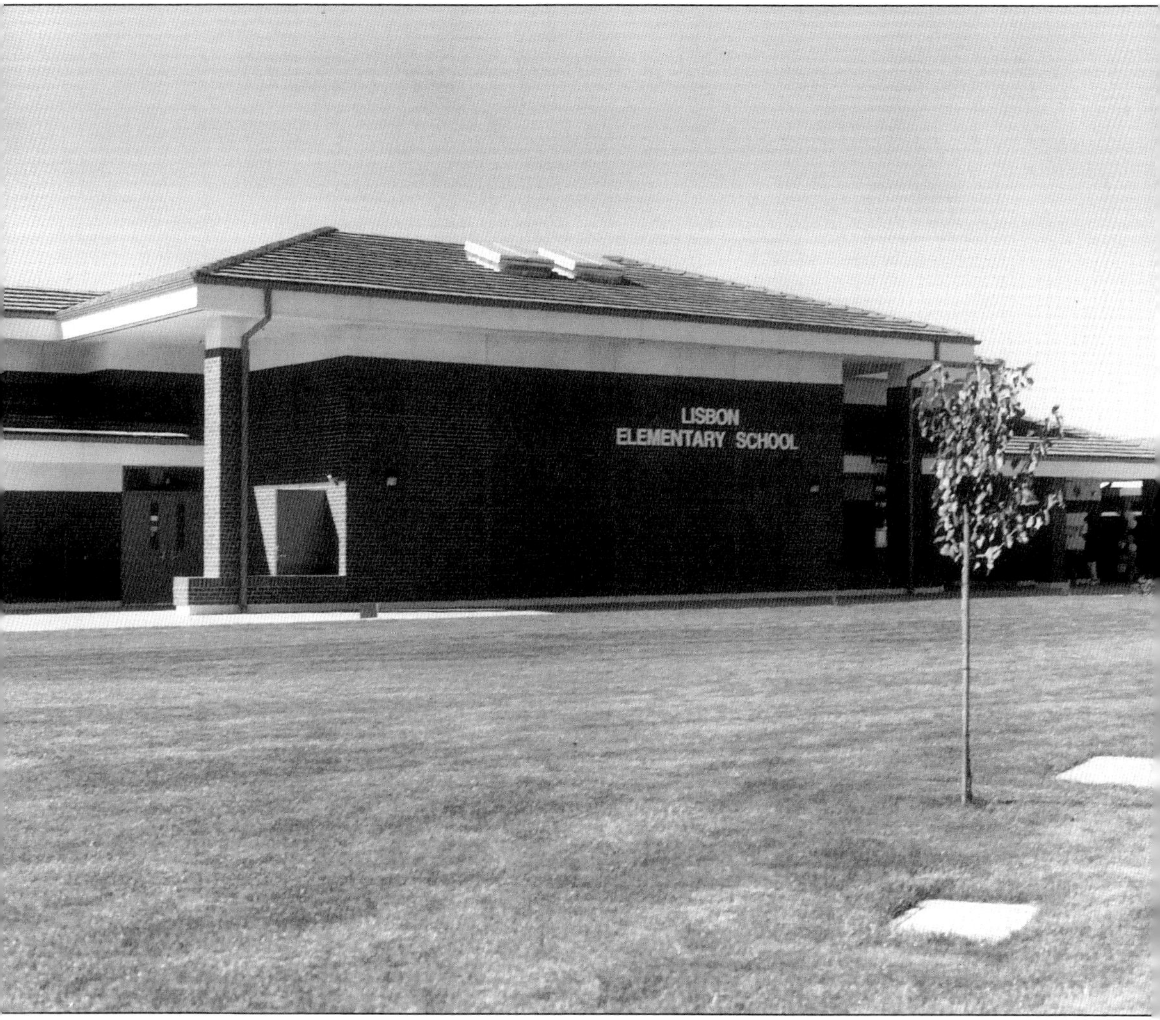

THE NEW LISBON ELEMENTARY SCHOOL IN THE SOUTH POCKET AREA, LOCATED TODAY ON 7555 SOUTH LAND PARK DRIVE. Dedicated in 1988, the school is one of the five public elementary schools found in the Greenhaven/Pocket area. It is named after the historic Portuguese-established Lisbon schools, one of the lobbying efforts that the Portuguese Historical and Cultural Society sought during the development of the area. At the dedication ceremonies, the oldest living student who attended the historic Lisbon schools, Mary "Milhomens" Silva Dutra, was present and received special recognition. The Portuguese Historical and Cultural Society also participated in the ceremonies. (Courtesy of P.H.C.S.)

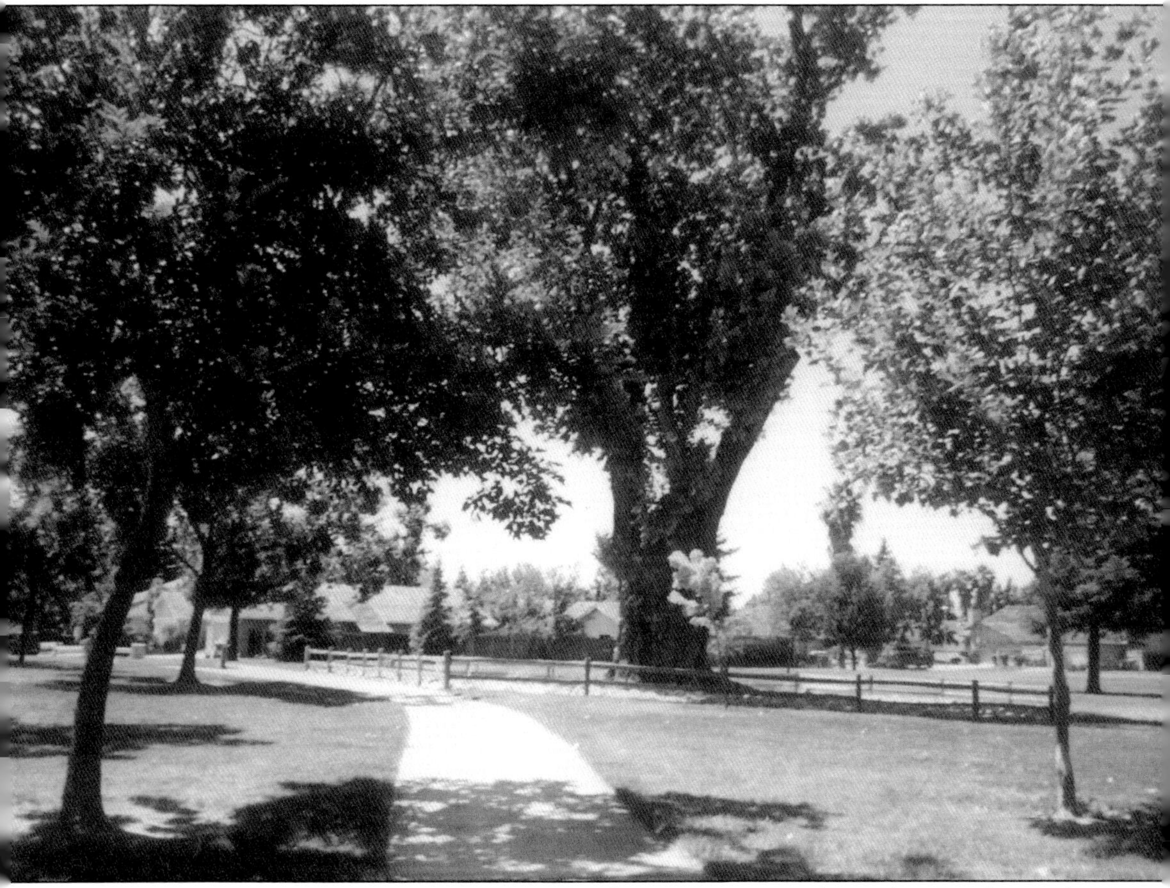

A Remnant of the Lewis Ranch. The old oak tree at center is located in Renfree Park, providing shade and character to the South Pocket area park, dedicated in 1986. A small plaque in the park located next to a park bench tells the story of the Lewis family and how their ranch was once located where this park is today.

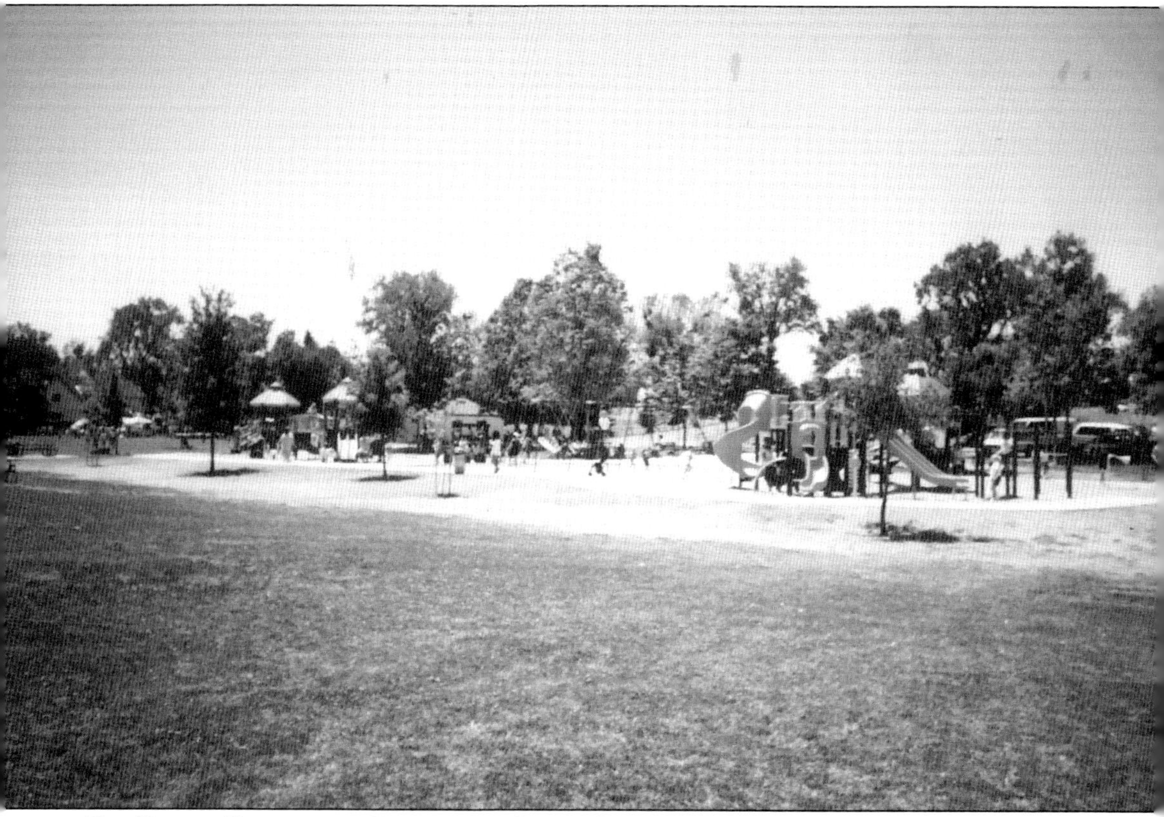

The Recent Playground Remodel of Garcia Bend Park in the South Pocket Area. All the parks in the Pocket area during the late 1990s received needed maintenance and repair by the City of Sacramento based on grants and passage of park measures.

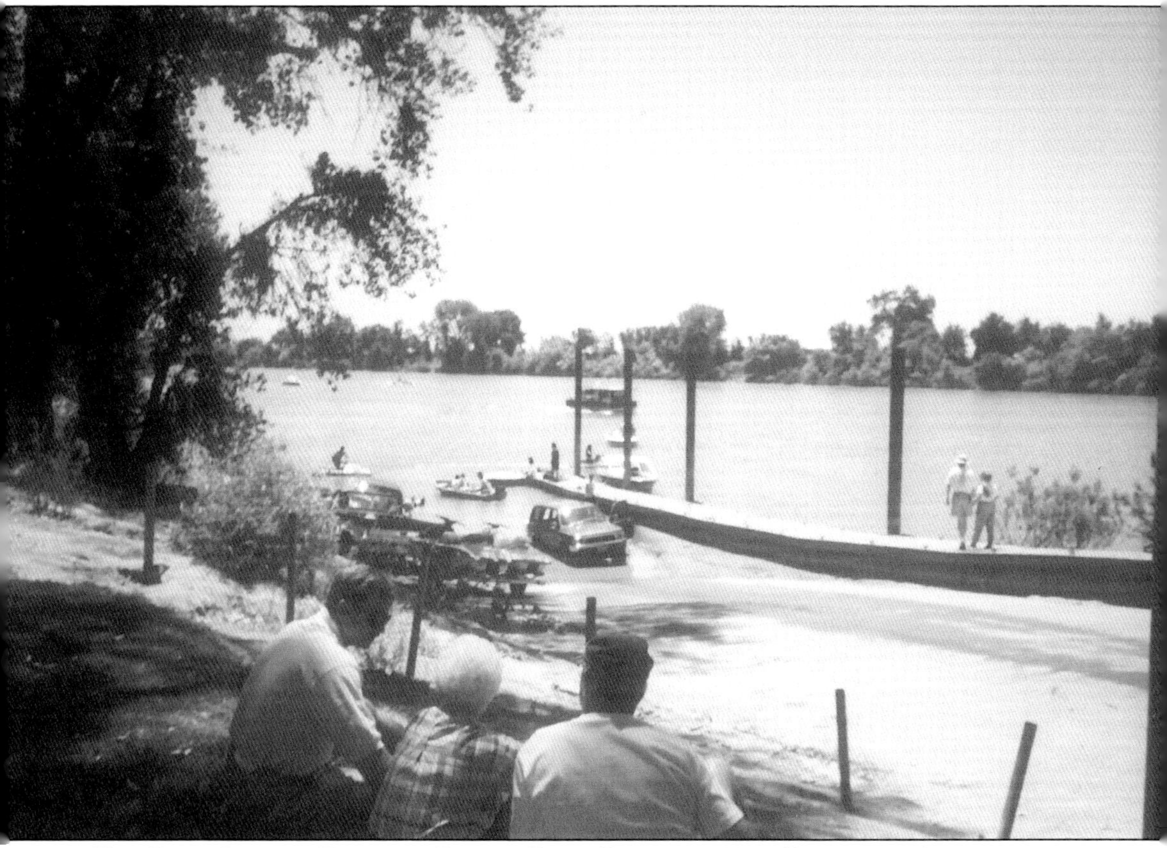

The Boat Launch Ramp at Garcia Bend Park in 1997, Providing Access to the Sacramento River. The Boat Launch is a popular place for recreational opportunity in the Pocket area and many who use it come from out of the area as well.

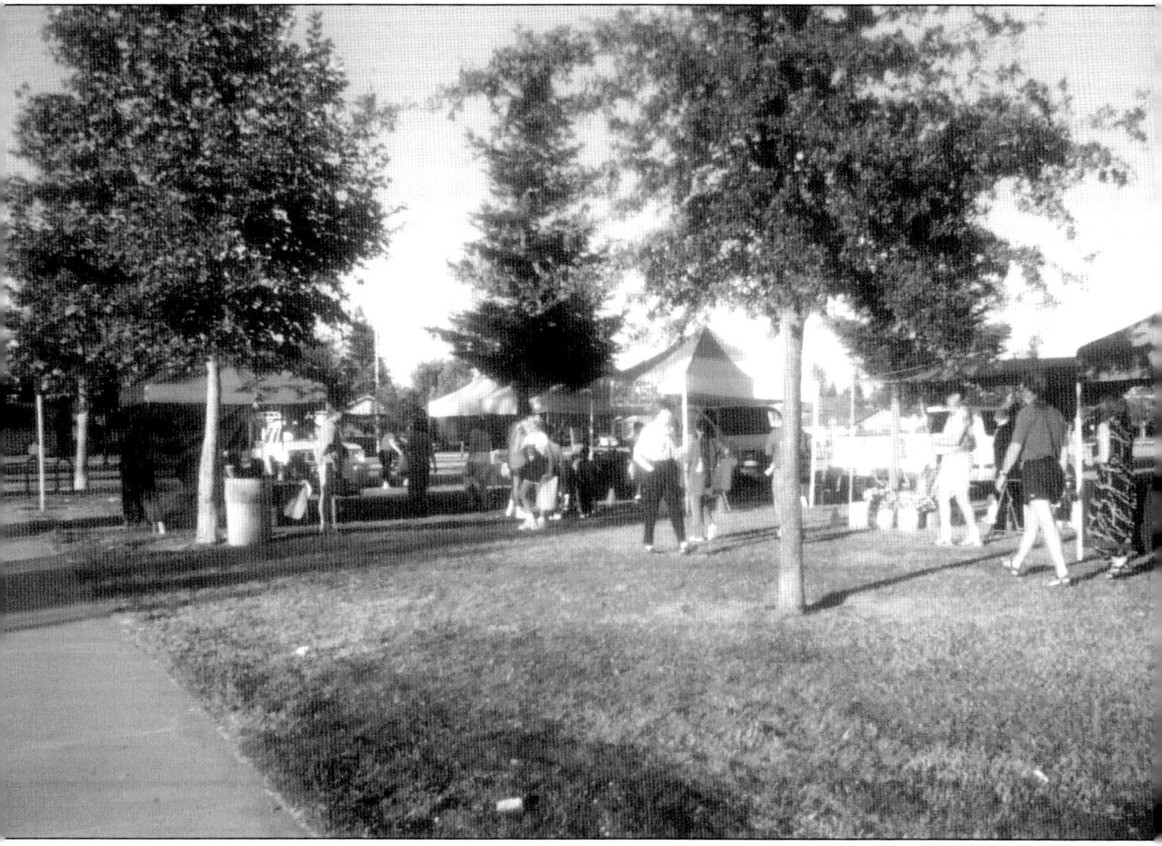

The Certified Farmers Market at Garcia Bend Park on June 7, 2001 For its Opening Day Season. The Farmers Market is held annually from June to September. The Farmers Market, along with the Pocket Fourth of July Parade and Fireworks celebration were community events established in the Pocket area in the late 1990s. The Farmers Market began in 1998 while the Fourth of July Celebration began a year earlier in 1997 by local community groups and volunteers.

References

Chandler, Barb. "Welcome to Pocket/Greenhaven!" (Research on John F. Kennedy High School). *Pocket/Greenhaven Business Directory 1999/2000*. Sacramento, CA: Valley Community Newspapers, 1999.

Gregory, Carol A. *Sacramento's Greenhaven/Pocket Area: History, Planning, Suburban Development, and Growth.* (Unpublished master thesis). Davis, CA: University of California at Davis, 1999.

Holmes, Lionel and D'Alessandro, Joseph. *Portuguese Pioneers of the Sacramento Area.* Sacramento, CA: Portuguese Historical and Cultural Society, 1990.